presents

XINJIANG

A Traveler's Guide to Far West China

By:

JOSH SUMMERS

FW FAR WEST
CHINA

Exploring Xinjiang and the Silk Road

Xinjiang | A Traveler's Guide to Far West China

By Josh Summers

Published by Go West Media

© 2019 Go West Ventures LLC

ISBN-13: 978-1-7321204-2-6

Cover Design: Anna Bryant

Map Designs: G.W. Fuqa

Table of Contents

City Guides

City Guides (con't)

EXTRA BONUS

This book comes with a number of free bonus materials including:

- High-resolution downloads of the Xinjiang maps in this book.
- HD Xinjiang Wallpaper
- Access to a private Facebook group
- Exclusive travel discounts

Take advantage of these free bonus materials by registering your copy of this Xinjiang travel guide here:

www.xjtravelguide.com/register

Dedicated to the special friends
who made Xinjiang my second home
for more than a decade.

Introduction to Xinjiang

Altay

G216

MONGOLIA

ay

G216

Urumqi

6

G30

Turpan

Hami

G314

G30

rla

XINJIANG
新疆

G218

5

CHINA

XINJIANG

CHINA

FW
CHINA

farwestchina.com

What Makes Xinjiang Special?

Xinjiang truly is a special place, unlike any other in the world. Few locations provide such variety of culture and scenery as China's far west region. Whether you're a history buff, an adventurer-seeker, a foodie or just a curious explorer, Xinjiang has much to offer.

The very fact that you've bought this book means I probably don't need to spend too much time convincing you that Xinjiang is a place worth visiting! The uniqueness of the Uyghur culture is more than enough reason to make a trip out to China's far west but if that isn't enough, consider these interesting facts:

- Xinjiang is so large that France could fit inside it...three times.
- Xinjiang is home both to China's 2nd largest desert (Taklamakan) as well as China's second tallest mountain (K2).
- Xinjiang makes up 1/6 of China's land mass and yet is home to only 1.5% of its population.
- Xinjiang borders 8 different countries, far more than any other region or province in China.
- Xinjiang is generally perceived as a poorer region; yet its mineral wealth and natural gas reserves make up 30% of the national total! The problem isn't money in the region, it's just the equal distribution of it.

Now, if that's not enough to convince you that Xinjiang is unique within China, visit the URL to the right to view a fun intro video or continue reading for a few more interesting Xinjiang facts.

Watch!

xjtravelguide.com/
xinjiang-facts

#1 Xinjiang is home to the only river in China whose water flows to the Arctic Ocean.

The Ertix River (额尔齐斯河), located in the Altay region of northern Xinjiang, exits Xinjiang into Kazakhstan and runs northward into the Arctic Ocean. The 546-kilometer river is actually the second longest river in Xinjiang in terms of water capacity and meets up with 5 other rivers before exiting the province.

#2 Xinjiang has the most airports of any Chinese province

Although the flights aren't always reliably available, airports are abundantly scattered throughout Xinjiang. As of 2019, there are 24 airports in Xinjiang, the most of any Chinese region, and there are more planned over the next few years. Most of these airports, however, have only one destination: the regional capital, Urumqi.

An example of one of these small airports is the Cherchen (Qiemo) Airport opened in the summer of 2016. It's a tiny airport with flights only to Urumqi and yet it cuts a 12-hour journey on land to less than 2.5 hours by air.

#3 Xinjiang houses China's only beaver natural reserve

Odd, but true. In the early 1980's the government established the Bulgan Beaver Nature Reserve, a 5,000-hectare natural reserve in northern Xinjiang, to help protect the beaver in Green River County.

Unfortunately, their efforts haven't been successful. The population has dropped from 1,000 in 1980 to only 500 as of 2007. Most of this can be blamed on droughts over the past decade, while some blame can also be placed on "ecological changes" (i.e. diverted water sources).

#4 Xinjiang has the largest mosque in China

Ok, so maybe this one isn't as obscure. The Id Kah Mosque, the famous yellow-brick building in the heart of Kashgar, may look small on the outside but actually takes up quite a large amount of space - 16,800 square meters to be exact.

I've been there during Eid al-Fitr, one of the largest Muslim holidays, and it is absolutely unbelievable how many people they can cram into (and around) that place - some estimate close to 30,000 worshippers!

Watch!

xjtravelguide.com/
kashgar-prayers-video

#5 People eat more fruit in Xinjiang than any other province in China

I believe the correct way to say this is that Xinjiang has the "highest consumption of fruits per capita" in China, but you get the idea.

The reason for this is the incredible amount of fruit grown here, many of which have become famous in their respective regions (i.e. Hami melons, Korla pears, Turpan grapes, etc.). In contrast, it is interesting to note that two of our three provincial neighbors, Tibet and Qinghai, have a difficult time producing fruit and therefore have the lowest fruit consumption in China.

#6 Xinjiang has the highest road in the world

First opened to the public in 1986, the Xinjiang-Tibet highway (also known as National Highway 219) is the highest road in the world. Its pass through the Kunlun Mountains to the Tibetan Plateau reaches over 6,000m in elevation and is arguably one of the most arduous routes to travel from Xinjiang to Tibet because much of it isn't paved.

As a side note, part of this road passes into the "disputed zone" between China and India (i.e. both countries claim the land to be theirs).

#7 Home to China's only Wild Camel Reserve

The two-humped camel, also called the Bactrian camel, is currently found wild in only three places in the world: the Taklamakan Desert, Lop Nur, and a part of the China/Mongolia border - all within Xinjiang.

The Wild Camel Reserve was established in 1999 and covers 65,000 square kilometers of barren nothing-ness. Thankfully, camels seem to be immune to the effects of nuclear radiation since this reserve sits next to what used to be China's nuclear testing grounds.

#8 You've probably seen it in a movie theatre

Xinjiang has been the setting for quite a few Chinese films, but more than likely you haven't seen any of them. There are, however, a few movies you probably have seen that you may not realize were filmed in Xinjiang.

"The Kite Runner" was entirely filmed in Kashgar, a city on the western tip of Xinjiang, while a scene from "Crouching Tiger, Hidden Dragon" was filmed at the Karamay Ghost City in the north.

#9 Bill Gates spent his honeymoon here

Ok, so not all of his honeymoon, but he did stop here. For those who have read Oracle Bones by Peter Hessler, this fact won't come as much of a shock but what's interesting is that I can find no other sources to corroborate Hessler's claim. Regardless, it's a fun trivia fact.

According to Hessler, the Gates only spent a few hours in Urumqi checking out the Xinjiang museum mummies and meeting with a woman who is now a Uyghur activist in Washington, D.C. and the Xinjiang government's #1 enemy.

#10 Home to the oldest Chinese paper cut

Apparently, an ancient Chinese soldier got pretty bored while being stationed in one of the garrison towns along the Silk Road. His paper creation was found and dated back to the 5th or 6th century, during the Southern and Northern dynasties.

The Peoples of Xinjiang

Xinjiang Ethnic Groups

Of course, all the fun trivia and Silk Road history you can imagine doesn't equal the one thing that makes Xinjiang one of my favorite places in the world: the people.

Partly due to its sheer size, the number of native ethnic groups that can be found within Xinjiang's borders is incredible. What's more, the geographic divides between each group can often be a surprisingly short distance.

For instance, a day spent in Kashgar will grant you a mostly Uyghur experience of Xinjiang. Drive a couple hours toward Karakul Lake, however, and suddenly a Uyghur is hard to find amid all the nomadic Kyrgyz herders. About an hour further down the road at Tashkorgan, most everybody you meet will be Tajik.

There's no doubt you'll notice the effects of the mass Han Chinese migration to Xinjiang over the past few decades, but if you look closely and step outside the comforts of the big city, there are a number of beautiful ethnic groups that would love to share their traditions with you.

According to official numbers released by the Statistics Bureau of Xinjiang in 2018, there are 24.45 million inhabitants of Xinjiang. This population is represented in majority by the following ethnic groups ordered from largest to smallest:

1. Uyghur People
2. Han Chinese
3. Kazakh People
4. Hui People
5. Kyrgyz People
6. Mongolian People
7. Tajik People
8. Xibe People
9. Manchu People
10. Uzbek People
11. Russian People
12. Daur People
13. Tartar People

1. Uyghur People

The Uyghur people of Xinjiang, the namesake of the "Uyghur Autonomous Region," are the largest ethnic group in the region, making up almost 50% of the population. While Uyghur can be found in most any town or city across Xinjiang, the majority reside south of the TianShan mountain range in areas like Kashgar, Aksu and Hotan.

Population: 11.27 million
Percentage: 49.04%

The Uyghur have their own Turkic language completely unrelated to Mandarin, with a writing system based on Arabic script. Even within Xinjiang, a number of different Uyghur dialects exist, although for the most part they can each understand each other.

Religion: Uyghur identity is closely tied with Islam, although the level of devotion to the religion varies from place to place, particularly under the current political environment. A report released by China in early 2015 boasted that Xinjiang is home to 20,000 mosques, most of which serve the Uyghur community. Despite this, religion among the Uyghur is heavily oppressed and that which does exist is closely monitored. China enforces bans on wearing head coverings, students attending mosque and fasting during Ramadan, among many others.

Culture: I find it extremely difficult to sum up Uyghur culture in a paragraph considering how much I have yet to learn, even after many years of living among them! In my experience, the culture best expresses itself through holiday festivities, family celebrations, food, dancing and music, all of which are in stark contrast to the Han Chinese culture. If you have the opportunity to attend a Uyghur wedding, you will learn more in this one experience than weeks of walking through the streets. Likewise, an opportunity to hear or see a performance of Uyghur muqam gives insight into an incredibly important part of their music tradition.

Festivals & Holidays: Uyghur celebrate most of the major Islamic festivals, of which the two most important are Rosa (known internationally as Eid al-Fitr) following the month of Ramadan, and Corban (known internationally as Eid al-Adha) 70 days following Rosa. Being around Kashgar's Id Kah Mosque or any other big mosques in Xinjiang during these festival times is a treat, as tens of thousands of Uyghur gather together in worship. Uyghur also celebrate the spring festival of Nowruz around the 21st of March, although time off usually isn't given for this smaller holiday as it is for the two larger ones.

2. Han Chinese

The Han Chinese of Xinjiang are a growing segment of the Xinjiang population that reside throughout the region. There's not much that

Population: 8.59 million
Percentage: 37.4%

separates the culture and customs of Xinjiang's Han from that of the rest of China, although there is a bit of a "Xinjiang hua" dialect that includes specific words and phrases not used anywhere else in China.

Wherever you go in Xinjiang, there will be plenty of traditional Chinese food options to eat and all of the major holidays like Spring Festival, Tomb Sweeping Day, National Day and others are celebrated.

Religion: The majority of Han Chinese are atheists, although remnants of Buddhism still remain part of their thinking. A few government-approved Christian churches exist, called "Three-Self Churches," where Han Christians meet as well as an approved Russian Orthodox and a small Catholic church.

Culture: Han Chinese have deep cultural roots and take great pride in tracing back their history thousands of years. Although Xinjiang is not the ideal place to view popular aspects of this culture, such as Beijing opera, acrobatics, lion dances and traditional Chinese architecture, they all exist here to a smaller degree.

Festivals and Holidays: Just as with the rest of China, the Han Chinese in Xinjiang celebrate holidays such as Spring Festival (January/February), National Day (October 1) and May Holiday (May 1) among a few other smaller holidays. Time off is usually given for each day, with Spring Festival being the longest.

3. Kazakh People

The Kazakh people are a distant third when it comes to population percentages. The majority of this 1.59 million Kazakh group reside in Xinjiang's

Population: 1.59 million
Percentage: 6.92%

Yili, Tacheng and Altay regions, all of which not-so-coincidentally border Kazakhstan. Most Xinjiang Kazakh speak both Mandarin and Kazakh, the latter of which has an Arabic-based script.

Religion: Most Kazakh will call themselves Muslim, although as with most Islamic practice in the north of Xinjiang, it is more of a cultural identity than a religion.

Culture: The Kazakh people of Xinjiang are historically nomadic herders who have only recently begun to urbanize. Horses have been a central part of the Kazakh culture which includes everything from breeding and riding them to using them for traditional sports like buzkashi or even as food. In addition to their beautiful horses, other characteristics of their culture include song, dance, wrestling, and traditional yurt homes, all of which are best seen when visiting the Yili grasslands during the major Muslim festivals.

Festivals & Holidays: Although the Kazakh celebrate all of the same holidays as the Uyghur, they do so quite differently. Aside from the fact that they place heavier emphasis on the Nowruz festival, their strong nomadic culture means that celebrations take place mostly outside and would not be complete without entertaining sports.

4. Hui People

Although the majority of China's ethnic Hui people fill up regions like Ningxia and Gansu to the east, they are still over a million-strong here in

Population: 1.06 million
Percentage: 4.61%

Xinjiang. Outsiders often assume the Hui to be Han Chinese because of their similar language, writing and looks. Even for locals, it can be difficult to distinguish the two.

There is much that differentiates the Han and Hui, however. Not only are the Hui ethnically separate from the Han Chinese (with more Mongol and Turkic ancestry), they are also separated by diet, religion and general demeanor.

The Hui are a very low-key people who can be hard to get to know. Most of the population lives in one of the five "Hui Autonomous Counties," including Changji (near Urumqi), Yanqi (near Korla) and three others.

Religion: The Hui are a Muslim people who usually worship in their own mosques separate from the Uyghur. Being generally conservative and pious, they have never been known to bear extremist Islamic beliefs. For this reason, the local security officials historically haven't restricted or monitored religious activities with the Hui to the same degree they have the Uyghur. Lately, though, this seems to be changing.

Culture: The staple food for the Hui is wheat flour, which they use to produce some of the best-tasting noodle dishes in the region. They are extremely family oriented and, although they likely won't be the first to invite you to their home, you can expect wonderful hospitality when they do. In addition, the Hui boast a very colorful heritage of poems and folk songs, although it is difficult to experience this when just traveling through Xinjiang.

Festivals & Holidays: As with all the Muslim groups, the Hui celebrate Rosa, Corban and Nowruz festivals.

5. Kyrgyz People

The Kyrgyz people of Xinjiang are another nomadic group that are found mostly in the mountainous regions of Xinjiang. The majority of the Kyrgyz live within the

Population: 202,400
Percentage: 0.88%

Kizilsu Kirghiz Autonomous Prefecture that surrounds Kashgar in western Xinjiang.

The Kyrgyz have their own Turkic-based language. While many of them have been educated in Mandarin, others who live far from the city have not.

Culture: The Kyrgyz culture is very similar to the Kazakh in many regards including dress, trade skills and even history. Milk tea with added salt is a favorite and the Kyrgyz women are often extremely adept at embroidery.

Festivals & Holidays: As with all the Muslim groups, the Kyrgyz celebrate Rosa, Corban and Nowruz festivals.

6. Mongolian People

The majority of Xinjiang's Mongolian ethnic group live in the Bortala and Bayingolin Mongolian Autonomous Prefectures, both of which ironically are on

Population: 185,300
Percentage: 0.81%

the west side of Xinjiang not even close to the Mongolian border. Like their Kazakh neighbors, most Mongolians in Xinjiang live as nomadic herders and farmers.

Xinjiang Mongols speak the Uirad (Oirat) dialect of the Mongol language, which is a member of the Altaic language family.

Religion: The Mongols of Xinjiang are heavily influenced by a strain of Shamanism, a common spiritual belief system of many Mongolian and Turkic peoples in Central Asia.

Culture: Much of the Mongol culture in Xinjiang is similar to Kazakh. Their traditional nomadic home, called a ger, resembles the Kazakh yurt and the Mongol music utilizes similar instruments and styles. The beautiful horse-head violin is a traditional instrument that has become the pride of Mongol musicians.

Festivals & Holidays: Mongols traditionally place high importance on the Nadaam (July-August) and Nowruz (mid-March) festivals, celebrated by joyous music, dancing and competitions on horseback.

7. Tajik People

Any visit to Tashkorgan, a small town on the Karakoram Highway between Kashgar and the Pakistani border, will give you an opportunity to observe the Tajik

Population: 50,100
Percentage: 0.22%

people. The physical features of the Tajik are striking, especially in contrast to most of the Central Asian ethnicities in Xinjiang. These features which you'll likely notice immediately include lighter hair, fair skin and colorful eyes.

The Tajik have their own Sarikol language which interestingly has no formal written form. Over half of them speak Uyghur and there are a number in Tashkorgan who speak Mandarin.

According to local tradition, Tajik people descend from the eagle and the majestic bird remains an important part of their culture. Hunting with eagles, the Tajik "eagle dance" and the "eagle flute" are just a few examples. The main intersection in Tashkorgan even has a monument topped by an eagle, a nod to the Tajik majority there.

8. Xibe People

The Xibe people of Xinjiang, also spelled "Xibo," inhabit their own autonomous region near Yili (Yining). Most Xibe live as farmers in the region and have done an

Population: 43,500
Percentage: 0.19%

admirable job retaining their culture despite small numbers within Xinjiang.

The Xibe were transplanted to this part of the world back in the 1760s by the Chinese Emperor Qianlong to help garrison the border and plant crops. Even today, they are known as proficient horsemen and excellent marksmen.

Although they are heavily influenced by the Manchu, the Xibe have their own dialect and their own mixture of Shamanism and Buddhism. You probably won't realize you've run into a Xibe community unless you happen to travel during the 18th day of the 4th lunar month. This is a festive holiday which they celebrate to commemorate when they were first transplanted to Xinjiang in the 1760s, a festival marked by singing, dancing, horse racing and plenty of food.

9. Manchu People

Manchu people, another people group transferred to Xinjiang for the purpose of creating a garrison along the border, has remained a very small minority here.

Population: 28,100
Percentage: 0.12%

Most are found in small communities around Urumqi, Yili and Hami.

Although they historically have their own Manchu language, the majority of the Manchu in Xinjiang today speak, read and write Mandarin.

The Manchu tend to celebrate both Spring Festival and Mid-Autumn Festival with the Han Chinese, but they still hold onto their own traditional holiday known as the Banjin Festival. It is on this day, the 13th day of the 10th lunar month that they celebrate their self-naming of "Manchu" back in 1635. Prior to that year they had been referred to as the "Nuzhen."

10. Uzbek People

A small population of Uzbek reside within Xinjiang, although they aren't concentrated in one single area. There are some which still act in the more

Population: 18,500
Percentage: 0.08%

traditional role of farmer while most have moved to the city to take up business.

Most Uzbeks associate themselves with Islam and are often confused with the Uyghur among whom they live. They have distinguished themselves in the embroidery business, as both the men and women are known for making and wearing intricately embroidered caps, shirts, dresses and scarves.

11. Russian People

Walking through the streets in southern Urumqi, there have been multiple times when I, a white American male, have been mistaken for a Russian.

Population: 12,000
Percentage: 0.05%

While there are some Russians that still live out on the farms of northern Xinjiang, a large concentration is found in southern Urumqi where the Russian market runs strong.

These Russian communities were once immigrants to Xinjiang in the 18th and 19th centuries but have managed to retain their language, culture and Eastern Orthodox religion. For this reason, they celebrate Easter and Christmas over the more traditional Chinese holidays.

12. Daur People

The Daur people, most of whom reside in the Tacheng region, first arrived in Xinjiang during the 1680s. They, like the Xibe and Manchu who came later, were sent here

Population: 6,900
Percentage: 0.03%

on garrison duty to suppress any rebellions in the region. When their duty was complete, they settled in the area.

The Xinjiang Daur speak their own dialect of Mongolian, although most have adapted to their surroundings by learning the appropriate language of trade, be it Uyghur, Kazakh or Mandarin.

Similar to the customs of their Kazakh neighbors across the border, the Daur entertainment is a mix of wrestling, horseback riding and even field hockey.

13. Tartar People

The Tartar are the smallest recognized minority in Xinjiang and are found mostly in the southern portion of the region. The Tartar language, which has an

Population: 5,100
Percentage: 0.02%

Arabic-based script, is still alive, although most Tartars speak either Uyghur or Kazakh with more frequency.

As Muslims, Tartars celebrate the traditional Islamic festivals such as Rosa, Corban and Nowruz, but they also have their own festival known as the "Saban" or Plough-Head Festival. Although there's no set date, the festival is usually celebrated sometime in June or July. During the festival, the small Tartar community gets together to sing, dance and enjoy the entertainment of traditional outdoor sports.

Planning Your Xinjiang Trip

Itineraries

<--->

One of the most common emails I receive regarding Xinjiang travel has to do with planning itineraries. Creating an itinerary for a place you've never visited is incredibly difficult, so don't be discouraged if you're having trouble!

There are three reasons that planning your travel to Xinjiang can be challenging:

1. Xinjiang is bigger than you realize: Unless you have the budget to fly everywhere you want to go, most travelers underestimate travel time when planning their itinerary. Taking a bus or train between Urumqi and Kashgar is at least 18-22 hours!

2. Xinjiang is still developing: Not all roads are smooth, or even paved for that matter. For this reason, throughout this guide you'll notice I am careful to use actual distances (i.e. 60 kilometers) instead of units of time (i.e. 1 hour) to address travel between two places.

3. In Xinjiang, expect the unexpected: Security checkpoints, sandstorms, rockslides and even a closed border crossing have all been the cause of travel delays for me. There are a number of things you just can't predict during your journey to Xinjiang.

Again, don't be discouraged, just prepare yourself to be flexible with your itinerary. This is especially true in southern Xinjiang where security checkpoints are more common and stricter.

For your travel, I want to list a number of itinerary options based on time and interest. Almost all of these itineraries can be accomplished whether you travel on a budget or with 5-star tastes, although the latter usually requires the assistance of a tour agency. I will address specifics of both luxury and budget travel in a further chapter. For now, look through the itinerary suggestions below and use this to build your own custom trip to Xinjiang!

1st Time Visitor Itinerary

Let's say this is your first time to visit Xinjiang and likely the only chance you'll ever have to come. You want to experience the best of what Xinjiang has to offer but limited time to explore the massive region. If this describes you, here are my suggestions.

For most travelers, the three most important cities to put on your itinerary are Urumqi, Turpan and Kashgar. You don't need to plan to spend more than a day in Urumqi; however, I advise at least two days in both Turpan and Kashgar, if not more. This will allow time for a good dose of history as well as immersion into Uyghur culture.

Beyond this, if you have extra time you'll not regret planning a trip along the Karakoram Highway where you will enjoy some of the best natural scenery that Xinjiang has to offer. Finish your trip with a visit down to Hotan, where the old town and market are reminiscent of the ancient Silk Road. From Hotan you can take a cross-desert bus back to Urumqi for your flight home.

For most travelers I don't even mention heading up north to Altay or Ili. While I highly recommend both regions, unless you have the time to travel or money for the extra flights, they aren't convenient.

An example of a first-time visitor itinerary would be the following, which should be tweaked according to your preferences:

Day 1: Arrive in Urumqi, visit the Xinjiang Museum (note: closed on Mondays).

Day 2: Take the high-speed train to Turpan and explore within the city.

Day 3: Hire a car to take you to see places outside of Turpan; grab an overnight train to Kashgar.

Day 4: Train travel, arriving in Kashgar that afternoon/evening (it's an 18-22 hr train ride!).

Day 5: Explore Kashgar and wander through the Old City.

Day 6: Hire a car to take you up the Karakoram Highway. Stop at Karakul Lake for lunch/dinner and then head to Tashkorgan.

Day 7: Explore the Stone Fort and grasslands of Tashkorgan in the morning before driving back to Kashgar.

Day 8: Take a bus or train to Hotan and explore the city.

Day 9: Continue to look around Hotan then take an overnight bus through the Taklamakan to Urumqi.

Day 10: Arrive in Urumqi and prepare to head home.

You can shorten this itinerary by either flying between Kashgar and Urumqi or skipping a city altogether. While some people might be inclined to skip Turpan, I would recommend you consider Hotan be cut out of the itinerary first.

Silk Road History Itinerary

For those seeking to retrace the ancient Silk Road, most of your time should be spent in southern Xinjiang. Hami will be your first destination in Xinjiang followed by Turpan, both of which are most conveniently connected by high speed train.

From Turpan you can head south through Korla where you have the option to choose the northern Taklamakan route or the southern Taklamakan route through Charkhlik (Ruoqiang). The northern route is more popular but the southern route is less developed and has a more authentic feel.

Note on the Southern Route: In many cases, over the most recent couple years, foreign travelers have not been permitted to cross the highway between Korla and Charkhlik (Ruoqiang). As with many things in Xinjiang, it's unclear if this is a hard-and-fast rule or just isolated incidents. In either case, it might be safer to fly from Urumqi to Cherchen (Qiemo) to begin your southern route journey.

On the northern route you'll certainly want to make a stop at Kuqa (Kuche) with its caves and ancient city ruins. From here you can continue to Kashgar or take the cross-desert highway to Hotan.

On the southern Taklamakan route you can leisurely make your way to Chechen (Qiemo), Niya (Minfeng), and Keriya (Yutian) before you hit Hotan. While there are a number of ancient ruins around this region, most require a high permit fee and are very difficult for the average tourist to visit. For this reason, visits to these smaller southern cities should be considered more for the purpose of experiencing the culture and way of life. Hotan is where you can finally explore some Silk Road desert ruins.

Between Hotan and Kashgar there are a number of interesting stops including the cities of Yengisar, home of the once-famous Uyghur knife, and Yarkand (Shache) with its Old City and Sunday Bazaar. Visiting one of these bazaars should be a priority. Even if you won't be around on Sunday there are still a number of bazaars that occur throughout the week in and around Kashgar. (see Kashgar Nearby Village Markets)

While a Silk Road itinerary can be approached from various directions with a number of different turns, here is one example that falls under 10 days.

Day 1: Arrive in Hami, quickly visit the Tombs of the Hami Kings then grab the high-speed train to Turpan where you can stay the night.

Day 2: Spend the day exploring Turpan.

Day 3: Hire a car to take you to see places outside of Turpan; grab a train that night to Kuqa.

Day 4: Arrive in Kuqa and explore the Kizil Caves.

Day 5: Continue your visit in Kuqa until you can grab a bus that evening to Hotan.

Day 6: Arrive in Hotan where you can explore and stay the night.

Day 7: From Hotan take the bus or train to Yarkand or Yengisar to stay the night.

Day 8: Continue on to Kashgar where you can explore and stay the night.

Day 9: Hire a car to take you to a nearby bazaar depending on which day it is.

Day 10: Depart for Urumqi and head home.

Obviously, I've skipped a large portion of the southern Taklamakan Desert in this itinerary; it requires more time than a 10-day itinerary can afford. Trains haven't yet extended all along the southern rim of the Taklamakan so bus or private car travel are often your best options, which is time prohibitive.

Should you have two weeks or more, another option would be to essentially circle the Taklamakan Desert with a short detour along the Karakoram Highway while in Kashgar.

Scenic Nature Itinerary

If Uyghur culture and Silk Road history don't interest you as much as the sight of beautiful mountains, verdant grasslands and barren deserts, you should probably take a different direction with your itinerary.

The natural beauty of Xinjiang is mostly found in the region's northern half, although there are still plenty of reasons to travel south. Areas around Altay, including a couple of Xinjiang's national parks, offer plenty of opportunities to hike and enjoy nature.

After Altay, the next top spot for scenic tourism is Ili (Yili), where lakes, mountains and grasslands stretch for as far as the eye can see. During certain times of the year you can also be amazed by fields of purple lavender, pink apricot trees or yellow rapeseed.

In southern Xinjiang, the scenic nature itinerary would take you along the Karakoram Highway, although a number of different poplar parks within the Taklamakan are an excellent sight during the fall season.

Since I've already covered a couple itinerary options in the south, the example below focuses more on the northern side of Xinjiang, although I would certainly recommend adding a trip to the south if you can manage.

Day 1: Arrive in Urumqi, visit the Xinjiang Museum and then take a plane to Fuyun.

Day 2: Spend the day hiking around Keketuohai National Park.

Day 3: Take a bus or car from Fuyun to Buerjin.

Day 4: Travel up to Kanas Lake National Park where you'll stay the night near Kanas Lake.

Day 5: Hike or take a bus from Kanas Lake to Hemu Village, returning to Buerjin for the night.

Day 6: After a quick visit to the Five Colored Hills, get an overnight bus to Ili.

Day 7: Disembark the bus before arriving in Ili at Salimu Lake where you can explore and find overnight accommodation in a yurt.

Day 8: Take a bus or hire private car to Yining City where you can explore and stay the night.

Day 9: Hire a car to take you to the Nalati Grasslands where you can again stay the night in a yurt.

Day 10: Return to Yining City where you can board a flight back to Urumqi.

A lot of time can be spent in both the Altay and Ili regions, but the above itinerary hits the highlights. The beautiful Barkol Lake and grassland near Hami may be a good alternative if you're entering by train from the east and don't have the time to head further north.

Photographer's Itinerary

A number of different Xinjiang expeditions dedicated to photography have become popular over the years. Most of these expeditions have a set itinerary with a private car and driver since the needs of a photographer are different than those of the average tourist.

For this reason, I won't lay out a specific itinerary for photographers, rather I will highlight here some of the most beautiful photographic opportunities Xinjiang offers.

For nature scenery, some of the most interesting places include the numerous Ghost Cities (the one at Wuerhe near Karamay is the biggest and most popular), Kuqa's TianShan Grand Canyon (similar to Antelope Canyon in Arizona), Shipton's Arch (the tallest natural arch in the world) and the Five Colored Hills, a wonderful mixture of rock, desert and water.

The Keketuohai National Park and the Kanas Lake Nature Reserve are both excellent places to hike about and take pictures, especially the nearby Hemu and Baihaba Villages. The area is home to a booming tourist industry that may hamper your ability to capture the natural environment but that's something you'll have to work around. The grasslands around Ili, including Nalati Grasslands and Bayinbulak Grasslands are both gorgeous, especially during festival season (June/July).

Speaking of seasons, there are certain months of the year that dictate the best places to visit. Springtime in Ili offers incredible fields of apricot blossoms (April/May), rows of lavender (June), and cultural festivities (July/August). During the fall months, the golden yellow leaves of the poplar forests along the Tarim River are spectacular (see Tarim River Park in the Korla chapter), as are the changing colors present all throughout Altay and Ili.

For cultural scenery, wandering the streets of Kashgar's Old City - or any of the smaller towns that dot the edges of the Taklamakan Desert - is a gold mine of photo opportunities. I recommend visiting one of the many bazaars that happen around Kashgar (see Nearby Village Markets in the Kashgar chapter) since the Sunday bazaar and livestock market are often filled with tourists.

Finally, a word of caution for photographers: carrying a large camera isn't a problem but pointing it at any sort of local military can be an issue. I've known photographers whose entire memory cards were confiscated or wiped just because they decided to snap a picture of the military patrolling the street.

Luxury Travel Tips

A decade ago, the idea of luxury travel in Xinjiang was almost laughable. Now, it is not only possible to travel in comfort, it's surprisingly easy to do so if you have the money.

Lodging

Legitimate, internationally-recognized 5-star hotels exist in Urumqi (Sheraton, Hilton) and in Kashgar (Raddison Blu) while the less-expensive - and less comfortable - Chinese 5-star hotels can be found in most any other city. Smaller boutique hotels exist in some areas such as The Silk Road Lodge in Turpan, which offers comfort, air conditioning and a beautiful local atmosphere.

Transportation

The most comfortable luxury travel around Xinjiang will take place either in the air or in a private car. You'll want to steer clear of the buses and trains; even the best beds in a Chinese train may be considered uncomfortable by some standards. The new-high speed train is an exception in terms of comfort, although the experience of getting through any Chinese train station is a nightmare you'll prefer to avoid.

It is possible to arrange a car that you can drive yourself (see Renting Your Own Car) but I believe it is best to go through a travel agency to hire a car and driver who is familiar with the roads (see my list of Approved Travel Companies). Based on my experience I can tell you that it's very easy to get lost on these roads!

Tourist Sites

The majority of Xinjiang's tourism requires significant outdoor walking, which can be strenuous at times. Heat is always a concern, especially in summer. You will be grateful for an air-conditioned vehicle if you travel during this time of year. For locations high in the mountains, tourist sites like Heavenly Lake, Narat Grasslands, Kanas Lake and Koktokay Park cater to the tourist who doesn't want to hike much. You can walk, of course, but there are buses and shuttles that are available in these areas.

Budget Travel Tips

For most travelers, it's best to prepare to "rough it" a bit during your visit to Xinjiang. That wild aspect of travel is part of the allure of this region, in my opinion!

Lodging

Xinjiang boasts a number of different hostels in cities like Urumqi, Turpan, Kashgar, Tashkorgan, Yili and more, all of which are described in detail within the individual city chapters of this guide. Most of the travelers you meet will be Chinese and the facilities aren't always to the standard you'll find at other hostels around the world. Still, they offer a great environment and often an excellent location.

If possible, I would also recommend that you plan to spend at least one night in a traditional yurt. This usually costs the same as a hostel bed but allows you to experience the local culture in a unique way.

Transportation

Budget always comes at the expense of time no matter where you travel but this is true nowhere more so than Xinjiang. Because the region is so large, travel by any means other than airplane can mean excruciating hours spent on the road.

For this reason, I always recommend that travelers try to plan overnight bus or train trips. Not only does this save you the cost of a hotel, it also eliminates wasted time that you should be using to explore.

Having said that, don't be afraid to check airfare for each destination. There have been many times where a discounted flight is the same as a hard sleeper on the train, saving you precious time.

Tourist Sites

Unfortunately, the entrance fees for many of Xinjiang's tourist sites continue to climb and will often be your biggest budget expenditure. Not everything is worth the expense of its entrance fee, though. My recommendations should be helpful as you try to get the best value for your money.

For instance, in Kashgar there's no need to pay to enter the Id Kah Mosque when most tourist are perfectly content with a picture outside. Likewise, in Turpan, you don't have to pay to enter the Flaming Mountains tourist site when a simple photo from the highway does the trick.

Traveling with Kids

◄━━━━━━━━━━━━━━━━━━━━━━━━━━━━━━►

Another common question I receive has to do with those who will be traveling to Xinjiang with kids. At first glance, the region does not seem to be very "kid-friendly," but I've known a number of families who have successfully traveled Xinjiang with kids including my own family with my two sons under the age of six.

Traveling with kids provides a new perspective on Xinjiang and a level of hospitality that you wouldn't normally experience alone. The curiosity of kids and their ability to get away with asking candid questions are wonderful gifts to a traveling family.

To help make your travel to Xinjiang with kids more enjoyable, here are a few tips to consider:

- **Be Prepared:** Be familiar with the basic history of the region before arrival. For older kids, I think they might enjoy a book entitled Foreign Devils on the Silk Road. I also advise bringing a map or buying one when you arrive so as to allow them to keep track of where you've been and where you're headed.

- **Understand Your Religions:** A rudimentary understanding of Islam and Buddhism will go a long way here in Xinjiang. Temples and caves display the rich history of Buddhism and you will no doubt see many mosques where most of the ethnic groups currently practice Islam.

- **Be Aware of Etiquette:** There is a lot of forgiveness for foreigners, especially with kids, when it comes to cultural etiquette but this is a perfect opportunity to teach children what it means to respect somebody else's culture. For more details, read the chapter on Cultural Sensitivity or ask your tour guide.

- **Prepare Your Kids for Pictures:** My sons get photographed almost on a daily basis here in Xinjiang by locals who think their blond hair and blue eyes are just too cute to pass up. We've prepared them for it, though and they both know that all they have to do is say "no" and we will pull them away from any uncomfortable situation.

- **Prepare Your Kids for Dead Animals:** In Xinjiang, sheep can have their throat slit in the street and carcasses can be seen hanging in restaurants. This can traumatize children (and some adults), so take appropriate measures based on the sensitivity of your child. One mom even suggested making it game of trying to figure out what animal each carcass used to be.
- **Appropriate Transportation:** Make sure you know what your kids can handle before getting on any mode of transportation. Trains can be comfortable but some only offer squatty potties. Buses have bathrooms but even the locals refuse to use them in most cases and the bus usually won't stop for emergency potty breaks. The fact is that planes and private cars are the best way to travel with kids if you can afford them.
- **Always Have Tissue Paper:** Buy a whole bunch once you arrive and keep it in their backpack. Most restaurants won't give you napkins and most bathrooms don't have toilet paper. You'll be surprised how often you use the tissue paper.
- **Bring/Buy a Ball:** Soccer is a universal sport, even here in Xinjiang. A ball will not only provide your child with entertainment, it often opens the door for interaction with the locals, both young and old.
- **About Clothing:** Although it may be hot in summer, wearing long pants isn't a bad idea for kids when outside the big cities. Not only is it culturally appropriate to wear long pants, your kids may notice the fact that nobody else is wearing shorts, causing them to shy away from local interaction.
- **About Hotels:** Chinese hotels are made for 3-member families (two parents and one child) and so they don't accommodate larger families well. You can ask for an extra bed if they have one, otherwise for families of 4+, you might be forced to purchase two or more rooms.

Special thanks to Kim Boughey who graciously shared what she learned while traveling in Xinjiang with her kids.

Weather in Xinjiang

◄──────────────────────────────►

I have to laugh a little every time I receive an email from a traveler asking me what to expect in terms of weather in Xinjiang.

You see, Xinjiang is home to the world's second-lowest point in the world, the Turpan Depression, as well as the second-highest point in the world, K2. The difference in environment between these two places is almost as vast as the region itself! How do you answer such a question?

I'll dive into specifics in a moment but as a general rule the two best times to visit Xinjiang are May-June and September-October. These times work best with most any location you want to visit but don't be discouraged if you already plan to travel during a different season. Here's a look at each season in further detail:

Spring Season (March to June)

The spring is a wonderful time to visit Xinjiang, with its cool weather and gradually longer days. The beginning of spring can still be quite cold in many areas of Xinjiang, particularly up in the north and in the higher elevations, so you'll need to be prepared with warmer clothing. It is likely that snow won't be completely melted in many places until well into April and sometimes even May.

In April, you begin to see a number of different fields bloom into beautiful seas of color, particularly around the Ili region. In late April into early May, the apricot blossoms fill the hills near the Nalati Grasslands with a beautiful shade of pink, while in June you'll see lavender fields outside of Yining City burst with majestic purple.

The southern regions like Turpan, Kuqa, Kashgar and all around the Taklamakan Desert are excellent to visit during these months as they are usually the first to welcome spring. It does get windy, though, so don't be surprised if you get caught in a sandstorm.

Summer Season (June to August)

As you may have heard, summer gets pretty hot in Xinjiang! Few regions of Xinjiang are exempt from this intense heat; although air conditioning is becoming more common, especially in hotels, you can't count on it.

Places in southern Xinjiang - Turpan, Kashgar, Hotan, etc. - will be even hotter than most places in northern Xinjiang at higher elevation. When planning summer travel to Xinjiang, expect to do your sightseeing in the cool mornings and late evenings. Keep in mind that even the locals take a "siesta" during the heat of the afternoon!

Despite the heat, travel during the summer will be rewarded with beautiful wildflowers and a tasty array of fresh fruits such as grapes and melons.

Fall Season (September to November)

The fall season is probably my favorite season to travel around Xinjiang, as it offers a wonderful mix of cooler weather, long days and colorful scenery.

There isn't a bad place to visit during the fall as long as you remember that temperatures can drop drastically in the evening and snow is always a possibility as the season progresses. The further you get into the fall, the more likely that many of the border crossings are at risk to suddenly close for the season.

Winter Season (December to March)

Winter in Xinjiang is bitter cold and unfortunately very long. I've put December to March here, but the reality is that in some regions of Xinjiang winter begins in October and lasts into April. In most cases, transportation still runs and most tourist sites are surprisingly still open, although you won't want to stay outside in the cold for long periods of time.

Skiing and other winter sports are an option (see A Guide to Skiing in Xinjiang). Since it's the off season, flights around Xinjiang can be purchased at a bargain.

Be advised that required clothing during winter includes long underwear, gloves, glove liners, a cap and sometimes even a face mask.

Festivals and Holidays in Xinjiang

One of my favorite ways to experience Xinjiang is through the festivals of its many ethnic groups. Often, they are the only opportunities to get a glimpse into the local culture and, thankfully, most people are very hospitable when it comes to foreigners joining their celebrations.

Major Holidays

Chinese Spring Festival (aka "Chinese New Year"): As is the custom all across the country, everything in Xinjiang shuts down for a week every year during Spring Festival, also known as the Chinese New Year. Most ethnic minorities don't celebrate this holiday, but you'll hear plenty of firecrackers throughout the night in every city. This holiday, based on the lunar calendar, usually occurs sometime between January and February. To find the exact date, check this link:

www.xjtravlguide.com/spring-festival-dates

National Day (Chinese): This holiday marks the founding of the People's Republic of China on October 1, 1949. Don't expect celebrations you can join; expect more travelers to join you since they have time off. This holiday takes place each year for the first few days of October.

Corban Festival (Islamic): The Corban Festival (also spelled "Korban" and known globally as Eid-al-Adha) is the largest and most important holiday celebrated by each of the Muslim ethnic groups including the Uyghur, Kazakh, Hui and others. During this time, truckloads of sheep are herded into the cities and sold for sacrifice. Although it can be bloody, it's amazing to watch the sacrificial process. If you have the pleasure of an invitation into a local home, it's a wonderful time of celebration between friends and family. Visit a mosque early on the morning of Corban Festival and you will see thousands, if not tens of thousands of worshippers join together to pray. Learn more about Eid al-Adha and approximate dates here:

www.xjtravelguide.com/eid-al-adha

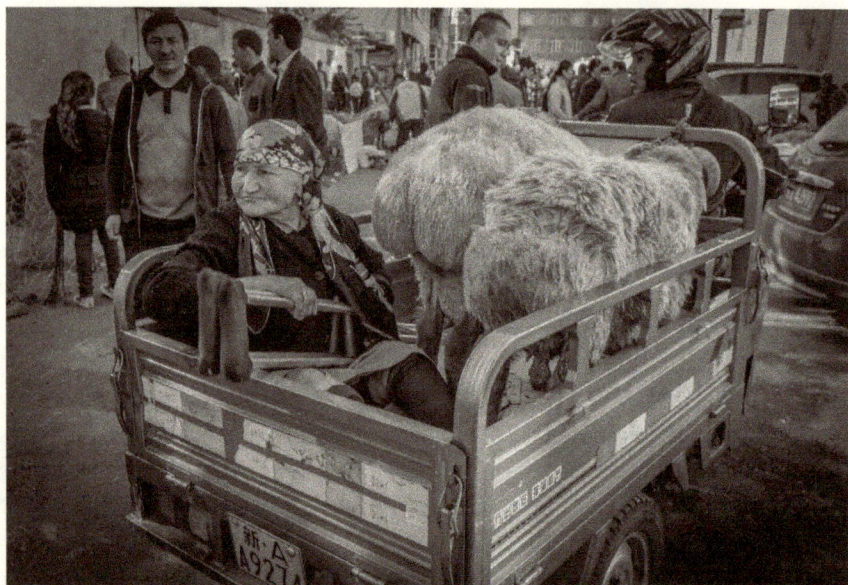

Rosa Festival (Islamic): Immediately following the Muslim fasting month of Ramadan, the fast-breaking festival of Rosa (also spelled "Roz" and known globally as Eid-al-Fitr) is a smaller festival celebrated by all of the Muslim ethnic groups in Xinjiang. The morning after the last day of the Ramadan fast, all Muslim men gather at the mosque for final prayer. The most popular place to observe this spectacle is at Kashgar's Id Kah Mosque where over 20,000 people come from all over to worship. Following the prayers, families and communities celebrate together with massive meals and plenty of singing and dancing (where permitted). More information and dates for this festival can be found here:

www.xjtravelguide.com/eid-al-fitr

Nowruz Festival (Islamic): The Nowruz festival, traditionally known as the Iranian New Year, is recognized by many of the minority ethnic groups in Xinjiang but isn't nearly as large a celebration as Corban or Rosa.

Minor Holidays

Nadam Festival (Nomadic Peoples): The Nadam festival, which is a major holiday in Mongolia, is relatively small here in Xinjiang, but still celebrated among the nomadic groups of Kazakh, Mongol and Kyrgyz. For those travelers who will be near Sayram Lake, Nalati Grasslands or other parts of the Ili region during this late July/early August holiday, you can look forward to entertaining music, dance, horse racing, buzkashi, wrestling tournaments and even archery.

Grape Festival (Turpan): Every year toward the end of July and throughout the month of August, Turpan celebrates the Grape Festival. Grapes are so abundant during this season that clusters hang on vines in literally every corner of the city. Performances are held at the Grape Valley; mass Uyghur weddings are organized and vendors line the streets selling boxes full of grapes. The festival occurs between August 20th and September 5th every year

Migration Festival (Xibe): This minor festival celebrated by the small Xibe community near Yili occurs on the 18th day of the 4th lunar month (usually sometime between April and May). The celebration usually includes music, dancing and archery competitions.

Banjin Festival (Manchu): Only celebrated by the Manchu communities near Ili and Hami, the Banjin Festival occurs on the 13th day of the 10th lunar month (usually between October and November). Traditional clothing is worn, traditional dances are performed and folk songs are sung. It's mostly a government-sponsored event now, but is still interesting to observe.

Crossing the Xinjiang Border

◄──────────────────────►

There are a number of travelers who use Xinjiang as a jumping off point into Central Asia where they will continue their adventure along the Silk Road. If this is you, make sure that you have determined what you need to have in terms of visas or permits before you arrive at the border.

There are numerous entrance/exit points for travelers in Xinjiang, three of them leading to other regions of China and the remainder passing into one of the eight other countries that border the region.

To Gansu (China)

The Gansu/Xinjiang border is the largest entry/exit point, encompassing two major highways and two train lines. No visa or special permit is required and rarely do you encounter any provincial checkpoint to cross here.

To Qinghai (China)

The seldom used Qinghai entry/exit point follows Highway 315 along a southern portion of the Silk Road. There is no special visa or permit necessary to make this trip. You will, however, need a private car; a train is currently under construction for this route but will not be operational for a number of years.

To Tibet (China)

I receive a number of questions from travelers who want to make the journey from Xinjiang into Tibet via Highway 219 in Karghalik (Yecheng). This is not an easy journey nor is it cheap as it requires a 4WD and a special permit. Even with a permit, border guards who are having a bad day have been known to turn away travelers for no good reason. The best advice I can give is to contact a Xinjiang travel agent before considering such a journey.

To Kazakhstan

A cross into Kazakhstan can be made via the Alashankou and Horgas Ports, both of which are on the border near the Yili region. Other border crossings exist, including ports at Tacheng and Jeminay, but they aren't convenient, nor have they been reliably open for travelers. The Alashankou Port is the most widely used although the Horgas Port offers the quickest transfer to Almaty. Both ports can be accessed by train from Urumqi. Visas must be in order, unless the country from which your passport is issued has an agreement with Kazakhstan to offer a VOA (visa on arrival). Thankfully, Kazakhstan offers most travelers a 15-day VOA but it is best to check your specific country requirements to be sure.

To Kyrgyzstan

Both the Irkeshtam Pass and Torugart Pass connect Xinjiang and Kyrgyzstan, although local buses only travel through the Irkeshtam. Kyrgyzstan offers most international travelers a 60-day VOA but check your country requirements to be sure. You can find specific instructions on how to cross the Irkeshtam border here:

www.xjtravelguide.com/irkeshtam

Crossing the Torugart Pass is unfortunately a much more expensive affair, with some reports indicating a total transportation price tag of US$500. It's best to work with a travel agent in Kashgar or Naryn (Kyrgyz side) to arrange the drivers and any permits you might need. On the positive side, the road on both the Chinese and Kyrgyz side is very scenic.

To Pakistan

The Khunjerab Pass, which divides the Karakoram Highway between its China and Pakistani side, is the highest paved border crossings in the world. Arrangements can be made to cross this border, although you must have your paperwork ready before you start the journey. Visas are not issued on arrival and must be arranged prior to travel.

Note on Tajikistan: While the Kulma Pass exists between Xinjiang and Tajikistan along the Karakoram Highway, it isn't an often-used crossing. While I've been told it's closed to foreigners, I also know many solo foreign travelers who have made the crossing. This is only advised for those adventurous travelers who are willing to get turned around at the border.

Arranging Transportation

When it comes to arranging transportation, I find that there are two types of travelers: those who like to have everything ironed out before they leave and those who prefer to be spontaneous for the sake of flexibility. Xinjiang travel tends to favor the latter, although over the past decade it has become easier to make reservations in advance.

Below I will discuss the advantages of every available mode of transportation so that you can get an idea of what is possible here in Xinjiang.

Air Travel

Air travel in Xinjiang resembles air travel in any other part of China - or the world for that matter. Tickets can be purchased online using your foreign credit card and passport. The process of checking in luggage and boarding your plane, even in smaller airports, are exactly as you would expect.

While travel agents can arrange your tickets, I find that searching online can be just as easy and often cheaper. Instead of using well-known global brands like Expedia, Orbitz, etc., search on China-based sites like Trip.com, a favorite among the expats in China because it's cheap. You can view the site in English and there are even English-speaking representatives if you have a problem and need to call.

Charter flights can be arranged through Chinese travel agencies if needed, although this is seldom done unless you're traveling with a larger group that doesn't mind paying extra.

Please note that security is a bit tighter in Xinjiang airports, so expect to put your bags through metal detectors before you even step into the building, in addition to other possible security measures they may have in place.

Luggage Restrictions

Most domestic flights in China allow for one checked bag per ticket weighing no more than **20 kg (44 lbs.)**. Carry ons have been a big hassle the past couple years, with most airports limiting carry-on weight to only 5 kg (11 lbs.). Roller luggage invites the most scrutiny so if you can fit it into a backpack, you can usually get away with more than 5 kg.

Train Travel

Thanks to a new rule implemented back in 2014, purchase of China train tickets can be made up to 60 days in advance, which makes planning your travel easier. You can rely on your travel agent to arrange the tickets for you or you can opt to do it yourself. I recommend you purchase train tickets at least a week in advance, otherwise you may get stuck with the uncomfortable hard seat or, worse yet, standing tickets. Believe it or not, train tickets get bought up pretty fast.

Thankfully, purchasing a ticket is not that difficult. My advice to any traveler in China is to download an app from China Highlights called China Train Booking. The app allows you to find up-to-the-minute information on train schedules and available tickets in English. If you like, you can even purchase the tickets through the app and have them delivered to your hotel (for a small fee), although the delivery option requires you to purchase at least 9 days in advance.

If you decide to purchase train tickets on your own there is a way to do it online, although you will need to be able to read Mandarin and have a Chinese debit card. For more details and a tutorial on how to do this, read my article online entitled How to Buy Chinese Train Tickets Online.

www.xjtravelguide.com/train-ticket-tutorial

Of course, you can always just stand in line to buy tickets at the train station ticket hall or at one of the many train ticket offices in each city (referred to as 火车售票店/Huǒchē shòupiào diàn). This is, for many travelers, the least-complicated option although lines can be long. The purchase of train tickets does require the passport for each traveler, so make sure you have either the physical passport or a copy of the passport with you to purchase.

Luggage Restrictions

Although there are luggage restrictions in place on trains (20 kg or 44 lbs per piece), I have never known bags to be weighed in a Chinese train station. Your biggest concern is space, as there isn't much storage on trains for large luggage and the luggage racks gets filled fast.

Bus Travel

In some areas of Xinjiang, travel by bus will be your only option. Tickets can usually be purchased the day of your departure, although I recommend buying tickets one day in advance if possible. You will need to present your passport to purchase a bus ticket.

The challenge with bus travel is that larger cities like Urumqi and Kashgar have multiple bus stations that service different locations. I will go into further detail in each city chapter, but you should check with your hotel or hostel to make sure that you're going to the right bus station.

Buses are usually prompt to leave, so be sure you arrive at least 20-30 minutes prior to your scheduled departure.

Luggage Restrictions

There are no published luggage restrictions for China buses but it's worth noting that all luggage is usually stored under the bus and out of your reach, so choose carefully what you keep with you and what you put below deck.

Private Car Hire

Transport by private car hire is another popular option and is sometimes not much more expensive than a bus. To clarify, "private car hire" is a car that goes from point A to point B and is usually shared by multiple travelers. If you desire to rent a vehicle, skip to the next chapter on Renting Your Own Vehicle.

Private car hire is harder to book in advance, but it is possible. Most private cars can be found outside the bus station where you'll likely be bombarded by men shouting out the location where they want to go. You can negotiate for same-day travel or for a near-future date.

Private car hire is economical for people that travel in groups of 4 or less. As a single traveler, you might find yourself sitting in the private car waiting for up to an hour or more as the driver seeks additional passengers. Unless you hire the entire vehicle, you're at the mercy of the driver.

Renting Your Own Vehicle or Bike

For those of you who have the budget and desire the independence, there are a few options for renting your own vehicle in Xinjiang.

Renting a Car

I'm happy to report that renting a car is not difficult, although not practical for most short-term travelers. If you're renting both a car and driver, it's especially easy and can be set up through a tourist agency.

If you want to rent and drive the car yourself, the first step is to make sure you have a Chinese driver's license. It's a somewhat complicated process if you don't already have it, but if you've already obtained one, there are numerous car rentals scattered throughout Urumqi and various other cities (look for the characters 租车 /Zūchē).

I must forewarn you, however, that it's not a streamlined process here in Xinjiang like it is elsewhere in China. Consider this:

- **There are no "big name" rental companies**: Don't expect to find Hertz or Enterprise at the airport. Rental companies here are mostly all privately owned.
- **Rental companies expect a sizable deposit**: I had to put down about US$1,000 to rent a car. In most cases it has to be cash since very few Xinjiang car rental companies accept foreign credit cards.
- **Rental companies hold 2,000 RMB for 30 days after drop off**: They do this in case you get a traffic ticket in the mail. I had to pick up my security deposit personally, but they can direct deposit into your Chinese bank account if you have one.
- **Most rental cars have distance limits**: Almost every company I've come across here in Xinjiang limits cars to at most 300km per day, which isn't much considering the size of this region. Every kilometer over 300 will cost you 1 RMB.
- **Wrecks: it's always the foreigner's fault**: This isn't a foregone conclusion, but I've seen it happen time and again with foreigners who own cars here in Xinjiang and get into a wreck.

- **It's hard to get gas**: New rules have made it very difficult to get gas if you're a foreigner. Technically, you're supposed to be able to purchase gas using your passport (Chinese people are required to present their I.D. Card), but many of the smaller gas stations don't understand this. In these cases, you might need to find a local to fill up with gas for you.

That's the bad news. Here's the good news: it is possible to rent a vehicle without distance limits using a foreign credit card. There are two methods I'm aware of which I'll share here.

First, there is a growing Chinese company known as "eHi" that allows for reservation of a car through their website. Cars are picked up near Terminal 1 of the Urumqi airport and returned there as well. Search for the eHi website but be warned that it is in Chinese and the English version isn't reliable.

The second option is to rent directly through a travel agency. You're limited to the vehicles that they personally own but in this way, you don't have to rent from Urumqi if you only want to drive around Kashgar.

Both of these options will usually be more expensive than renting through one of the many other car rental companies in Xinjiang (average about 300-500 RMB/day) but again, they offer unlimited mileage and the ability to pay with a foreign credit card.

Bicycles and Motorcycles

I've owned a motorcycle and a bicycle here in Xinjiang for many years and have loved every minute of it. Unfortunately, it's not always the easiest option for a short-term traveler.

Motorcycles

The biggest hurdle to using a motorcycle is needing a Chinese license. International licenses are not accepted and they are pretty strict about that here in Xinjiang. I was stopped numerous times on my motorcycle and asked to present proper documentation.

I get a lot of people asking me about motorcycle rentals or driving their motorcycle from outside the country into China through Xinjiang. The answer to the first question is that as far as I know there is no place to rent a motorcycle despite the plethora places to buy one.

As far as driving your motorcycle - or any vehicle for that matter - across the border into Xinjiang, you need to arrange that ahead of time with a travel agency that can run all the paperwork for you. It's an expensive process, I'm sorry to say, but it is possible.

It's worth noting that some cities like Urumqi technically don't allow motorcycles on the road. Other cities like Kashgar are chock full of scooters, but have no place to formally rent them.

Bicycles

For tourists, renting a bicycle in smaller cities like Kashgar or Turpan can be done at most hostels and is a wonderful option. Urumqi isn't a very bike-friendly city and I have yet to find a hostel that rents bikes in the city.

For those who are biking across Xinjiang, all three of these cities (Urumqi, Kashgar, Turpan) offer a number of stores to supply you with tires and any maintenance tools you might need. For more information, see A Guide to Cycling in Xinjiang.

Safety Concerns

It may come as no surprise to you that the #1 question I am most frequently asked by travelers is in reference to safety. "Is it still safe to travel to Xinjiang?"

Some people tend to shy away from visiting Xinjiang on the basis of safety concerns. Oppression and ethnic conflict, the only two news items from the province to reach the international press, paint Xinjiang as a dangerous and crazy region. The truth is that all of the extra security in Xinjiang make it probably one of the safest places to travel in China.

Still, it is a good idea to be alert – not paranoid – about potential problems, and to take measures to ensure a safe trip to China. The following are a few ideas for travelers to Xinjiang or any other part of the country.

Watch!

xjtravelguide.com/
xinjiang-safety-video

- **Take care of your belongings:** The most common problem you are likely to face anywhere in China is that of theft. If you are traveling by train, never leave your luggage alone. While at the hotel, take all your valuables along with you when you leave. Pickpockets are also the norm, so watch your wallet and bring along a purse that can be zipped closed or a special passport pouch.

- **Over-identify yourself:** There are two primary ways in which the average traveler has noticed a change in Xinjiang since the riots of 2009: more military and more checkpoints. I recommend you keep a copy of your passport, visa, and the embassy contact numbers in case you need them, preferably in a different place than where you keep the actual documents. Carrying extra ID isn't necessary, but it doesn't hurt.
- **Watch where you point your camera:** The fastest way to get your camera confiscated or memory card wiped is to point it toward a group of military or police personnel. If you do run across any sort of protest or political gathering (which you probably won't!), resist the urge to pull out your camera.
- **It's hot, but be modest:** Although Xinjiang is predominantly Muslim, it is not necessary to fully cover your whole body and head when traveling. Be modest and you'll be fine.
- **Use common sense:** If it feels scary for you to walk outside at night, then don't. Chances are that in Xinjiang you'll be perfectly safe, but use common sense. Don't go out alone as a woman and keep your distance from any suspicious situations.

I also want to take a moment to address foreign travelers of Han Chinese ancestry. Many Han Chinese-appearing travelers have expressed concern over visiting predominantly Uyghur parts of Xinjiang, which I completely understand due to ethnic tensions.

I have not received any reports of Han-looking tourists being singled out over other tourists. What travelers do report is the feeling of being glared at or outright ignored, neither of which presents any sort of physical safety concern.

My advice is not only to use common sense but also to smile. This simple gesture is one that gets lost in the ethnic conflict between Han and Uyghur and is often disarming even to the most cynical of people.

Adventure
Travel

Hiking and Camping

As someone who loves the outdoors, I find it hard to resist the unadulterated, untamed natural beauty that Xinjiang offers. There are no dedicated campgrounds in Xinjiang, nor are there any published trail guides in English or Mandarin that I have found. It is simply nature at its best and (usually) least commercialized. It is possible to hike for days without another human being in sight.

Before I get into some of the ins and outs of enjoying the great outdoors in Xinjiang, let's get a few very important points out of the way:

- **Unregistered lodging is illegal:** According to Chinese law, foreigners must be registered with the local authorities for every night they reside in China. This means that unless you are being accompanied by or permitted through a local tourist agency, you are technically supposed to register with the police wherever you sleep.
- **Xinjiang is not leisure-camping friendly:** There are no "campgrounds" as you may find in other parts of the world. If you've never set up your tent in the wilderness where bathroom facilities and electricity are unavailable, Xinjiang might not be the best place for you to start. There are no "park rangers" who are a phone call away to help when you're in trouble.

- **Xinjiang is still sensitive:** There are a number of stories told about hikers who have accidentally stumbled upon military installations in Xinjiang. This is possible and you need to be observant wherever you go, particularly near the border.

If this has not successfully discouraged you from hiking and camping in Xinjiang, congratulations! Read on.

Camping/Hiking Gear

The Xinjiang outdoor industry is young but is quickly growing in popularity. Hiking groups, comprised of mostly Han Chinese, have sprung up over the past decade and the industry has grown up with them to accommodate their needs.

There are a number of small outdoor stores south of the People's Square in Urumqi that sell all sorts of camping gear, ranging from compasses to tents, fuel tanks to sleeping bags. The gear isn't cheap, though, so the better option is to bring your own if possible.

Note: Keep in mind that due to Xinjiang's heightened security, you won't be allowed to take fuel tanks on buses and trains. You either need to take private transportation to get to your trailhead or purchase your fuel near your destination. I have found fuel sold at outdoor stores in Urumqi, Kashgar, Yili and Buerjin. Ask around for a 户外店/Hùwài diàn, the stores where these will most likely be found.

To rent camping gear, there is a place in Urumqi near Hong Shan Park that rents out sleeping bags (10 RMB/day), tents (15 RMB/day) and sleeping pads (5 RMB/day) on a first-come first-serve basis. The small shop is located on the western side of Youhao Road across the street from the China Southern Hotel. Most of the sign is in Chinese but in the upper-right hand corner you'll see English that says "Outdoor Equipment".

Best Places to Hike

The list of places to hike in Xinjiang are truly endless. I have personally set up my tent at the base of Muzataghata, a mountain along the Karakoram Highway, as well as within the sand dunes of the Kumtagh Desert. Be cautious, though: after a decade in Xinjiang I have an intimate knowledge of this place and, at least according to my wife, I'm a little bit crazy.

The biggest hurdle you'll face when hiking and camping in Xinjiang is getting to and from your start point. For this reason, my list below will hone in on the locations that have transportation naturally built in: tourist-friendly parks and lakes.

- **Heavenly Lake Nature Preserve:** The area around Heavenly Lake offers some beautiful hiking without having to travel too far. The park is 1.5 hours from Urumqi and once you're inside you're free to roam all around the lake, up the mountains and through the various valleys.
- **NanShan Scenic Area:** Equally close by Urumqi is NanShan, a place which can accommodate both day and overnight hikes. Buses and taxis to and from Urumqi make the area accessible and it's not hard to find a path that has already been used by either local herdsmen or previous travelers.
- **Kanas Lake Nature Preserve:** The Kanas Lake Nature Preserve is massive - far bigger than you'll ever have time to hike. Within the preserve, the best places to hike are around the lake to the north, toward Baihaba Village to the west or toward Black Lake and Hemu Village in the east.
- **Keketuohai National Park:** Paved roads can get you a good distance into the park, providing plenty of opportunity to hike from there.
- **Karakul Lake:** The area around Karakul is ripe for hiking. Although the lake itself is small and won't take long to circumnavigate, the nearby hills provide an excellent view of the lake, village and Muztaghata mountain. Speaking of which, hiking up toward Base Camp at Muztaghata has been another great option for experienced hikers, although you technically need a permit once you hit the base of the mountain. Note: Local police have explicitly asked me to hike on the east side of the highway and to avoid the west side that begins to run up against the Tajikistan border.
- **Ili Grasslands:** Whether you're at Narat (Nalati), Bayinbulak, or any of the other smaller grasslands throughout Ili, there is plenty of opportunity to explore and find a place to set up camp. Officially, you're supposed to stay near the locally-owned yurts, which will likely ask you to pay a fee.
- **Sayram Lake/Fruit Valley:** On the way to Yining City, you can stop to hike around Sayram Lake and the nearby Fruit Valley. Both offer incredible views and camping opportunities without veering too far away from the highway and civilization.

None of these locations have trails which are officially marked or pre-arranged campsites. Also, this is a very limited array of options that doesn't even begin to cover the breadth of Xinjiang's hiking opportunities. I encourage you to explore or even hire a tour guide to take you to a secluded area to hike as long as it's still permitted.

Tips for Successful Camping

As I mentioned earlier, unregistered lodging is illegal for foreigners in China, so anything you decide to do is at your own risk. Camping happens all over China without consequence for foreigners, but the fact that this is Xinjiang means there is a stronger adherence to the letter of the law and therefore always risk involved.

The best way to avoid trouble is to avoid contact with other people. Setting up camp right next to the lake shore (unless that's acceptable, as is the case at Sayram Lake) or in the middle of a pasture is an invitation for somebody to come find you and tell you to leave. Taking a few extra minutes to hike further in and find a secluded place to camp will be worth the time.

Speaking of people finding you, don't be surprised if some locals come to you claiming to own the land you've set up camp on (they don't) and demanding some sort of fee. You're welcome to fight the extortion, as I have tried, but they always have one advantage over you: they can call on the local-friendly authorities to forcibly remove you. Sometimes it's worth the 50 RMB to pacify them or if you have time, just move camp.

Before you even leave the big city, whether that be Urumqi, Kashgar or any others, make sure that you are fully stocked up with all the food and water you'll need for the entire trip. Grocery stores in the small towns near all of the above-mentioned parks won't have everything you need. Once you actually enter the parks, everything, including water, is triple or quadruple the regular price.

I recommend that all outdoor lovers be careful about using a professional GPS system within Xinjiang. Now that smartphones can double as a GPS, it's best to use this instead of a dedicated GPS unit, although both could get you in trouble. In 2011, one foreigner was fined US$3,000 while hiking in Xinjiang for "illegal surveying activities." In reality, he was just using a GPS unit to make sure he didn't get lost but that's not how the authorities saw it. My advice is to avoid the risk altogether.

Finally, and MOST IMPORTANT, please don't attempt anything for which you are not qualified. There's no embarrassment in hiring an experienced, local guide. In fact, I highly recommend it. Every year there are reports of people who attempt outdoor activities in Xinjiang without the proper experience or equipment and end up losing a limb or even their life. This happens to both foreigners and Chinese alike, so don't think that you're exempt.

Homestays in Xinjiang

←――――――――――――――――――→

Some of my best memories have come as a guest in the home of a local here in Xinjiang. Not only does it provide a rare glimpse into the local culture unavailable at a hotel, it is also a wonderful chance to get to know the people here on a more personal level.

The problem with a homestay in Xinjiang is the same problem presented by camping: foreigners must be registered wherever they stay the night. Registering isn't difficult, but you always run the risk that the local authorities decide you can only stay in a hotel, which has happened to me a number of times. It's the classic dilemma of choosing permission or forgiveness.

Certain parts of Xinjiang are more sensitive than others, so while I've been able to do a homestay in the Ili or Turpan areas, I've never been able to stay at a local home in Kashgar due to the higher security of the region.

This leaves you with two primary options for a homestay in Xinjiang:

- **Tourist-Friendly Homes:** This category includes all of the yurts in the grasslands and log cabins in the Altay villages. Authorities may or may not come by to request a look at your passport, but these are recognized as official tourist lodging and there is very little chance that you'll be asked to leave.

- **Agency-Approved Homes:** Many of the local agencies listed in the Approved Tourist Agencies portion of this book are capable of setting up a homestay for travelers. These are usually traditional homes that are still being lived in that allow you the opportunity to experience life with the locals. In many cases, expect to sleep on a hard bed under the stars and use an outhouse. Also, don't be surprised to learn that a homestay isn't allowed anymore - these regulations change regularly.

For those who are coming to Xinjiang on an invitation from a friend, you'll want to have this friend accompany you to the local police station to present your official identification. They will likely ask you where you're staying, how many days you will be here and the purpose of your visit. Whether they permit you to stay is up to the official's discretion, but you won't help matters by arguing an unfavorable decision. The best tools you have at your disposal are your smile, your ignorance and your willingness to cooperate.

Camel Treks

A desert camel trek into one of Xinjiang's deserts is a memorable and thankfully simple adventure to arrange. From Turpan all the way to Kashgar, there are a number of picturesque sand dunes to choose from.

While it's possible to pay for a short ride or picture on a camel, many travelers ask about overnight treks into the desert. These treks usually involve hiring a guide along with multiple camels used to transport your party and all your gear. They can last from a single night to a full week or more depending on where you want to go.

Costs for this kind of desert adventure can add up quick, but here's a basic breakdown: camels are usually rented out at a rate of around 300 RMB/day, and 3-4 camels are required for every 2 people depending on the length of the journey. Additionally, a camel guide is required for every 4 camels which usually cost about 200 RMB/day.

Once you factor in the cost of private transportation to the desert, which can range from 500-1200 RMB round trip from a major city, you can see why this isn't a cheap adventure.

However, having participated in an overnight camel trek, I can tell you that it's an excellent adventure that makes for incredible pictures and a great story to tell your grandkids one day!

It is possible to enter the desert at literally thousands of points all around the Taklamakan and Kumtag deserts in Xinjiang, but for the average traveler there are only a couple places I recommend to begin a camel trek.

Kumtagh Desert at Shanshan

Approximately two hours east of Turpan, the little town of Shanshan rests beside sand dunes whose towering size and scope rival those of Dunhuang in neighboring Gansu province.

Considering its relative convenience and beauty, this is probably the best place to consider any kind of camel trek. All it takes is about 3km before you're surrounded on all sides by sand dunes.

You'll need to pay an entrance fee for the Sand Dunes Park but they can help you connect with a camel herder and rent you a tent for the day. I had the camels drop my group off for the evening and then pick us up in the morning.

Taklamakan Desert in Hotan

Equally impressive are the endless sand dunes of the Taklamakan Desert near Hotan. The only downside is the time and expense required to get there.

From here travelers can follow the footsteps of explorers like Aurel Stein and Sven Hedin, both of whom spent months in these desert sands excavating ancient cities. While you probably won't be able to visit these ancient ruins (see Ancient Cities Surrounding Hotan for why) you'll still get to experience life in a desert.

There is no entrance fee for this portion of the Taklamakan Desert, but hiring a private car from Hotan is quoted at least 1000-1200 RMB round trip for a sedan.

Taklamakan Desert near Kashgar

Finally, I'll mention the portion of the desert most easily accessible from Kashgar. It's not quite as picturesque as what you'll find near Hotan but it's more convenient.

The Dawakul Lake Desert Park is located 130km southeast of Kashgar, which takes a little less than two hours' drive. The area has been heavily commercialized but they do offer an authentic camel experience and camels that are always ready for tourists.

A Guide to Cycling in Xinjiang

Over the past few years, cycling has become my favorite mode of transport here in Xinjiang, despite it being slow and inefficient.

Due to Xinjiang's sheer size, long-distance cycling should only be attempted by those experienced and well-equipped. However, that doesn't mean that the casual cyclist can't enjoy a unique travel experience in the region.

Cycling for the Casual Cyclist

Whether you're bringing your own bike or renting a bike once you get here, the biggest hurdle for the casual cyclist is transporting the bicycle.

For instance, you can rent a bike in Kashgar, but it's difficult to get it on public transportation to Tashkorgan in order to cycle down the Karakoram Highway. The alternative - cycling UP the Karakoram Highway - is quite daunting!

So where does that leave you? At this point, you're left with either day trips from a single point of origin or working with a travel company to arrange a support vehicle. It's not a cheap option, but you can connect with a local travel agency to get a quote.

Cycling for the Serious Cyclist

By Eleanor Moseman

Xinjiang is surely one of the most exhilarating, exciting, and most diverse provinces of China to cycle through. You can spend weeks in vast and empty deserts such as the Taklamakan and the edge of the Gobi, venture to the contrasting mountains of the Altay region, Tianshan range, Tashkorgan, or skim the Kunlun Mountains that separate Xinjiang from mystical Tibet.

As a cyclist, your two major concerns will be dealing with authorities and water supplies, while winds will follow these 2 issues closely.

It is legally required to be registered with a police station every night when traveling through China. There may be moments you find an unmarked police car following you through towns and then escorting you to the edge and encouraging you to continue on your way. There have been people removed from camping in the desert during the middle of the night to be relocated to a hotel room or sleep in a police station. It is also possible that police may request money for breaking the laws. In some of these cases they have been known to take the offender's photograph and demand their signature on papers acknowledging their crime with verbal threat that they will be reported to Beijing authorities.

Be prepared for police checkpoints where you will be asked for your passport. If you hold a Work and/or Residence Visa, this will help you move through some areas without difficulty. It's recommended you keep note of any politically sensitive areas and stay away from these areas to avoid trouble.

If camping is your only option, it's recommended to get as far from towns, cities, and out of the sight of people (for more, see the chapter on Hiking and Camping). Sometimes it may just be best to sleep under the highways and in culverts to avoid being noticed by the authorities. Also, be aware that the winds can really pick up so take care when breaking down your tent and setting up, as a good gust can have you running and leaping over sand dunes to retain your home for the future.

Coming from Central Asia to China, you will notice a drastic change in local hospitality. Don't count on locals to house or feed you and always be prepared to find lodging for the evening on your own.

Ideally, travel with at least 3 days of water. You can generally find water once a day, but if you were to be hit by a sand or wind storm, this could stop you in your tracks for a day without being able to replenish your water supply.

Depending on your direction and route, winds can be a huge factor throughout the journey. Winds can slow you down to cycling at 4km/hour and the peak times of the day for these winds seem to be between 4-11pm.

Along the southern Silk Road route, there is the old road that runs parallel to the newly paved highway of G315 where you can cycle without any traffic. Sometimes this is a good option if you need to cycle through the night to make up distance after spending the afternoon with headwinds.

Cycling G315 could be one of your greatest stretches of road throughout your tour. The tarmac is smooth and black without a lot of traffic. Be very aware of speeding vehicles that would cause instant death if you were to collide with one. The closer you get to Kashgar on this road, specifically from Hotan, the traffic gets extremely hectic and sometimes seeing 5 lines of traffic on a two-lane road ranging from tanker trucks, cars, buses, motorcycles and donkey carts.

Kashgar and Urumqi both have excellent bike shops and you can find the locations by talking to locals employed at hostels, other cyclists residing there or find an address online through Giant bicycles website (Mandarin). Most employees can't speak English, but basic hand gestures will work and you should be able to find all basic supplies and tools.

Most cyclists attempt to cross from China to Kyrgyzstan along A371. You must get your Passport Exit Stamp approximately 160 km east of the China border. The city is called "Wuqia" and you must go through the Exit/Entry Station. You will be required to load your bicycle in a truck or some other mode of transportation to get it to the border crossing with Kyrgyzstan. Because the truck drivers do not care about the safety of your bicycle and gear, I would personally recommend finding a small group and hiring a truck or taxi service to drive you to the border. There is no way to avoid this government enforced policy; you will not be allowed to cycle to the border.

This crossing is closed on the weekends and there is very little to purchase in regard to supplies at the border. I suggest that you carry 3 days' worth of supplies. This should get you to Sary-Tash, Kyrgyzstan if the weather is good.

Coming from Kyrgyzstan into China, trying to get your Chinese visa in Bishkek has caused a lot of trouble for cyclists over the past few years. It's recommended that if you plan on crossing into China along A371 from Bishkek, that you obtain your visa ahead of time. The Chinese Embassy is very sensitive to tourists, especially cyclists, coming over the border into a politically sensitive province.

Xinjiang can be one of the most splendid places to cycle but the first rule to follow would be to avoid police and authorities as this could change your adventure drastically.

About Eleanor: Eleanor Moseman cycled China and Central Asia from 2010-2012. She traversed over 1,500 miles through Xinjiang and spent an additional 6 months living with and photographing Uyghur life.

www.eleanormoseman.com

A Guide to Snow Skiing

By Siv Sears

◄──────────────►

Xinjiang, being a mountainous region in the cold north of China, is well suited to skiing and snowboarding. While resorts and facilities are not quite on the scale of Europe or North America (even the biggest Xinjiang resorts have less than 15 km of pistes), some decent options exist with a range of challenges available.

Silk Road and Altay resorts rank among the top ten skiing areas in China. The Silk Road and Tianchi resorts even hosted ski and snowboarding events for the 2016 national winter games.

At all the resorts below, skiers and snowboarders can rent equipment and clothing on site. A set of pants and jacket is usually 20 RMB while helmets are around 10 RMB. Goggles, hats and gloves are available to buy at slightly inflated cost compared in the city.

Resorts are open from late November to late March; Silk Road is usually open a couple of weeks later than Heavenly Lake and Altay. Some tougher pistes (ski runs) are only open in December.

丝绸之路国际度假区
Sīchóuzhīlù Guójì Dùjiàqū

Price: 200-400 元
(0991) 591-1111

Silk Road International Ski Resort

As an Urumqi resident, Silk Road is the core of my winter sports experience. A 40-minute drive or 1-hour bus ride out of Urumqi to Nanshan, this resort has established itself as the number one option for winter sports in the Urumqi area. The resort, set within the mountains of Nanshan, hosted the skiing events for the 2016 national winter games and some ultra-modern buildings have been erected close by to host events such as curling and ice-hockey. There is also a good and growing community of both skiers and snowboarders here.

Clothing, equipment and ski pass for a full day will cost 200-300 RMB as long as you don't go during Spring Festival. Accommodations range from windowless twins to piste-side 12-berth wooden cabins equipped with wifi and hot showers (230 RMB - 1,580 RMB). Rooms are usually available upon arrival at the resort, but you may want to book ahead by calling them on weekends or holidays. A cabin for New Year or Christmas is a good option.

Public buses with just 2 or 3 stops run up at 9:40am from the Huanghe Road bus stop in Urumqi (黄河路) until between 4pm and 6pm from the resort, time depending on the month. The bus will cost 12 RMB each way while the journey takes about 70 minutes.

Altay Ski Resort

From just 60 RMB for a whole days skiing (10:30-18:00) and return flights from Urumqi costing as little as 300 RMB, Altay is worth considering for a ski trip. The resort is on a par with Silk Road for quality, and it is close to Altay City with its cheap hotel options. This place really is a winner.

> 阿勒泰将军山滑雪
> Ālēitài Jiāngjūnshān Huáxuěchǎng
> **Price:** 60 元
> (0906) 213-9999

The airport is only a 20-minute cab ride away from the resort. Hit the pistes a stone's throw away from Kazakhstan, Mongolia and Russia up in the far northwest tip of China. Night skiing is available. I highly recommended it either as a change from the norm back in Urumqi or as a dedicated trip destination.

Ground has just been broken on a new 500 million RMB ski resort near Altay that will be vying for the title of "Best in Asia." While it won't be able to compete with the powder in Japan, it will be interesting to see what size of resort will result.

Tianshan Tianchi International Ski Field

It takes about 1.5 hours to get from Urumqi to the Tianchi Ski Resort, which is located just below the famous Heavenly Lake. While smaller than the Silk Road Resort, this place is up and coming and hosted the snowboarding events for the 2016 National Winter Games.

> 天山天池国际滑雪场
> Tiānshān Tiānchí Guójì Huáxuěchǎng
> **Price:** 150-250 元
> (0906) 323-1238

Free private buses run to the resort and back every day of the week from outside of the Hongshan and Ergong stadiums (红山体育馆 Hóngshān Tǐyùguǎn). No need to book ahead; just show up. The bus can take your board or skis if bringing your own. Full day passes cost about 150 RMB weekdays, 200 RMB weekends. Accommodations are available.

Other Skiing Options

It is worth pointing out that there are numerous smaller, cheaper resorts around Xinjiang. Urumqi has at least four within the city itself; the one at West spa (维斯特 0991-488-6088) is the best of the bunch. Karamay, for example, also has its own small piste. Each of these smaller resorts offer a very rudimentary ski experience, can be very crowded and are mostly full of first-timers falling over.

Other Adventure Options

In addition to hiking, camping, cycling and skiing, there are a number of different adventure options available in Xinjiang. Most are either cost- or time-prohibitive, but I want to at least list them for your consideration.

Mountain Climbing

A number of different sizable and difficult mountains within Xinjiang present a formidable challenge for even the most experienced mountaineer. Whether you want to climb Muztaghata near the Karakoram Highway, Bogda near Urumqi or K2 along the Pakistani border, you'll need to connect with a travel agency to arrange the appropriate permits and equipment that you'll need (see the list of Approved Xinjiang Travel Agencies).

Locals maintain that the fatality rate on many of these mountains is higher than average. Although I can't verify this, those seeking to climb Xinjiang's mountains should heed the warnings and make sure to connect with a reputable, experienced agency to make the climb.

Costs start at US$2,000 and quickly go up for such expeditions, depending on the mountain and your equipment needs.

River rafting (Ili, Altay, Hotan)

River rafting is a little-known adventure activity for which reliable information is hard to find. Some of these areas, such as Kanas and Bayinbulak are set up to accommodate limited rafting for tourists (far from "whitewater"), while other places, such as the river near Hotan is extremely hard to arrange.

A few groups have brought in their own rafting equipment. Before you consider such a trip, make sure you contact a local travel agency first.

Paragliding / Parasailing

Finally, you may run across the opportunity to do paragliding near Kanas Lake, which was home to the 2012 National Paragliding Championships. Paragliding can be a challenge to arrange. There are clubs that come here from across the country, but it's best to attempt to arrange any such adventures through a local agency.

Parasailing around Urumqi's NanShan, on the other hand, is much easier. Parasailing caters to the tourists who want a quick adrenaline rush and will cost at least 100 RMB or more.

Traveler Tips

Staying Connected in Xinjiang

One of the things I love most about Xinjiang is the sense of adventure that comes from being in such a remote part of the world. This is also something that gives me (and my family) the most grief. Whether you want to make a simple phone call or access the internet, things are a bit different here in Xinjiang.

Using a Cell Phone

Unless your cell phone from home is unlocked, you won't be able to use it here in China. And if you don't know what I mean when I say "unlocked," then chances are it probably isn't. Check with your local carrier to determine roaming rates and to find out whether or not you can unlock your phone to use a cheaper China SIM card.

Most China Mobile or China Unicom stores will sell you a phone or SIM card to use in Xinjiang but the purchase will require a copy of your passport and about an hour of your time. What you can do is purchase a pre-paid China SIM card to put in your phone. You'll be required to submit a copy of your passport for verification, but it's much easier to do this than to try to get a SIM card upon arrival.

www.xjtravelguide.com/china-sim-card

The good news is that cell coverage is amazing throughout Xinjiang. I've been in remote villages or hiking in the mountains and maintained a good signal. However, what you're able to do with the internet is restricted by the powers that be.

The Internet: What Works and What Doesn't

China is famous for its censorship of the internet, censorship that bans access to sites like Facebook, Instagram, Twitter, Youtube, Gmail and many, many more.... including FarWestChina.com! In addition to this censorship, the Xinjiang region also suffers from slower internet speeds than the rest of the country. Believe it or not, you can live life without social media and email for a couple weeks, but I completely understand if you don't want to.

Skype has been hit-or-miss over the past year. FaceTime and iMessage can work well at times but are unreliable.

Bottom line: If staying connected via email or VoIP is a priority for you, you have two options:

1. **Download WeChat**, a popular messaging service that isn't blocked in China. You can message, voice call and video call through the app. Unfortunately, you'll have to convince everybody else who you want to stay in contact with to download WeChat as well.
2. **Get a VPN** (Virtual Private Network) so that you can use reliably use Skype and FaceTime. See my recommendations below. Watch a video explanation:

www.xjtravelguide.com/what-is-vpn

Virtual Private Networks

The first thing I always tell people who are either traveling or moving out here to Xinjiang is to consider investing in a Virtual Private Network, better known as a "VPN". This is helpful all over China but especially so here in Xinjiang.

A VPN allows you to tunnel past the censorship to access sites that are blocked in China both on your computer and your phone. It's quite simple to set up, even if you're not "tech-savvy," and trust me when I say that it's worth the $5-$10 per month.

Personally, I recommend either ExpressVPN or NordVPN as reliable options here in Xinjiang. Check out both options here:

- **ExpressVPN**: www.xjtravelguide.com/expressvpn
- **NordVPN:** www.xjtravelguide.com/nordvpn

Money Issues

Xinjiang uses the Chinese Renminbi (shortened to RMB) as its currency of exchange. You'll notice as you travel around China that cash quickly being replaced by the rise of mobile payments, the most popular of which are WeChat and Alipay. Payment is as simple as scanning your phone!

Unfortunately, the current reality is that mobile payment isn't available for foreign travelers. Setup requires a Chinese bank account, which is time prohibitive and not worth the effort. This leaves you with pretty much one option: cash.

Most shops, hotels and restaurants throughout Xinjiang don't accept Visa or MasterCard. Thankfully, there are a few other options you have to choose from:

- **Bank ATM Machines:** Bank ATMs are plentiful throughout every city and most will allow you to withdraw money using a Visa or MasterCard for a small fee (plus whatever your bank at home charges you). This, in my opinion, is the best way to obtain cash while traveling in Xinjiang. Depending on the bank, you will be allowed to withdraw between 2,000 to 3,000 RMB per day.

- **UnionPay Card:** While Visa and MasterCard aren't accepted in Xinjiang, UnionPay is accepted *everywhere*. For those travelers from the U.S.A. who are interested, there is an option to receive a pre-paid UnionPay card through a company known as eCard. You can add a balance to the card through your US bank and then use the card to pay for things directly or get a better ATM exchange rate than your Visa/MasterCard. This is a newer option that I've really enjoyed using this past year. Apply for free here:

www.xjtravelguide.com/ecard

- **Exchanging Cash:** Exchanging cash can be done at the Urumqi Airport, although if you arrive too early in the morning or late at night the kiosk may not be open. An alternative solution is to make your way to the Bank of China near Urumqi's People's Square or the one near NanMen in Urumqi. Before you even reach the doors of the bank you'll have money changers asking you if you want to change your dollars for yuan. It seems shady but if you know a fair exchange rate before you arrive it can be a quick and painless transaction. Otherwise, exchange your cash inside the bank.

Visa Issues | FAQ

In regard to visas and permits, there are a number of common questions that I receive on a weekly basis that I want to cover here.

Do I need a special permit to enter Xinjiang?

No, you don't. Prior to your arrival in Xinjiang, make sure to have your passport and Chinese visa in order, but other than that there are no additional permits or fees for entering Xinjiang (unlike Tibet).

Should I mention my trip to Xinjiang on my China visa application?

Some travelers suggest that any mention of your planned visit to Xinjiang be omitted when applying for your Chinese visa. There seems to be some merit to this thought, even though the Chinese government would never admit to discriminating against travelers to Xinjiang.

Put Xinjiang on your itinerary or not - it's completely your call. That said, there will be no one at your port of entry in Xinjiang asking to see your official itinerary. If you come to China and decide on a whim to make a trip to Xinjiang, your Chinese visa gives you the right to do so.

Can I do a visa extension in Xinjiang?

While you are in Xinjiang, any Chinese visa problems or visa extension requests should be directed to the Public Security Bureau. Xinjiang does not have consulates for the United States, the United Kingdom, Australia or any other "western" country, so any such passport problems will need to be addressed elsewhere within China.

Where do I get visas to travel into Xinjiang's bordering countries?

Arrangements will need to be made either prior to your arrival or in the case of Kazakhstan or Kyrgyzstan, while you're in Urumqi. The closest embassies will be in Beijing.

Do your homework before you arrive. Many Central Asian countries such as Kazakhstan and Kyrgyzstan are now offering VOA (Visa on Arrival) for many passports, so you may not even need to get a visa.

- **Pakistan:** The closest embassy is in Beijing and can be reached by phone at (010) 6523-3504 or you can find information on their website in English here: www.pakbj.org

- **Tajikistan:** The closest embassy is in Beijing and can be reached by phone at (010) 6532-2598 or you can find information on their website (Mandarin / Tajik only) here: www.tajikembassychina.org
- **Kazakhstan:** While there is a Kazakhstan Visa Office in Urumqi, visas require at least 4-5 days to process. I recommend you try to work out your visa at the embassies in Beijing or Shanghai prior to arrival. The Urumqi visa office (哈萨克斯坦驻乌鲁木齐签证代办点) is located on 216 Kunming Rd next to the large, black Yuma building. You can try to call them at (0991) 381-5796 but they rarely answer the phone.
- **Kyrgyzstan:** The closest Kyrgyz embassy is located in Beijing and although I've heard there is a visa office here in Urumqi, I have yet to find it. The Beijing Embassy can be reached at (010) 6468-1348.

If you need a visa and would rather avoid the headache of contacting the embassy or driving to the nearest consulate, I have used and trust Passport Visas Express:

www.xjtravelguide.com/passport-visa-express

Souvenirs

←——————————————————→

While you're in Xinjiang, no doubt you're going to want to pick up a few souvenirs to remember your journey. Places to buy such souvenirs are usually limited to tourist sites and markets, although I prefer small shops with homemade handcrafts when possible. Here is my suggestion: if you see something you like, buy it when you see it. Chances are you won't find it again. Here are some souvenirs I recommend.

Yengisar Knife

Watch!

xjtravelguide.com/
yengisar-knife

The Yengisar Knife is one of the most popular souvenirs from Xinjiang. Originally handcrafted by the Uyghur people near the small town of Yengisar, the sad truth is that most of what you'll see in the big markets is now mass-produced in a factory. A single stall will usually carry between 100-500 different versions of these knives, so there are plenty of options.

WARNING: Taking these knives onto buses, trains and sometimes even within your checked luggage on an airplane is strictly forbidden. For this reason, these knives are often hard to get home. Some sellers at the Urumqi International Grand Bazaar can ship them internationally, but it's not guaranteed that it will make it through customs.

Suggested Price: Small: 20-40 RMB; Large 50-500 RMB.

Uyghur Musical Instruments

You will find quite a few different varieties of Uyghur musical instruments, but the most popular is the rawap, a long-necked stringed piece similar to a number of different Central Asian instruments. These wooden instruments can be either 3-stringed (ancient practice) or 5-stringed (modern practice) and usually have an animal skin covering the sound box.

In addition to the rawap, you can also find a dutar (2-stringed lute), a dap (beautifully decorated drum) or a variety of other instruments. Each of these traditional instruments can be purchased as a small tourist trinket or as an actual, playable instrument. Pricing matches quality.

Suggested Price: Varies greatly depending on quality and size.

Dopa Hats

Wherever you travel in Xinjiang you are bound to run into a number of Uyghur men wearing a hat known as a "dopa" or "doppa." They are usually brightly colored and embroidered with beautiful beads. They have come to be known as a symbol of the Uyghur people and are easily acquired at most markets.

The best part is that they are collapsible for easy transport. These hats are not a symbol of Islam, although most people who wear them are Muslim.

Suggested Price: 20-50 RMB.

Raisins, Nuts and Fruits

Xinjiang is well known for its delicious nuts and fruits, and it's amazing to see how many different colors of raisins are available! Open-air stalls are great to pick up snacks for a long trip, while grocery stores offer great packaged goods that can make it across international borders. Don't purchase these at a transportation hub (airport, train station, etc.) where the prices are inflated two to three times or more.

Suggested Price: 2-10 RMB per kilogram.

Silk and Carpets

The carpets and silk products of Xinjiang are valued for their artistic design and craftsmanship. Stores selling carpets can be found primarily around Kashgar, Hotan and the southwestern region of Xinjiang, although there are stores selling carpets around Urumqi's International Bazaar and Erdaoqiao Market. Many of the cheaper carpets you'll find are actually produced outside the country, unfortunately, but it is still possible to locate authentic, handmade Xinjiang carpets.

As for silk, a variety of products are available in all of the markets across the region. The colorful atlas pattern is popular among the Uyghur people and can be found on dresses, scarves, and decor.

Suggested Price: Pricing varies based on size and quality.

Hotan Jade

Stores all across Xinjiang sell intricate carvings of Hotan's most famous export: jade. Jade is best known for its light green shade, although there are numerous varieties, the most valuable of which is white jade. Be wary of street sellers who are likely hawking fake rocks; stick with the larger, more reputable markets if authenticity is your priority. Due to high demand, Hotan jade can be extremely expensive, even in Hotan city itself.

Suggested Price: 200 RMB for a small piece up to tens of thousands of RMB.

Xinjiang Pottery

As you walk around the Old City in Kashgar, particularly on the eastern edge of the city, you'll notice some colorful pottery on display. Most of this pottery is handmade and hand-painted, making it an excellent gift to bring home. I've learned the hard way that these pieces can break easily during travel, so you'll want to pack it carefully.

Suggested Price: 20-100 RMB.

Bargaining in Xinjiang

Bargaining is a necessary part of shopping here in Xinjiang. In general, vendors in Xinjiang might raise the price slightly because you are a foreigner, but not to the absurd extent that you'll find in larger tourist cities like Beijing or Shanghai. You are expected to participate in bargaining as a natural part of the purchasing process.

The most common way to bargain among locals here is to simply ask "Is that the lowest price?" A smile can help the process tremendously; arguing can shut down negotiations altogether.

The best advice I ever received about bargaining in China was this: determine what you're willing to pay. Be willing to walk away if the seller doesn't budge and be satisfied if they do. Finally, and most importantly, never, ever, EVER respond when somebody later asks you "So how much did you pay for that?" Nothing kills the satisfaction of a purchase faster than the feeling that you've been swindled and if you're satisfied with the price you got, then you weren't swindled!

How to Use Public Transportation

I'm not going to try to sugarcoat it...public transportation throughout Xinjiang sucks in general. As with most areas around China, the cars are numerous, taxis are too few, roads are unkept and buses are too old.

To make matters worse, unless you can read Chinese characters, using public transport can be challenging. Public buses don't post their schedules in English or Pinyin.

Here's a quick tip: I highly recommend you download the free Baidu map app on your phone (search "Baidu map" in iOS and Android). If you can pinpoint where you're headed - and the app often does accept English searches for locations - it will tell you which number buses can get you there.

It's not 100% accurate based on my experience, but for most travelers it will work wonders and it is far more reliable than trying to use Google Maps or Apple Maps, both of which are blocked in China.

Subway/Metro - Urumqi only

Starting in late 2018, Urumqi christened its first subway line that runs from the airport all the way to the south of the city in a north-south direction. It's the fastest way to get into the center of the city, particularly during rush hour, but it does get packed.

Unlike the rest of China, the Urumqi metro system runs on a real-name ticketing system. That means that in order to purchase a ticket, you'll need to show your passport at the ticket window. It's inconvenient as a foreign traveler, since the automatic teller machines don't read passports.

As of 2019, there is only one metro line, although they are aggressively building more over the next decade.

Bus Rapid Transit (BRT) - Urumqi only

Until all subway lines are completed in Urumqi, the best form of public transportation in the city is the BRT bus system. The cost is just 1 RMB per person and since these buses often have dedicated lanes, traffic usually isn't an issue. The only issue, especially during rush hour, is an overcrowded bus.

My suggestion is that if you're going to be making a long jaunt across town, check to see if the BRT goes anywhere near where you're headed and try to use it. One way to do this would be to type in "BRT-1," "BRT-2," "BRT-3," "BRT-5," or "BRT-7" in the Baidu map app mentioned above. Maps are also posted at each BRT station.

Note: Before entering a BRT station, be prepared to open your bag for a security officer to check. Currently, no liquids of any kind are allowed.

City Buses

City buses in every city throughout Xinjiang are also just 1 RMB per person and reach most any place you'd want to go. Buses don't give change so make sure you keep plenty of 1 RMB notes handy if you plan to take the bus often.

I never rely on the city buses to get me somewhere on time but in some cases, they will be your only option if taxis are hard to find.

Taxis & Black Taxis

Taxis are usually the fastest way to get from point A to point B. The difficulty, at times, is finding one.

When you hail a taxi, make sure you have the driver start the meter, which start at 5-15 RMB depending on the city. Legally, they are supposed to start the meter for each trip but there are instances, especially in the evenings, when a taxi driver will attempt to negotiate a price. Stand your ground and if they don't budge, your only recourse is to threaten to leave and write down their information posted on the dashboard.

In certain parts of the city or at certain times of the day, official taxis are a rare commodity. In this case you'll probably have a lot of cars honking at you or blinking their headlights if they see you on the side of the road. These cars come in many shapes and colors but are collectively referred to as "black taxis". Technically they're illegal but practically, they are indispensable.

Wave them down and they'll drop their window to ask where you're headed. This is important: Tell them where you want to go and then ask how much they'll charge. You must get the price negotiated before you jump in the car or you're just asking for problems down the road.

Cultural Sensitivity

As a foreign tourist, the expectations in terms of your cultural IQ aren't high and most of the time you'll be forgiven for any mistakes you make. However, you can earn a high level of respect from locals by honoring their culture and religious practices.

Below are just a few of the best ways that you can display your cultural sensitivity toward the people of Xinjiang.

Understanding Islam in Xinjiang

Starting in the 11th century, Islam began to spread through Xinjiang at a rapid pace. In Xinjiang today, Islam could be considered more of a cultural identity than a religion but interestingly it is not a uniting force.

In other words, the Islamic identity of a Uyghur Muslim doesn't necessarily signify a kinship with Kazakh Muslims or Hui Muslims. Mosques are often segregated along ethnic lines and while inter-ethnic marriages happen, they aren't the norm.

Even the Uyghur in the north of Xinjiang differ greatly from the Uyghur in Xinjiang's south. Often, the only outward sign of similarity between Muslims of different ethnic groups in Xinjiang is their refusal to eat pork or anything else that isn't "halal", although the even the definition of what is halal is debated.

As a traveler, this means that you shouldn't assume that all expressions of Islamic faith in Xinjiang are the same. Be prepared to see Muslim men smoke and drink at the bar.

Respecting the Mosque

Entering a place of worship, no matter where you are in the world, can be a tricky thing. Xinjiang and its mosques are no different.

There have been a number of times when I, a conservatively-dressed man, have been respectfully asked not to enter or point my camera at a mosque. Through multiple experiences like these, I have learned to be sensitive to the locals, many of whom already feel like their times of worship have been invaded by too much oversight.

There are a number of mosques in Xinjiang that generate income from tourists and having foreigners walking around is common. They allow women to enter, except during Friday prayers, and normally won't even make a fuss about their attire.

To be respectful, it is recommended that you try to dress modestly or at least bring something to cover up while you are inside the mosque. When entering any prayer halls, remember to take off your shoes and try not to point your camera directly at somebody who is praying.

Cross-gender Interactions

When it comes to cross-gender interactions, Xinjiang isn't much different than the rest of Central Asia. It is against social protocol for men to hug or even touch a woman who isn't their wife and women shouldn't attempt to make contact, even to shake hands, unless a man initiates.

Men usually greet men with a two-handed shake and an exchange of greetings, while women can often be seen greeting by touching cheeks on both sides. This courtesy isn't expected of travelers passing through, but can be an easy way to endear yourself to a host who may take you into their home.

Being a Guest in a Local Home

For those who have the privilege of entering the home of a Uyghur, Hui, Kazakh or any other ethnic minority here in Xinjiang, there are a number of small courtesies you can do that can show your respect for your host.

- Take off your shoes when you enter the home. Often, they will offer you slippers.
- Don't wear the slippers on the carpet. You'll notice everybody else slipping them off at the edge of any carpet they step on.
- Bring a gift. You should never arrive to a house empty-handed. Appropriate gifts include fruits, Uyghur bread or bricks of tea.
- Women shouldn't cross their legs especially in front of men.
- Always stand and greet when somebody new enters the home.
- Eat slowly...the meal will likely be much larger than you anticipate!

Appropriate Attire

As you walk the streets of any big city in Xinjiang, you'll wonder if there really is an appropriate way to dress considering that some women wear veils while others walk around in tight jeans. Throw in the fact that the younger generation of Han Chinese often dress as provocatively as westerners (at least in the eyes of conservative Muslims), it's easy to get confused with what is ok to wear and what isn't.

My suggestion is to dress as modestly as you can, particularly in the southern half of Xinjiang. Long pants or a skirt in the middle of summer may seem like torture but it is appropriate.

Will anything happen if you wear shorts and a sleeveless shirt? Not at all. Thousands of foreign tourists have done it before and many will continue to do so. However, being appropriately dressed not only shows respect to the local culture, it also increases your chances of getting invited over to a local home or local event.

Regarding Alcohol and Cigarettes

Finally, while Islam frowns upon the consumption of alcohol and smoking of cigarettes, you will find plenty of both in Xinjiang.

Some Muslim restaurants and hotels do not allow alcohol within their establishment so make sure you check before taking anything in. The same goes for smoking, although smoking is a more accepted practice throughout Xinjiang.

A Note on "Xinjiang Time"

It's a well-known fact that the Xinjiang region in China operates on a two-time zone system: the official "Beijing Time" and the unofficial "Xinjiang time" or "local time" which is a two-hour time difference.

As you travel through Xinjiang, you'll notice that all state-owned enterprises and areas populated mostly by Han Chinese will show Beijing time, whereas Uyghur-run stores and Uyghur-populated areas will show local time. The use of Xinjiang time, although practical in some cases, is often a minor form of rebellion for a portion of the local Uyghur population.

At first it may seem confusing but you quickly forget the time paradox even exists once you arrive.

I recommend that travelers set their watch to Beijing time, because any transportation you use – from buses to trains to airplanes – runs on official time. I've known people to miss their flight just because they confused time zones. Don't let that be you!

Keep in mind that generally speaking, most Han Chinese will speak to you using Beijing time while the Uyghur, particularly in southern Xinjiang, will speak to you in local Xinjiang time. It's best to clarify, of course, with a simple "北京时或新疆时?" or "Běijīngshí huò Xīnjiāngshí?" (Beijing or Xinjiang time?).

Other Tips

Before we move on to the actual travel guides, I want to cover a few more commonly asked questions about travel around Xinjiang.

What about tipping in Xinjiang?

In general, no tipping is necessary. I've even stayed at 5-star hotels in Xinjiang where tips were not expected. It's not rude when it's not expected.

The only exception would be with a personal travel guide. If you think that a travel guide or personal driver did an especially good job showing you around, a tip is a polite way to say "thank you." I usually tip 50-100 RMB per day for a driver or tour guide.

How do I send letters or postcards?

Mailing letters is as simple as finding a China Post (中国邮政/Zhōngguó Yóuzhèng) and purchasing a stamp. Postcards can be bought at most large Xinhua Bookstores or at a limited number of tourist spots.

Do I need a plug outlet converter?

Electrical outlets in Xinjiang are the same as the rest of China. Outlets run 220V and almost all of them can be used with the two-prong plugs found on most phone and tablet chargers (with the exception of the two prong plugs with different sized prongs). Three-prong plugs with a ground can't be plugged into the wall but you should be able to easily find a power strip that will do the trick.

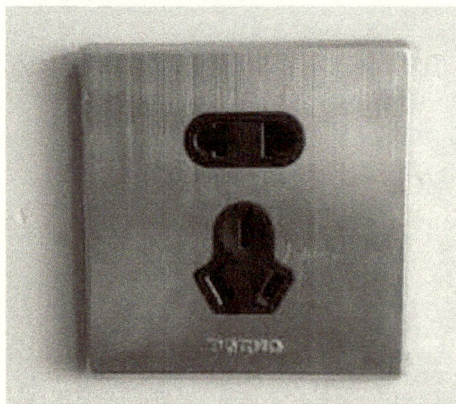

Bringing along plug adapters isn't a bad idea but personally I haven't found much need for them here.

How are the hospitals in Xinjiang?

In most cases I advise against visiting a hospital here unless absolutely necessary. Most of the foreigners who live here, including myself, prefer to travel elsewhere for any major medical issues.

I recommend that you consider purchasing travel health insurance prior to your trip that provides evacuation in the case of a serious medical emergency. This may seem like an extraneous purchase, but as with all insurance, you never appreciate it until you actually use it.

To find out how much travel insurance would cost for you, get a quote using the well-respected World Nomads service:

www.xjtravelguide.com/travel-insurance

City Guides

Urumqi

乌鲁木齐

Urumqi Top Sights

International Grand Bazaar – Pg 104

Although not a particularly new building, the International Bazaar is a great place to eat, walk around and even buy some souvenirs.

City View from Hong Shan Park – Pg 110

On a clear day, the view of Urumqi's business district from the top of Hong Shan Park can be worth the short hike.

Heavenly Lake – Pg 117
A simple day-trip outside Urumqi, the beautiful Heavenly Lake can be crowded with tourists but it's not hard to get away and enjoy the scenery.

Urumqi Number 1 Glacier – Pg 121
The journey through the Tianshan mountains is rough, but the reward is a beautiful view of the world's closest glacier to a major city.

Introduction to Urumqi 乌鲁木齐

Welcome to Urumqi, Xinjiang's capital and largest city! Most travelers I speak with dread coming to Urumqi. I used to be one of them and then for some reason I moved here.

There's no getting around the fact that Urumqi is a massive Chinese city: big buildings, far too many cars and very few parks. However, having lived here for a few years, I learned to appreciate what the capital of Xinjiang has to offer.

If your time in the city is limited, there are only two places I think are truly worth seeing within the city limits: The **International Grand Bazaar** and the **Xinjiang Autonomous Region Museum**. These two places will set the stage for your adventures throughout the entire region.

For those of you who will be spending more time around Urumqi, there are a number of things you can consider:

- **Day Trips:** There are day trips to Nanshan to the south or Heavenly Lake to the east, both beautiful nature spots within a two-hour drive. Even the city of Turpan is a day trip thanks to the new high-speed train.
- **City Parks:** Panoramic views of Urumqi can be had from the top of HongShan Park in the middle of the city or, if you're willing to take on a more strenuous hike, from Yamalike Hill (羊山湾畔) behind the old south train station.
- **Shopping:** Beyond what you can find at the International Grand Bazaar, there are some fun alleys to browse if you're willing to do some walking.

Before you jump to conclusions about Urumqi, take a moment to check out what there is to do around town. I wouldn't recommend allotting extra days but don't despair if you have an extended layover!

Historical Perspective of Urumqi

◀━━━━━━━━━━━━━━━▶

Urumqi. Wulumuqi. Ürümqi. Dihua. Tihwa. Luntai. The names given to this area of Xinjiang are almost as numerous as the ethnic groups that populate it. The city is strategically located on a pass in the TianShan which separates the Tarim and Dzungaria basins, a positioning that has helped build Urumqi into one of the most important trade centers of Central Asia.

It hasn't always been this way. When compared to many of the Silk Road cities throughout Central Asia, Urumqi is a relatively young establishment. It's only been in the past century that the city has grown to become a powerful player in the Asian market.

A Closer Look at Urumqi

It used to be that Urumqi's concrete jungle was full of beautiful green pastures populated by nomadic herders. The name "Urumqi" is a Mongolian word that means "a beautiful pasture land," but those days are long gone.

The most logical way to break down Urumqi's history is to follow the changes in its name that marked turning points in the region's history. Although nomads have roamed this land for centuries, the best place to begin is a Tang military garrison located 10km south of Urumqi.

Luntai / Beshbaliq (7th century to 18th century)

Although China had stationed troops in this area intermittently throughout the Han Dynasty (206 B.C. to 24 A.D.), it wasn't until the Tang Dynasty in 640 A.D. that an official prefecture was established. The area was named "Luntai County" and was an important Tang military outpost whose income was generated via taxes collected from caravans that passed along the northern arm of what is now referred to as the "Silk Road."

Very little is written about this period in Urumqi's history. Following the Tang Dynasty fall and retreat in 755 A.D., Central Asian powers became entangled in a complex tug-of-war for control of the area until a mass migration of Uyghur people set up their winter capital at Beshbaliq.

Beshbaliq (known in Chinese as Beiting) is located northeast of present-day Urumqi, nowhere near the ruins of Luntai, but this demonstrates the fluid nature that is characteristic of Xinjiang history. From the 9th to the 13th centuries, this city remained a part of the Uyghur state until pressure from Mongolian invasions forced the rulers to retreat to Gansu. The Uyghur people who remained pledged allegiance to the Mongol state.

This very scattered history of Urumqi was finally unified when the Qing Dynasty marched into Xinjiang to stake their claim.

Dihua (1763 to 1954)

Once the Qing troops marched through in 1750 and brutally exterminated all opposition, they quickly set up state farms to take advantage of Urumqi's green pastures. In 1763, the old town of Luntai was officially expanded north and renamed "Dihua" meaning "guided to civilization."

Because Dihua was a relatively new town, most of its inhabitants were Han Chinese as opposed to Uyghur. Rapid development stimulated population growth and by 1884 Dihua was named the capital of the newly formed, yet still unstable, Xinjiang region.

A wall was built around the city and much of the surrounding land was used for agriculture. Due to constant wars and poverty in the south, many Uyghur began to migrate to the fertile lands of Dihua, most of them setting up outside the South Gate of the Dihua walls – an area which is still predominantly Uyghur today.

As growth continued, international trade became a permanent part of Dihua's economy. American and Soviet Consuls were set up in the city and large bazaars attracted foreign and local merchants to buy and trade goods.

By this time the Qing Dynasty had collapsed with little effect on Xinjiang. Chinese generals maintained a struggle for power in Dihua.

These struggles continued throughout the 1940's when the Guomingdang (GMD) rose to power, and finally came to a head in 1949 when the Chinese Communist Party (CCP) marched into Dihua and finally "liberated" Xinjiang.

Urumqi (1954 to present)

For five years the CCP maintained the name "Dihua" for its Xinjiang capital as it struggled to maintain control of the region. It wasn't until February 1, 1954 that the city was officially changed to the Mongol name Urumqi, a move that reflected the government's early attempt to promote autonomy in the region.

Over the next half a century, Urumqi outgrew its walls, which were eventually torn down, and continued to expand to the north. Today the terms "North Gate" (北门), "Big West Gate" (大西门) and "South Gate" (南门) still indicate approximately where these gates once stood, but the towers that marked the entrance to the city were demolished decades ago.

Today, very few historical buildings remain in Urumqi, but in continuing with historical precedent, its location as a central hub for economic development and tourism ensures that almost everybody entering Xinjiang will most likely step foot inside Urumqi.

Getting to/from Urumqi

Urumqi Airport Guide

The Urumqi Diwopu International Airport (乌鲁木齐地窝铺国际机场) is the region's primary airport and is an important hub for transportation both within the province and around China.

What to Expect at the Urumqi Airport

Most travelers fly into and out of either Terminal 2 or the newer Terminal 3 (pictured above). Most signs are in English and the bathrooms are (usually) clean.

The food options in both airport terminals are terrible, so don't expect to eat well. Terminal 2 and Terminal 3 both have a Best Food Burger on the upper level and a KFC, which although not great, are your cheapest and most recognizable options.

Coffee shops are scattered throughout both terminals, but expect to pay Starbucks prices for convenience store coffee. Finally, the airport offers free wifi if you have a Chinese phone number (they use text messaging to provide a unique wifi password).

To/From the Urumqi Airport

Unless you have a friend or travel agency picking you up at the airport you might understandably be nervous about transportation into the city. It doesn't help that you get swarmed by private drivers when you first exit the baggage claim area, your foreign face screaming "I'm a traveler with money!" My suggestion is to avoid these people. Nine times out of ten they will cheat you out of every yuan you have. Just push them away and say "No."

A few better options are available to travelers when you first arrive at the Urumqi airport:

- **Subway / Metro:** Urumqi's new Metro Line 1 starts at the airport and travels south into the center of the city. This will be the easiest and fastest mode of transportation, although you'll have to go through airport-level security to use it and your passport is required to purchase tickets.

- **Private Car:** Those who arrive with a larger group or extra-large baggage may wish to have a private car or van. Inquire about what is available at the service desk near the baggage hall's main exit or call ahead to one of the travel agencies who can have a driver pick you up.
- **Taxi:** A special taxi lane is located just outside the main exit from both terminals and is usually full of waiting taxis. Approximately 50 RMB is a fair price for a trip to the city center, but it's best to insist that they start the meter.
- **Shuttle Bus:** There are shuttle buses just outside the terminal that can take you toward the train station with multiple stops in between. The shuttle costs 10 RMB and there's no need to buy a ticket inside. Just have your money ready as you board the shuttle.
- **City Bus:** A city bus stop is located under the approach bridge between Terminal 2 and Terminal 3. There are a couple buses that leave from here but the best one is bus 51 that makes a direct line down to the south of town. This is an extremely slow option but it only costs 1 RMB.

By far the easiest way to get to the airport is either by metro or by taxi. The average taxi rate to the airport should end up being around 35-60 RMB depending on where you are coming from. There is also a shuttle that runs every half hour between 7am and 10pm Beijing time from the China Southern Hotel on Youhao Nan Lu. Cost for the shuttle is only 15RMB.

Flights to/from Urumqi International Airport

From Urumqi you can get daily flights to almost every airport in Xinjiang including Kashgar, Hotan, Ili, and Altay. Some cities, like Kashgar, have multiple flights per day throughout the year while others, like Kanas Airport, run only during the summer.

Throughout the rest of China, Urumqi connects to every major airport multiple times per day, often directly but sometimes with a layover.

Flying internationally, from Urumqi travelers can fly directly to/from:

- Taipei (Taiwan)
- Seoul (South Korea) – seasonal
- Bangkok (Thailand)
- Istanbul (Turkey)
- Sharjah (UAE)

- Moscow (Russia)
- Almaty (Kazakhstan)
- Bishkek (Kyrgyzstan)
- Baku (Azerbaijan)
- Dushanbe (Tajikistan)

For up-to-date flight schedules and ticket prices, I recommend that you search Chinese travel booking site Trip: **www.xjtravelguide.com/trip-flights**

Urumqi Train Station Guide

There are two train stations in Urumqi, the Urumqi South Station (乌鲁木齐南站/Nánzhàn) and the Urumqi High Speed Station (乌鲁木齐高铁站/Gāotiě zhàn). As the names suggest, the High-Speed Station in the north services all high-speed trains (marked by a "D" on your ticket) while the south station services all other trains.

Urumqi South Station

Urumqi High Speed Station

Urumqi High Speed Station | What to Expect
乌鲁木齐站 / Wūlǔmùqí Zhàn

The new(er) high speed train station, opened in 2016, is a beautiful new building set in the heart of "new Urumqi". If you've been to other Chinese train stations across the country, this design will feel familiar.

Ticket halls are located on the first floor of the structure with window number 5 designated as the "bilingual window". You'll have to go through a bit of security to access the ticket hall in addition to another set of security checks to enter the 2nd floor waiting hall, which are divided into section "A" and section "B".

Before you enter those two sections, you'll see a number of fast food restaurants serving food on the raised level and seating scattered throughout (before you get through the second level of security). There are ATMs should you need cash and hot water dispensers for drinkable water.

There are plenty of digital signs that switch between Mandarin, Uyghur and English, so you shouldn't have a difficult time figuring out which platform is yours. The easiest way to find your gate is to look on the upper-right hand corner of your ticket.

To/From Urumqi High Speed Station

The advantage of building this new station from the ground up is that city planners had a chance to ease the congestion that plagues the South Station (see below). It's much easier to access the station by taxi or bus. The BRT-5 will be your cheapest option but there are many other city buses that terminate at the station.

When exiting the train station, you'll be directed to the north square where you'll find buses, taxis and even long-distance buses to other parts of the region. Eventually, a subway/metro station will open up here.

South Station | What to Expect
乌鲁木齐南站 / Wūlǔmùqí Nánzhàn

Security is incredibly high at both train stations, and at the South Station you should expect to go through 3-4 checkpoints and X-ray machines before you even enter the main building. I usually budget at least 30 minutes to get through security on a normal day. During the holidays it's much, much longer.

You'll find the train ticket hall is on the left side of the main building, which requires you to go through only one security checkpoint. The ticket hall is open from 5:30am to 12:30am (Beijing time). The main building is broken out into three floors with waiting halls on each side. If you feel confused, there is an info desk to ask directions immediately after you enter the station doors.

If you are looking to stock up on food and drinks before you depart, there are a number of mini-marts all around the train station that are open throughout the day as well as a few smaller (and more expensive) stores once you get inside.

To/From Urumqi South Station

Unlike the airport, which is far to the northwest of town, Urumqi's South Station is located not far from the city center in the southwest corner. Despite a good location, travelers still often complain of difficulty leaving the station. To make it simple, there are three primary means of transportation away from the train stations.

- **Taxi:** Directly in front of the station exit there is a taxi lane where you can find transportation. Another option, should there be no taxis available, is to walk east toward the street where taxis drop passengers off.
- **Shuttle:** Near the taxi lane there is usually a shuttle bus parked that heads toward the Urumqi airport. The shuttle costs 10 RMB per person but should not be relied upon if you're rushing to catch a flight.
- **Public Bus:** Taking the bus is by far the most common way to enter the city – that is, if you're willing to brave the system. As you exit the station you can head to the right (south), where all of the BRT buses start, or to the left (north) where the city buses begin. For the average traveler, the BRT buses will be the most convenient and reliable option.

Getting to the train station is fairly straightforward. Taxis are usually your fastest option while BRT 1 is a close second. There are a number of city buses whose route terminates at the train station including 52, 62, 906, 909, 914, 927 and many others. On the bus signs, look for 火车南站 as the final stop.

Buying Train Tickets in Urumqi

While I've already gone into detail about buying train tickets earlier in this guide, I'd like to make special note that unless you buy your train tickets online, I highly recommend you try to purchase your tickets through the many ticket resellers in the capital (search 火车售票站/Huǒchē Shòupiào Zhàn on Baidu maps).

There are quite a few in Urumqi, but the two most notable are the one off of Renmin Lu just west of Nanmen (South Gate) and on Xibei Lu just north of the regional Museum. You'll pay an extra 5 RMB service fee per ticket to use these resellers but often it's worth not having to travel to the train station and wait in long lines.

Trains within China

Trains in China are given multiple designations but for the sake of simplicity I will categorize them into one of two groups: high-speed trains and everything else.

High Speed Trains

Currently, the only high-speed rail line in Xinjiang goes from Urumqi through Hami onto Lanzhou. There are trains that leave to/from Lanzhou every morning (approx. 600 RMB, 12 hours) as well as multiple trains throughout the day that travel to/from Hami (approx. 170 RMB, 3.5 hours). Both of these service lines have stops in Turpan and Shanshan.

Currently, Xinjiang's high-speed trains only offer 1st and 2nd class options. First class has an aisle down the middle of the car with two wide seats on each side. There is plenty of leg room and even plug outlets at each seat for charging your computer or phone. Second class is similar except the seats are narrower, fitting three seats on one side and two on the other.

All Other Trains

From Urumqi there are three directions you can head using the regular service lines: south toward Kashgar/Hotan, west toward Ili/Kazakhstan and east toward the rest of China. Instead of listing all of the possible destinations throughout China, I will focus on Xinjiang's primary cities of interest:

- **Kashgar:** 135/262 RMB (hard seat/sleeper), 23 hrs
- **Turpan:** 23/69 RMB (hard seat/sleeper), 1.5 hrs
- **Ili:** 86/152 RMB (hard seat/sleeper), 10 hrs
- **Hotan:** 165/318 RMB (hard seat/sleeper), 31 hrs leaving only once per day.
- **Kuqa:** 102/178 RMB (hard seat/hard sleeper), 11 hours
- **Beitun (Altay):** 98/171 RMB (hard seat/sleeper), 12 hrs leaving only once per day
- **Hami:** 78/139 RMB (hard seat/hard sleeper), 5 hours

Trains to Kazakhstan

There are two trains per week that leave Urumqi for Almaty on Monday and Saturday at 11:58pm (K9795) and one that leaves for Astana every Thursday night at midnight (K9797) from the Urumqi South Station.

Tickets for both trains should run approximately 900-1100 RMB for a journey that takes around 30 hours, give or take a few hours depending on customs at the Alashankou port.

The tricky part about getting on these trains is buying the tickets. The only counter that sells tickets is in the lobby of the Ya'ou Hotel to the right (north) of the Urumqi South Train Station. You will need to pass through one level of security just to enter the hotel and the ticket counter is closed on Sunday, Tuesday and Friday.

Unfortunately, you can't hire a proxy service to buy these tickets for you. You must show up to the ticket counter in person with your passport in order to make a ticket purchase.

Urumqi Bus Station Guide

Taking a bus in Urumqi may not always be the cheapest option (the hard seat on a train is sometimes cheaper), but it will always be the easiest. Buses are frequent and require very little effort to purchase tickets.

The only drawback to taking a bus is determining which bus station to use. There are multiple stations throughout Urumqi and each of them serves a specific area – or a specific city - in Xinjiang.

Urumqi South Station
南郊客运站 / Nánjiāo Kèyùnzhàn

Urumqi South Bus Station is located a couple kilometers south of the International Bazaar. More than likely this will be the bus station you will be headed to. This transportation hub services:

- **Kashgar**: 260/280 RMB (top/bottom berth); multiple departures all day; 24 hrs
- **Hotan**: 370/390 RMB (top/bottom berth); afternoon departures; 24 hrs
- **Turpan**: 45 RMB; departures every 20 minutes; 2.5 hrs
- **Kuqa**: 145/155 RMB (top/bottom berth); frequent afternoon departures; 12 hrs

Nianzigou Bus Station
碾子沟客运站 / Niǎnzǐgōu Kèyùnzhàn

This particular bus station is located on Heilongjiang Road just a couple kilometers away from the Urumqi train station. From here you can grab a long-distance bus to cities in the north and south of Xinjiang such as:

- **Ili (Yining):** 193/203 RMB (top/bottom berth); departs hourly; 11 hours
- **Hami:** 150/160 RMB (top/bottom berth); departs 11am, 1pm & 8pm; 8 hours
- **Buerjin (Altay):** 178/188 (top/bottom berth); 11am, 8pm, 8:30pm; 12 hours

Mingyuan Station | Jungong Station
明园客运站 / Míngyuán & 军供 / Jungong

Mingyuan has hourly buses only to Karamay. Jungong, next door to the train station, services Shihezi and all the small towns along the way.

Buses to Kazakhstan

The Urumqi International Bus Station is located down a small alley behind the Nianzigou Bus Station on Heilongjiang Road. Buses to Almaty leave every evening at 7pm. Tickets cost 440/460 RMB (top/bottom berth) and the entire journey takes about 24 hours.

Transportation within Urumqi

Getting to Urumqi is the easy part. Unfortunately, maneuvering around the city is a bit trickier. As the city grows, the roads continue to become more congested, a fact that often takes away some of the joy of visiting Urumqi.

You need to get from point A to point B, though, so I'd like to offer a few tips before detailing your transportation options within the city.

My first and most important tip is to try to avoid being on the road between the hours of 9:30am-11am and 6:30pm-8pm Beijing time. This is "rush hour" and traffic is often at a standstill. I can walk home faster than a car can drive in most cases.

Second, don't be afraid to take what is known as a "black taxi" (see How to Use Public Transportation). Most of the time, they won't rip you off and often they are your only option.

Now, onto your options for transportation within the city.

Taking the Metro/Subway

The newest mode of transportation is the Urumqi metro, which we've already discussed. As of publication, only Line 1 is operational.

This line runs from the Urumqi International Airport in the north of the city all the way through the city center and into the southern portion of the city.

You should expect security entering each metro station to be ridiculous and you'll have to stand in line at the counter to purchase tickets with your passport since you as a foreigner can't use the automated machines.

Taking a Bus

Urumqi has an extensive bus system that covers the entire city. I've mentioned before the BRT system (Bus Rapid Transit) and it's worth doing some research to understand where it goes. The bus is broken up into different numbers (BRT-1, BRT-2, BRT-3, etc.) that reach different parts of the city. It can get crowded but since these buses often have their own lane, they can avoid a lot of the traffic that builds up.

Most buses only cost 1RMB to ride, with the exception of the big white "K" buses which are 5RMB. These "K" buses are nice and comfortable, but they generally don't stop where you'll want to go. Unless you're intimately familiar with Urumqi, I suggest you just avoid the K bus.

Finally, as I've mentioned before, I recommend you download the Baidu Maps app on your phone. Type the number of any bus to see its route or determine the best bus to get to your destination.

Taking a Taxi

Urumqi taxis are legally obligated to use their meters while taking passengers. When taking a taxi anywhere within the city, this won't be a problem. The only time you might need to force the taxi driver to use the meter is at the airport or train station. For some reason this is the only place I've noticed them try to take advantage of foreign travelers.

Riding a Bike

Unfortunately, Urumqi is not a very bike-friendly city. It's hard to rent a bike here and even if you did, there aren't great places to lock it up nor are there any bike lanes to use.

Oddly, there are now a few Chinese "bike share" companies that now operate in Urumqi. Using these services requires WeChat or the company's own app, both of which won't work unless you have a Chinese bank card.

What to do in Urumqi

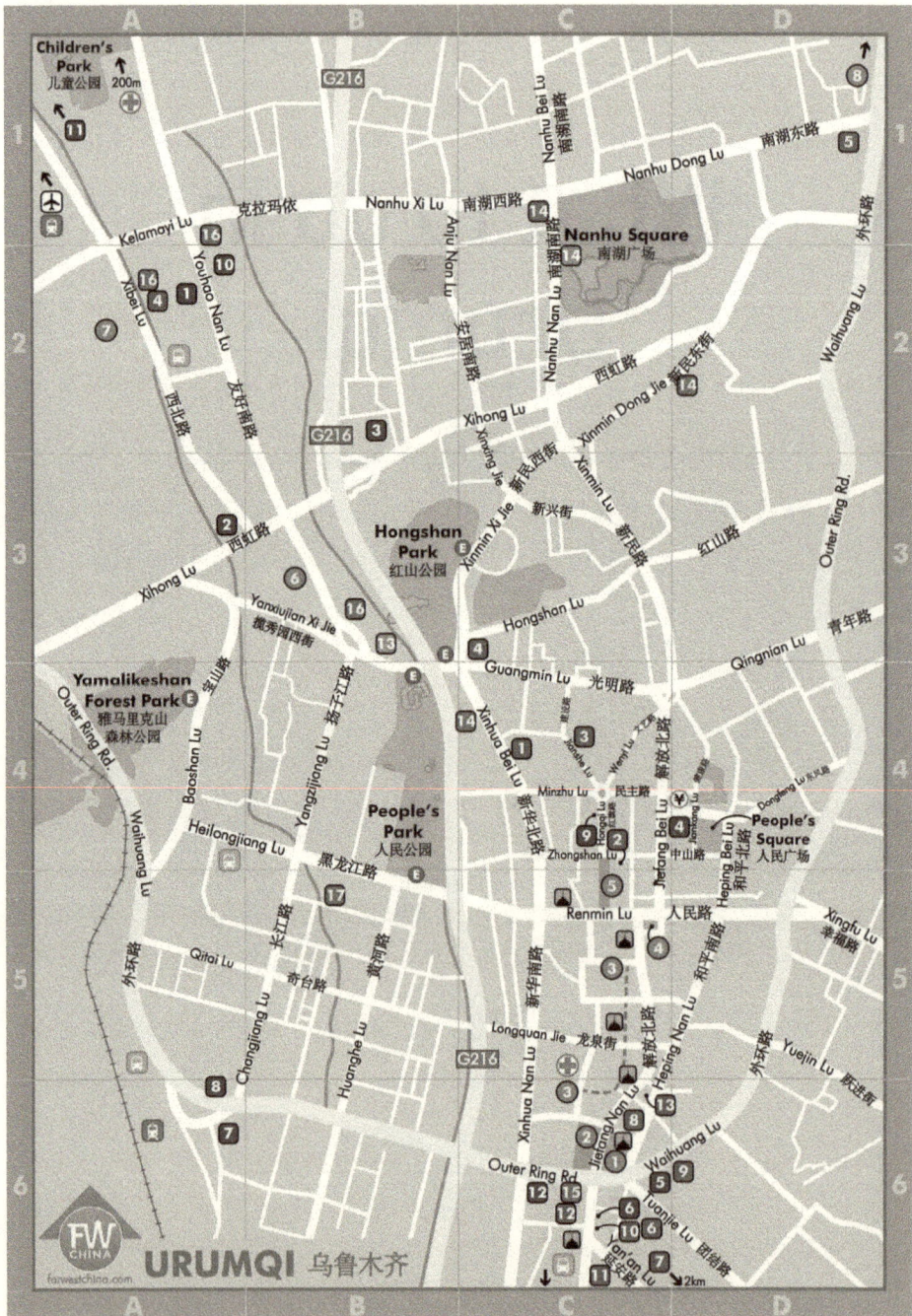

Children's Park
儿童公园

200m

Kelamayi Lu 克拉玛依

Nanhu Xi Lu 南湖西路

Nanhu Bei Lu 南湖北路

Nanhu Dong Lu

Nanhu Dong Lu 南湖东路

Nanhu Square
南湖广场

Youhao Nan Lu

Xibei Lu

Anju Nan Lu

Nanhu Nan Lu 南湖南路

Waihuang Lu 外环路

G216

Xihong Lu 西虹路

Xinmin Dong Jie 新民东街

Xinmin Dong Jie

Xinmin Lu

Xineng Jie

Xinmin Xi Jie 新民西街

新兴街

新民路

红山路

Hongshan Park
红山公园

Hongshan Lu 红山路

Qingnian Lu 青年路

Outer Ring Rd.

Yanxiujian Xi Jie
揽秀园西街

Xihong Lu

Yamalikeshan Forest Park
雅马里克山
森林公园

Baoshan Lu

宝山路

Yangzijiang Lu 扬子江路

Guangmin Lu 光明路

Xinhua Bei Lu

Zuzhiu Lu

Wenyi Lu

Jiefang Bei Lu

Dongfeng Lu 东风路

People's Square
人民广场

Heping Bei Lu 和平北路

Xingfu Lu 幸福路

Outer Ring Rd.

Heilongjiang Lu

Qitai Lu

Changjiang Lu

Huanghe Lu

Yangzijiang Lu

黑龙江路

People's Park
人民公园

Minzhu Lu 民主路

Zhongshan Lu

中山路

Renmin Lu 人民路

人民路

奇台路

武疆路

黄河路

长江路

G216

Longquan Jie 龙泉街

龙泉街

Xinhua Nan Lu

新华南路

Jiefang Nan Lu

解放南路

解放南路

Heping Nan Lu 和平南路

Waihuang Lu

Yuejin Lu 跃进路

跃进街

Outer Ring Rd.

Tuanjie Lu 团结路

贸结路

Waihuang Lu

Waihuang Lu

Outer Ring Rd.

2km

URUMQI 乌鲁木齐

FW CHINA
farwestchina.com

102

URUMQI 乌鲁木齐

RESTAURANTS

Foreign:
1. 9.9 Pizza -- C4
2. Pizza Hut -- C4
3. Aroma -- C4
4. Burger King -- C3, A2
5. Il Pjazza -- D1
6. Eden -- C6
7. Rendezvous -- C6

Local:
8. Castle (Uyghur) -- C6
9. Astana (Uyghur) -- D6
10. The Diplomat (Uyghur) -- C6
11. Herembag (Uyghur) -- C6
12. Food Court over Arman -- C6
13. Zam Zam -- C6

Coffee Shops:
14. Caffe Bene -- C1, C4, D2
15. Meseta Coffee -- C6
16. Tous le Jours -- A1, A2, B3
17. Cornerstone Cafe -- B5

HOTELS
1. Sheraton (5 Star) -- A2
2. Yin Du Hotel (5 Star) -- A3
3. Grand Mercure (5 Star) -- B2
4. Hoi Tak (5 Star) -- D4
5. Int'l Trade Grand Hotel -- C6
6. Aksaray -- C6
7. Super 8 -- A6
8. Kashgar Hotel -- A6
9. Lucky Chance Hotel -- C4
10. YouHao Hotel -- A2
11. Airport Hotel -- A1
12. Tumaris Hotel -- C6

Hostels:
13. MaiTian -- B3
14. White Birch -- C2

TRANSPORTATION
- Heilongjiang Bus Station -- A4
- South Bus Station -- C6
- Karamay Bus Station -- A2
- Shihezi Bus Station -- A5
- Train Station -- A1, A6
- Airport -- A1

CITY SIGHTS
1. Int'l Grand Bazaar -- C6
2. ErDaoQiao (shopping) -- C6
3. Uyghur Culture Walk -- C5-C6
4. NanMen -- C5
5. Computer Market -- C5
6. Camping Equip. Rental -- B3
7. Museum -- A2
8. City Visa Office -- D1

- Mosques
- Hospitals -- A1, C5
- Entrance
- Bank -- D4

PARKS
HongShan Park -- B3
People's Park -- B4
Yamalikeshan Forest Park -- A4
Children's Park -- A1
Nanhu Park & Square -- C1-C2
People's Square -- D4

See Map

To receive a free, full-resolution PDF version of this and all the maps in this guide, please register your book:
www.xjtravelguide.com/register

103

International Grand Bazaar

国际大巴扎/**Guójì Dàbāzā**

Price: Free to Enter
Rating: Recommended despite its "touristy" feel
Map: Urumqi Map C6 - 1

About a kilometer south of the city's NanMen, or "South Gate", is a popular tourist spot known as the International Grand Bazaar. This complex of 6 buildings covers an area of 100,000 sq/m and although it looks like a historical site, don't be fooled. It was first opened to the public on June 26th, 2003.

Inside the bazaar, described by Xinjiang tourist pamphlets as a "fantastic shoppers' emporium" you can get your fill of mass-produced souvenirs including Uyghur knives, musical instruments, a wide selection of Xinjiang fruits and, of course, jade jewelry. Also available for purchase are rugs similar to what you will find in Kashgar and Hotan (Khotan).

In the center of the Bazaar is a large minaret which, again, looks like an important Islamic building but is instead just a small viewing deck with an elevator. For a fee of 50 RMB you can take an elevator to the top and get a 360-degree view of Urumqi. No calls to prayer are made from this building and the windows at the top obviously haven't been cleaned for quite some time.

After spending some time at the Grand Bazaar you can either walk around to find a good place to eat or you can cross the street to continue your shopping at the Erdaoqiao Market.

Getting There: A new metro stop (二道桥/Èrdàoqiáo) conveniently puts you in the heart of the International Bazaar. City suses 61, 70, 104, 301 and 310 will also drop you off behind the bazaar.

Erdaoqiao Market

二道桥市场

Erdàoqiáo Shìchǎng

Price: Free to Enter
Rating: Touristy but worth a visit
Map: Urumqi Map C6 - 2

Across the street from the International Bazaar is the equally-popular, yet considerably smaller Erdaoqiao market. Although the building was renovated in 2002, this site and its name have long been synonymous with Xinjiang trade.

As early as the late 1800's during the Qing Dynasty, the Erdaoqiao Market was a well-known center for trade. Fast forward to today, this once important trade hub now primarily caters to the needs of tourist.

Most of what you'll find inside will be overpriced trinkets and the shops themselves don't usually reflect a "true" Xinjiang. Still, if you're looking for those last-minute souvenirs, this might not be a bad stop.

Getting There: Again, the fastest mode of transportation here is the new metro that has a stop ((二道桥 / Èrdàoqiáo). There are also a number of city buses and BRT buses that stop here.

Xinjiang Autonomous Region Museum

This Xinjiang museum is one of the few "must-see" tourist stops in Urumqi. Historical context is an important part of tourism in Xinjiang and this museum will give you a good, albeit slanted, framework to make sense out of it all before you

新疆自治区博物馆
Xīnjiāng Zìzhiqū Bówùguǎn
Hours: 10am-6pm; Closed Monday
Rating: Highly recommended
Map: Urumqi Map A2 - 7

travel. Among the 50,000 relics in their collection you'll find ancient pottery, manuscripts in various languages, and their most valuable archeological treasures: mummies.

The museum is divided into two levels that include the Exhibition Hall of Ancient Xinjiang Corpses (mummies), the Exhibition Hall of Historical Relics, the Exhibition Hall of Xinjiang Folk Custom and the Exhibition Hall of Ancient Xinjiang Costume. Thankfully, English translations can be found in each exhibit.

It will be obvious to any person who has studied Central Asian history that many of these exhibits were assembled for the purpose of proving China's claim on the Xinjiang region, but the artifacts still remain fascinating. Most interesting of all are the mummies, including the famous "Loulan Beauty" whose hair and eyelashes can still be seen. The museum curators acknowledge that these mummies are of "Europoid" descent, not Chinese – a fact that many have used to question China's rule over the province.

The museum is closed on Mondays and any national holiday. Hours are 10am-6pm (summer) and 10:30am-6pm (winter), but they close the gate for new visitors at 4:30pm.

Getting There: Numerous public buses stop at the 博物馆/Bówùguǎn bus stop, including the 51, 68, 303 and many others. Since there aren't any BRT stops directly near the museum, I usually recommend people take a taxi.

Other Urumqi Museums

Aside from the Xinjiang Autonomous Region Museum, there are a few additional museums in Urumqi that I want to mention as points of interest as well as a couple that are no longer in existence.

Xinjiang Geological and Mineral Museum

新疆地质矿产博物馆
Xīnjiāng Dìzhì Kuàngchǎn Bówùguǎn
Price: Free
Rating: Not unless you love rocks
Map: Urumqi Map A1 - Not listed

If, by chance, you like rocks and geology, this museum may be of interest to you. The most popular of its displays include the world's third-largest meteorite, an almost 6-foot long crystal, or a 102kg piece of copper.

The Xinjiang Geological and Mineral museum is located on the east side of Youhao Road next to the Youhao BRT bus stop. Even if you decide not to enter the museum, you can check out the large fossilized wood displayed in the front of the building.

Xinjiang Museum of Science and Technology

新疆科技馆 /**Xīnjiāng Kējìguǎn**
Price: Free
Rating: Not recommended unless your children are extremely bored
Map: Urumqi Map A1 - next to Children's Park

The four floors of the Xinjiang Museum of Science and Technology contain your typical science museum exhibits, which at one time was probably an incredibly fun place for children. Unfortunately, the years have not been kind to this building.

Exhibits look to be falling apart and some don't even work anymore. Schools still make guided trips to this museum but the average visitor won't find much worth seeing.

Urumqi Aquarium

Although not technically a "museum", the Urumqi Aquarium fits the same mold as the rest on this list. It's not particularly large but it does boast a small show and an "underwater tunnel". This isn't worth a second glance for any tourist, but for those who are spending an extended period of time in Urumqi with kids, this is an option.

乌鲁木齐海洋馆
Wūlǔmùqí Hǎiyáng Guǎn
Price: 50 RMB
Rating: Fun for kids but not a world-class facility
Map: Within the Urumqi Water Park (水上乐园) along South Dawan Rd.

Museums No Longer in Existence

If you're referencing older guides about Xinjiang or searching online, you might see mention of museums like the Silk Road Museum (丝绸之路博物馆) or the Urumqi City Museum (乌鲁木齐市博物馆). These museums no longer exist, so don't waste your time trying to find them.

Urumqi Mosques

During your trip through the southern portion of Urumqi to visit the International Grand Bazaar, you may as well walk by a few of the city's more beautiful buildings. Urumqi boasts quite a few mosques - many more than I can detail here! - so I will list the handful of mosques that are usually open for public viewing.

Southern Mosque

Due to its prominent location next to Nanmen, the Southern Mosque is the most familiar mosque in Urumqi today. Built in 1919 and remodeled in 2014, the architecture of the Southern Mosque has a heavy Uyghur influence on the outside with a large, beautiful prayer hall on the inside. The Southern Mosque is also referred to as the "Khantengri Mosque" or 汗腾格里清真寺/Hànténggélǐ Qīngzhēnsì.

Shaanxi Mosque

The Shaanxi Mosque or 陕西大寺/Shǎnxī Dàsì, located down an alley south of NanMen, is named after the Hui Muslims of Shaanxi province who donated money for its construction. It was built almost two decades ago with a distinctly Chinese architectural influence and is one of the largest mosques in the city.

Yanghang/Tartar Mosque

The twin spires of the Tartar Mosque (洋行清真寺/Yángháng Qīngzhēnsì) are a beautiful sight just south of the International Grand Bazaar on Jiefang Rd. It was built in 1897 from private donations by the Tartar community and thus follows their architectural influence (squared minarets). You're supposed to be able to wander in as a tourist, but security at the gate may or may not let you in.

Shows & Entertainment

The Uyghur culture is often a primary draw for people coming to visit Xinjiang yet, sadly, travelers often don't get a chance to witness the Uyghur arts such as music and dancing.

That's where these theater shows come in handy. They're a bit expensive in my opinion but you're guaranteed to witness the costume, dance and music not only of the Uyghur, but also of many other Xinjiang ethnic groups. Fair warning: these shows are usually attended by buses full of Chinese tourists.

Erdaoqiao Theater Show

The most convenient show is located on the upper level of the Erdaoqiao Market, entered through a separate set of doors in the back of the building. The show includes either a lunch or dinner and usually lasts and hour and a half.

Show times are listed below but you'll probably want to call (0991-286-8111) or visit ahead of time to reserve tickets, which cost around 300 RMB per person.

- **Showtimes**: 2pm, 4pm and 8pm Beijing time.
- **Address**: 二道桥大剧院/Èrdàoqiáo Dàjùyuàn

"Back to the Silk Road"
千回西城

To the north of Urumqi in the town of Changji, there is a production of a much grander scale that visitors are invited to watch. Known as "Back to the Silk Road" in English, the two-hour show features approximately one hundred performers and is very well-choreographed.

The biggest drawback to this show is that Changji is almost an hour from Urumqi by car. Ticket prices range from 280 RMB to 1,280 RMB per person. Performance times vary by season and it's good to book ahead of time (0994-816-6666).

- **Showtimes**: 5:30pm or 8:30pm Beijing time, depending on the season.
- **Address**: 昌吉市新疆大剧院/Chāngjíshì Xīnjiāng Dàjùyuàn

Parks & Squares

If you're looking for a place to hang out or just walk around while in Urumqi, there are a select few parks and traditional Chinese squares scattered throughout the city. Parks gates are usually opened in the early morning but often close by 6-7pm Beijing time.

Hong Shan Park

红山公园/**Hóngshān Gōngyuán**
Price: Free to enter, paid activities within
Rating: Good park with moderate climbs
Map: Urumqi Map B3

Hong Shan Park, or "Red Mountain" park, is located in the heart of the capital and covers a total area of 4,069 sq/m. The park itself was originally built in 1958 by the Chinese Red Army but incorporated older structures such as the pagoda first erected in 1788 and the Grand Buddha Temple finished in 1797.

Neither of these buildings makes the Hong Shan park a particular destination of interest, however. Most tourists who visit the park find the panoramic view of Urumqi more appealing, so take your camera if you arrive on a particularly clear day. The most popular panoramic photo can be had along the path to the pagoda where you'll find plenty of other people taking pictures.

Hong Shan Park is one of the few places in Urumqi that offers a respite from the noisy and dirty roads of the city. If you're feeling overwhelmed or just have extra free time, you might enjoy a visit to Hong Shan Park, but otherwise there's no reason to make a special stop here.

Getting There: Take buses 29, 35, 61, 62, 63 or 73 to the front gate of Hong Shan Park.

People's Park

人民公园 /**Rénmín Gōngyuán**
Price: Free to enter, paid activities within
Rating: Plenty of paths and mostly flat
Map: Urumqi Map B4

Not far from Hong Shan Park is the equally large People's Park to the southwest. With a flat topography, you might find this park less strenuous to navigate than the hills of Hong Shan.

Within People's Park there are amusement rides for children, people dancing to Uyghur music and places to picnic. During the winter, they even turn the small lake into an ice rink for skating.

It is here at both the north and south gates of People's Park that you can find a number of tour agencies to bring you all over the province. Buses to NanShan and Heavenly Lake leave from the gate on a daily basis.

Getting There: If taking a bus, the easiest way is via the park's south entrance where you can find a 44, 58, 308 and 903.

Children's Park

For those with kids and some extra time, a visit to the Children's Park near the Xinjiang Medical University is a nice diversion. While it's free to get in, every game, ride and little electric car rental you want to do will cost a little bit extra.

Getting There: This park is located next door to the new BaLou metro stop (八楼). You can also get here by taking the BRT-1 or BRT-2. You're looking for the "Er Tong Gong Yuan" stop.

人民广场 /Rénmín Guǎngchǎng
Price: Free to enter, paid activities within
Rating: Fun for young children
Map: Urumqi Map A1

Urumqi Water Park

Across the street from the south bus station, it's hard to miss the amusement park known oddly as the "Water Park". The entrance to the park is on the northwest side along South Dawan Road and it's from there that you'll see the large, man-made lake after which the park is named.

Inside the park you can board a boat, ride a roller coaster, play carnival games or even visit the Urumqi Aquarium. Everything comes at a price, although usually it's not too expensive.

水上乐园/Shuǐshàng Lèyuán
Price: Free to enter, plenty of paid activities
Rating: Plenty of walking and things to do
Map: Urumqi Map D4

People's Square

Although technically not a tourist destination, you'll probably run into this centrally-located square during your time in Urumqi. The 100-foot high monument in the middle, called the "Monument to the Peaceful Liberation of Xinjiang," was erected in 1995 to mark the 40th anniversary of the establishment of the Xinjiang Uyghur Autonomous Region.

人民广场/Rénmín Guǎngchǎng
Price: Free
Rating: Not much to see or do

The square itself isn't much to look at, but the shaded area on the western corner is a nice place to sit and rest your feet. A large TV screen usually plays a Chinese TV show and every once in a while, there will be a performance in the square.

Thanks to all the ethnic tensions and its close proximity to head government offices, you'll find plenty of security fences and military surrounding People's Square now.

Shuimo Gou Park

水磨沟公园 /Shuǐmógōu Gōngyuán
Price: Free to enter, paid activities within
Rating: Pleasant park if you're bored
Map: East of the current map boundaries

Far from a being tourist destination in Urumqi, the Shuimo Gou Park is still a well-kept park with cobblestone walkways and a fish-filled stream. Locals go here to get exercise and enjoy the peaceful surroundings away from the city noise and pollution.

Getting There: The 801 bus stop here, but since this park is a bit removed from the city, it's best to take a taxi.

Urumqi Botanical Gardens

植物园/Zhíwùyuán
Price: 5 元
Rating: Not much to see or do
Map: North of the current map boundaries; Address: 北京中路 916 号

In the far northern half of Urumqi a large plot of land has been reserved as a botanical garden. Built in 1986, this garden covers an area of more than 60 hectares and is advertised as featuring many rare breeds of China roses.

Unfortunately, unless you're a plant aficionado who knows the difference between an American rose and an almost extinct species of China rose, you won't find this garden any different than anywhere else in the world. In fact, I find it hard to differentiate this "garden" from any of the above-mentioned parks in Urumqi.

Getting There: Take either the metro Line 1 or the BRT-1 to the "Zhi wu yuan" bus stop.

Shopping

Like any major city in China, Urumqi offers plenty of places to shop for electronics, clothing and souvenirs. While these aren't bargain prices, shopping can still be something fun to pass the time within the city.

Computer and Camera Equipment

I don't recommend buying computers or phones in Urumqi, but if you're a photographer who needs to grab some extra gear, the place you'll want to head is the **Computer Market** (红旗路电脑城/Hóngqílù Diànnǎochéng; Map C5).

The first and second floors of this long market have quite a few shops that sell genuine Canon, Nikon and DJI products including lenses, bags, tripods, etc. If you're looking for even more specialized gear, there's a small shop about 200 meters west of the southern entrance on Renmin Lu (behind the bus stop) that sells lighting, filters and other such accessories.

Souvenir Shopping

As has been mentioned earlier, the best places to search for the tourist souvenir is at the International Grand Bazaar and the Erdaoqiao Market. A lot of these trinkets are mass-produced in places other than Xinjiang, believe it or not, but they can still make great gifts or keepsakes.

While you're souvenir shopping near Erdaoqiao, I recommend you take a side trip through the back alleys of Urumqi. These alleys are slowly being torn down but if you wander long enough, you're bound to find one.

For an example of what I'm referring to, watch this FarWestChina YouTube video:

www.xjtravelguide.com/urumqi-walking-street

Unfortunately, this particular street has already been torn down, but there are others you can still visit.

Clothing Shopping

In the same way I advise against buying computer gear here in Urumqi, I also don't recommend looking for bargain clothes. The knockoff clothing exists, you just won't get a good deal on it like you will in other major China cities.

Cheap clothing can be found in small shops all across the city, particularly near XiaoXi Men (the West Gate) and along ZhongShan Lu (中山路).

Another option if you have the time is to buy local cloth from the shops near Erdaoqiao Market and get a seamstress to make a dress or shirt. The cost is relatively low but you'll have a souvenir that you won't soon forget. The only downside is that the making of the dress or suit usually takes a few days to complete and is difficult to do if you don't have a translator with you to nail down the important details.

What to do Around Urumqi

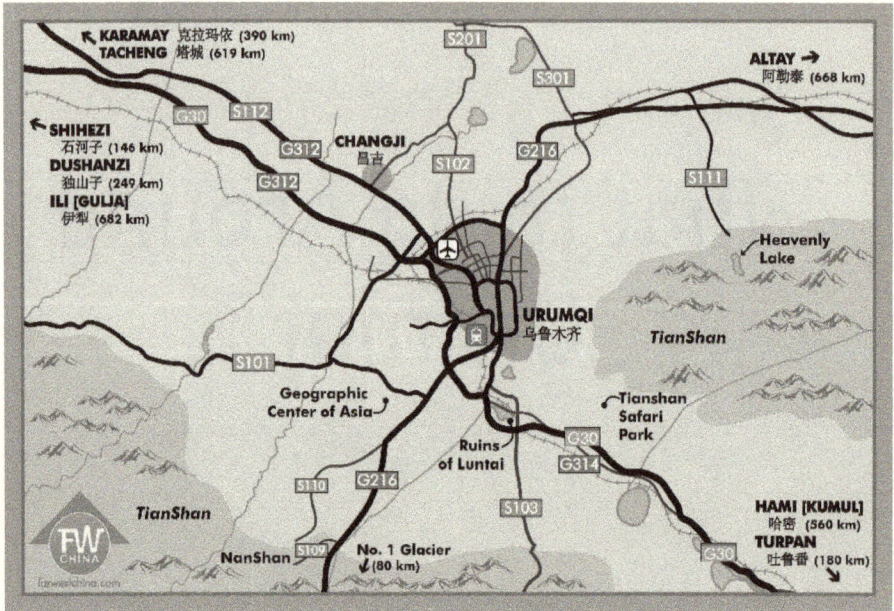

To receive a free, full-resolution PDF version of this and all the maps in this guide, please register your book:
www.xjtravelguide.com/register

Heavenly Lake

- **Name:** 天池/Tiānchí
- **Price:** 215 RMB (entrance & shuttle fee)
- **Rating:** Worth visiting if you can't visit Kanas or Karakul Lake
- **Map:** See Urumqi Area Map

Urumqi's Heavenly Lake is an excellent way to escape the city without going far. Although it's usually filled with tourists and the entrance fee is unbelievable, it provides a breath of clean air in contrast to the polluted capital city.

The beautiful, crystal-clear waters of Heavenly Lake are guarded by the Tianshan, a major mountain range dividing Xinjiang into northern and southern portions, and includes the majestic Bogda Feng (1,980m / 6,500ft).

It used to be that the lake was only accessible by off-road vehicles until a road was paved a few decades ago. The lake sits on an area known as the Tianchi Nature Reserve and in 2006 the entire park was closed to all vehicles except the new park buses and those cars owned by locals.

Tips for Tourist | Heavenly Lake

The most well-known view of Heavenly Lake can be seen from the northern edge where the crowds of tourist tend to gather. It is on this side of the lake where you can find restrooms, small shops and a boat dock for a ride on the lake (80-95 元 per person). There are even some nice areas to set up a picnic if you bring a blanket and food.

The key to enjoying Heavenly Lake, however, is to hike beyond the crowds of tourist. New wooden pathways surround the northern half of the lake but beyond these there is even more to see and few tourists who will join you.

Heading north down the mountains, paved walkways well-shaded by the trees run adjacent to beautiful waterfalls and smaller bodies of water. It's even possible to hike a few hours in this direction until you reach the old tourism gate where shuttle buses can be waved down.

It used to be that you could rent a yurt to stay the night at Heavenly Lake, but new policies seem to have made that difficult. If possible, expect to pay around 100 RMB per person, which may include one meal. Space is usually available upon arrival but I know that some people prefer to call ahead. I recommend you connect with a Kazakh, English-speaking gentleman named Rashit (138-9964-1550) who can arrange for you to stay in one of his yurts for the night. If you can't get a hold of Rashit, here are a few yurt owners you can call (all of whom usually speak broken Mandarin): 150-2618-1081 or 158-9927-1029 or 183-9990-1898.

Alternatively, if you have camping gear you can hike around and set up for the night (before you do, read Hiking and Camping in Xinjiang).

Finally, there are vehicles that will drive you even further up the mountain on steep but paved roads. You should expect to pay close to 120 RMB per person to get a higher elevation view of the lake.

Getting to Heavenly Lake

Most people choose to take the tourist buses to Heavenly Lake, which depart from the north gate of People's Park every day at 9am, returning somewhere between 5 and 7pm. It's best to confirm these times and purchase tickets a day in advance at the tour agencies near the gate. The journey takes approximately 2-3 hours and costs 50 RMB round trip.

The problem with these tour buses is that they are often known to stop multiple times at souvenir and refreshment stands along the way. An alternative is to take a public bus to Fukang (阜康) from Urumqi's 北客运站/Běikèyùnzhàn bus station. Once you arrive at Fukang station, you grab a mini-bus that runs every half hour to the entrance of Heavenly Lake. This method avoids most of the bogus tourism stops along the way.

Whichever method you choose, the bus will drop you off at a large tourist facility where you will be required to purchase an entrance ticket and tickets for yet another shuttle bus that will transport you 30 minutes up the mountain.

Believe it or not, this bus still doesn't drop you off at Heavenly Lake! At this point you have the choice to hike an additional kilometer up a paved road or pay 10 RMB per person for an electric golf cart.

NanShan Scenic Park

- **Name**: 南山牧场/Nánshān Mùchǎng
- **Price**: Free to enter
- **Rating**: A nice getaway from the big Chinese city but nothing spectacular
- **Map**: See Urumqi Area Map

If you're a hiker or outdoor-lover you might be interested in the Nanshan region. It offers some great mountain views and plenty of space to get away from the tourist crowds if you like. There's not much else to do besides enjoy nature out here, though.

The Kazakhs have set up quite a few yurts throughout Nanshan that have in the past offered overnight stays, BBQ and beer. You don't need to book ahead; once you arrive you'll find plenty of availability. The question is whether the local authorities will let you stay.

There are waterfalls and a couple short summit hikes that can be done in a day. For those of us who live here it's a nice little getaway but for the average tourist the scenery is nothing spectacular.

During the winter months there is snow skiing on these mountains (see A Guide to Skiing in Xinjiang) and you can take the bus from the People's Park or arrange for transportation through a tour company.

Getting to NanShan

Getting to NanShan from Urumqi isn't very convenient, but it's possible. Buses depart from a small station near the south gate of People's Park called 乌鲁木齐市郊客运中心站/Wūlǔmùqíshì Jiāokèyùn Zhōngxīn Zhàn. Heading east on Renmin Lu from the park, before you cross the bridge, turn off the main road right down a smaller alley known as 和天街/Hétiān Jiē. 50 meters later it will be on your left.

The problem with these buses is that they are slow to arrive at Nanshan and the last bus departs very early in the afternoon, giving you relatively little time to hike/explore. Make sure you don't miss that last bus!

Tianshan Safari Park

- **Name**: 新疆天山野生动物园/Xīnjiāng Tiānshān Yěshēng Dòngwùyuán
- **Price**: 70 元 entrance, 30 元 shuttle fee
- **Rating**: Possible fun for kids but is an all-day affair
- **Map**: See Urumqi Area Map

Up until 2005, visiting the zoo in Urumqi was an extremely depressing experience. The cramped park space in the southern portion of the city was far too small and none of the animals looked very happy.

Then in September of 2005, a new "safari park" was opened about 40 kilometers southwest of the city at the base of the TianShan range. Not only have they introduced a number of new species into the park but now with an area of 70 square kilometers, these animals have at least a little more space to roam freely. It's nowhere near a world-class zoo, but it's leaps and bounds better than the previous zoo.

Large tracts of land are set aside for camels, white tigers, black bears, ostriches, zebras and many more.

A decade is a long time in China, though. It is still fun to visit as a family but the facilities now look old and the road that leads to the park is laden with potholes. The animals seem to be taken care of for the most part, although there are still a few exhibits that will break your heart.

Tips for Tourists

For those who don't have a private car, city bus number 313 leaves Urumqi from the old zoo (南公园/Nángōngyuán) and takes about 1.5 hours to arrive at the safari park. The first bus leaves for the park at 10:50am Beijing time and the last bus leaves the park 3:30pm. It's a short trip but that should be all that you need.

Walking is only permitted in certain parts of the zoo, so in order to get in you'll need to either pay a fee for your private car (90 RMB) or get a ticket onto one of the zoo shuttles (30 RMB).

I suggest taking your own food for a picnic. There are a number of places where you can find a table to eat and it's much easier to do this than to purchase food when you are there.

Geographic Center of Asia

- **Name**: 亚洲大陆地理中心/Yàzhōu Dàlùdì Lǐzhōngxīn
- **Price**: 20 RMB
- **Rating**: Not a big deal
- **Map**: See Urumqi Area Map

The exact geographic center of Asia has been debated for quite some time but somehow Chinese cartographers conveniently decided that it should be located not far from Urumqi where they quickly built a tourist attraction.

Here you can take your picture next to a 22-meter high fixture with a golden globe on top. The circle surrounding the tower boasts a relief of all Asian flags as well as a map of the Asian continent.

Most tourists don't venture all the way out to this spot about 30 minutes south of the city but I could see it being an adventure if you happen to go during the annual Skydiving Championships (August/September).

Watch: Enjoy a look at this Center of Asia:
www.xjtravelguide.com/center-of-asia

Getting to the Center of Asia will require a private car hire, as there are no buses that come out in this direction.

Urumqi Number 1 Glacier

- **Name**: 一号冰川 Yīhào Bīngchuān
- **Price**: 50 RMB...or whatever the local gate guard asks
- **Rating**: Fun detour if you're headed to Korla on Highway G216
- **Map**: See Urumqi Area Map

South of Urumqi headed through the Tianshan toward Korla, it is possible to at least drive by the world's closest glacier to a major city. The No.1 Glacier is a gorgeous glacier and supplies the Urumqi River with much of its water. Geologists from all over the world are studying this glacier because it has significantly shrunk over the past three decades.

Currently the glacier measures 500 meters wide and about 2.4 kilometers in length. The glacier itself is great but the surrounding area, including Mount Tiangar, is incredibly scenic.

When I first made this trip, the road was unbelievably bumpy and slow. A new road has hopefully changed all of that. Unfortunately, because of the shrinking of glaciers all over China, the country has enacted a new policy banning tourists from getting near them. More than likely you won't be able to get as close as I once did in the video linked to below, but you can still see the beautiful glacier as you drive by.

Watch: Josh's road trip along Highway 216
www.xjtravelguide.com/highway-216

Ruins of Luntai City in Wulabo

⬅——————————➡

- **Name**: 乌拉泊古城/Wūlābó Gǔchéng
- **Price:** Free to enter
- **Rating**: Not worth a stop
- **Map**: See Urumqi Area Map

Back during the Tang Dynasty (or possibly earlier), this ancient city thrived as a part of the Silk Road. Thanks to the construction of the nearby reservoir in more recent times, ancient tombs full of various artifacts have been excavated. The area now sits as a protected historical site.

Historical relevance does not always convert to value in tourism, however. The grounds of this city are vast and the mounds of mud, with the exception of a few walls, are indistinguishable. The small exhibition hall (or "museum") isn't quite worth the money you'll pay to hire a car down to the city.

Spare yourself the disappointment and instead make a stop at the Silk Road town of Turpan, a wonderful town south of Urumqi. Here, there are a couple of ancient cities in much better condition and more interesting than Luntai.

Where to Stay in Urumqi

Urumqi Hotel Recommendations

- ✓ **Best hostel**: Maitian Youth Hostel
- ✓ **Best luxury hotel**: Sheraton Hotel
- ✓ **Best hotel(s) in the Uyghur side of town**: Aksaray and Tumaris Hotels
- ✓ **Best hotel in the center of town**: JinJiang Inn
- ✓ **Best High-Speed Train Station Hotel**: Wanda Vista
- ✓ **Best south train station hotels**: Super 8 & Kashgar Hotel
- ✓ **Best airport hotel**: Tianyuan Hotel

It's in your best interest to arrive in Urumqi with at least the address and phone number of the hotel you wish to stay, although I recommend you make some reservations if possible.

As is the case in all of China, only hotels rated with three stars or greater are officially allowed to accept foreigners. Oftentimes experienced travelers who speak Mandarin can get around this restriction to get "Chinese rates" at smaller hotels but thankfully the rates at all the government-approved hotels are cheaper or at least comparable to those in the rest of China.

I've already given you my specific recommendations above, but more detail is provided in the following pages, separated out into Budget, Mid-Range and Luxury hotels:

- Luxury Hotels in Urumqi
- Mid-Range Hotels in Urumqi
- Budget Hostels in Urumqi

Luxury Hotels in Urumqi

Urumqi Hotel (formerly Sheraton)

Considering location, the Urumqi Hotel is one of the best 5-star hotels in Urumqi and offers all the amenities you would expect from a (former) Sheraton – spa, pool, workout facilities, shopping, & incredibly comfortable beds. Prices will be higher than the average Urumqi hotel. This beautiful hotel is located in the trendy YouHao district next to plenty of shopping, eating and the Xinjiang museum.

> 喜来登/Xīláidēng
> **Address**: 669 Youhao Road (友好北路 669 号)
> **Phone**: (0991) 699-9999
> **Map**: Urumqi Map A2 – 1

Pictures, Pricing and Booking: **www.xjtravelguide.com/urumqi-sheraton**

Wanda Vista Hotel

As the newest hotel of this list, the Wanda Vista Hotel is the most pristine hotel. From here, you're walking distance from the high-speed train station, a large shopping center and plenty of other sections of Urumqi's new development zone. Pricing is high but the comfort level can't be beat in Urumqi.

> 万达文华酒店/Wàndá Wénhuá Jiǔdiàn
> **Address**: 777 Xuanwuhu Road (玄武湖路 777 号)
> **Phone**: (0991) 318-1111
> **Map**: Just west of high-speed train station

Pictures, Pricing and Booking: **www.xjtravelguide.com/urumqi-wanda**

Hoi Tak Hotel

The Hoi Tak, located right beside the People's Park, used to be the go-to Urumqi hotel for years, although it's starting to show its age. Like the Sheraton, it offers many amenities and is a bit pricey, but it's a great location to catch a bus anywhere in the city.

> 海德酒店/Hǎidé Jiǔdiàn
> **Address**: No 1 Dong Feng Road (东风路 1 号)
> **Phone**: (0991) 232-2828
> **Map**: Urumqi Map D4 – 4

Pictures, Pricing and Booking: **www.xjtravelguide.com/urumqi-hoitak**

YinDu Hotel

银都酒店/Yíndū Jiǔdiàn
Address: 179 East Xihong Road (西虹东路 179 号)
Phone: (0991) 453-6688
Map: Urumqi Map A3 – 2

The Yin Du Hotel is an excellent high-end option that is frequented by travelers, businessmen & (at least in the past) diplomats. It is located somewhat near Hong Shan Park, the Xinjiang Museum and lots of public transportation. There's plenty of shopping and restaurants nearby as well that will keep you busy.

Pictures, Pricing and Booking: **www.xjtravelguide.com/urumqi-yindu**

Grand Mercure Hotel

美爵大饭店/Měijué Dàfàndiàn
Address: 109 East Xihong Road (西虹东路 109 号)
Phone: (0991) 518-8888
Map: Urumqi Map B2 – 3

The Grand Mercure Hotel is an Accor-managed hotel that is the lowest-priced 5-star option I've found in Urumqi. It's location in the center of a trade center means that there's plenty of activity nearby although that also means that transportation can sometimes be hard to come by.

Pictures, Pricing and Booking: **www.xjtravelguide.com/urumqi-grand-mercure**

International Trade Grand Hotel

国际外贸大饭店/Guójì Wàimào Dàfàndiàn
Address: 389 Tuanjie Road (团结路 389 号)
Phone: (0991) 853-2222
Map: Urumqi Map C6 – 5

This hotel has one of the best locations in the south of Urumqi with incredible views of the city and the International Grand Bazaar. It caters to businessmen and luxury travelers, providing comfort and good service.

Pictures, Pricing and Booking: **Online booking unavailable in English**

Mid-Range Hotels in Urumqi

Aksaray Hotel

The Aksaray Hotel is a nice Uyghur-style hotel worth staying in the southern part of Urumqi. The location next to the International Grand Bazaar and near a BRT stop is excellent and there are plenty of food options nearby.

Pictures, Pricing and Booking:
www.xjtravelguide.com/urumqi-aksaray

> 阿迪力商厦 /**Ādílì Shāngshà**
> **Address:** 160 Shengli Road (胜利路 160 号)
> **Phone:** (0991) 288-6666
> **Map:** Urumqi Map C6 – 6

JinJiang Inn

The JinJiang Inn is a popular hotel chain you'll find anywhere you go in China. This particular hotel is located in the dead center of the former downtown next to plenty of great shopping, dining and transportation. I recommend this hotel for anybody who needs to split their time between the northern and southern parts of Urumqi.

> 锦江之星酒店/**Jǐnjiāng Zhīxīng Jiǔdiàn**
> **Address:** 93 Hongqi Road (红旗路 93 号)
> **Phone:** (0991) 281-5000
> **Map:** Urumqi Map C4 – 9

Pictures, Pricing and Booking: **www.xjtravelguide.com/jinjiang-urumqi**

Youhao Hotel

The Youhao Hotel, located across the street from the Urumqi Hotel (Sheraton), is a comfortable but much cheaper alternative if this is the area you want to be in. The hotel is within walking distance of the Xinjiang museum as well as plenty of shopping, dining and grocery stores.

> 友好大酒店/**Yǒuhào Dàjiǔdiàn**
> **Address:** 548 Youhao Road (友好路 548 号)
> **Phone:** (0991) 483-6888
> **Map:** Urumqi Map A2 – 10

Pictures, Pricing and Booking: **www.xjtravelguide.com/urumqi-youhao**

Tumaris Hotel

突玛丽斯大饭店/Tūmǎlìsī Dàfàndiàn
Address: 618 South Xinhua Road (新华南路 618 号)
Phone: (0991) 852-5555
Map: Urumqi Map C6 – 12

This beautiful 4-star hotel is located in the Uyghur heart of Urumqi. It's less than 100 meters away from the International Bazaar and all the major Uyghur shopping options. What's cool about this hotel, though, is the beautiful ethnic influences in the architecture and interior design. It's not a luxury hotel, but it's definitely an experience that you'll enjoy.

Pictures, Pricing and Booking: **Online booking not available**

Super 8 Hotel

速 8 酒店/Sùbā Jiǔdiàn
Address: 508 Qiantangjiang Road (钱塘江路 508 号) - Near Train Station
Phone: (0991) 562-5888
Map: Urumqi Map A6 – 7

The great thing about the Super 8 chain is the price, which is quite cheap, and the fact that they have multiple locations throughout the city. These locations include a spot near the train station, next to the People's Park and near the city center. Be aware: they've been known to turn away foreigners so you might have to go elsewhere.

Pictures and Pricing: **Online booking unavailable**

Kashgar International Hotel

喀什国际酒店/Kāshi Guójì Jiǔdiàn
Address: 419 Qiantangjiang Road (钱塘江路 419 号) - Near Train Station
Phone: (0991) 557-3333
Map: Urumqi Map A6 – 8

The Kashgar International Hotel is across the street from the Super 8 and a step above in terms of comfort. The pricing will also be slightly higher, but it's a great place to stay if you get in late or leave early from the old Urumqi train station.

Pictures and Pricing: **Online booking unavailable in English**

Tianyuan Airport Hotel

With its prominent location across from the Urumqi International Airport, the Tianyuan Hotel is a perfect option for anybody who needs to get up early for a flight out. It's a "luxury" hotel based on star ratings but it's usually reasonably priced and within walking distance of the airport. Other, cheaper airport hotels are further south if this ends up being beyond your price point.

天緣酒店 /**Tiānyuán Jiǔdiàn**
Address: 1341 Yingbin Road (迎賓路 1341 号)
Phone: (0991) 761-1111
Map: Urumqi Map A1 - 11

Pictures, Pricing and Booking: **www.xjtravelguide.com/urumqi-tianyuan**

Budget Hostels in Urumqi

⟵――――――――――――⟶

Maitian Youth Hostel

The MaiTian is currently one of the best youth hostels in terms of location and one of the only ones that can be booked online. It's situated right next to HongShan Park, a large grocery store and plenty of good transportation. The rooms are clean and wifi is included. This hostel is tucked away in a small alley, so check the map carefully and don't get discouraged if it takes a moment to find.

麦田国际青年旅馆/**Màitián Guójì Qīngniánlǚguǎn**
Address: 726 South Youhao Road (友好南路 726 号)
Phone: (0991) 459-1488
Map: Urumqi Map B3 - 13

Pictures, Pricing and Booking: **www.xjtravelguide.com/urumqi-maitian**

White Birch Hostel

The White Birch is a good hostel with an unfortunate location. You'll find the rooms and pricing to be good but with the current subway construction and the sealing off of the Nanhu Park, this hostel is not conveniently located in the city anymore.

白桦林国际青年旅舍 **Báihuà Línguójì Qīngniánlǚshè**
Address: 186 Nanhu Road (南湖路 186 号)
Phone: (0991) 488-1428
Map: Urumqi Map C2 - 14

Pictures, Pricing and Booking: **www.xjtravelguide.com/urumqi-white-birch**

Where to eat in Urumqi

As one might expect, Urumqi offers the widest variety of dining options in Xinjiang, more than can be mentioned here. What you'll find on this page are recommendations for stable, higher-end Uyghur restaurants as well as western fare and coffee shops.

However, you should take time to wander the streets and pop into one of the hundreds of small shops that sell noodles, Uyghur cuisine, and Chinese dishes. Recommendations of this kind are hard to make and part of the joy of eating at a hole-in-the-wall is the process of discovery.

Uyghur Cuisine

Instead of attempting the impossible feat of naming hundreds of Uyghur restaurants in Urumqi, I will just name a few of the higher-end restaurants around the International Bazaar.

- **Zamzam Restaurant** (Urumqi Map C6 - 13): located behind and a little north of the Grand Bazaar on Heping Nan Lu, this Uyghur restaurant (and others nearby) serves great traditional food (0991-853-0555).
- **Astana Restaurant** (Urumqi Map D6 - 9): An upscale Uyghur restaurant that has some outdoor seating during the summer months (0991-288-5899).
- **Herembag, aka "Eden Cafe"** (Urumqi Map C6 - 11): A chain of nice Uyghur restaurants, this one can be found on Tuanjie Road just south of the International Bazaar (0991-852-7444).
- **The Diplomat** (Urumqi Map C6 - 10): A Uyghur/Turkish restaurant connected to the Aksaray Hotel (0991-285-8588).
- **Food Court over Arman** (Urumqi Map C6 - 12): A Uyghur/Turkish food court is located on the second floor over the Arman grocery store. The food is good but the view of the Tartar Mosque is even better, especially during Friday prayers.

Foreign Cuisine

There are only three big western fast-food chains in Urumqi: **Burger King**, **Pizza Hut**, and **KFC**. While locations for the first two have been noted on the map, I won't go into detail about them.

There used to be a number of foreign-run restaurants in Urumqi that are still listed in some of the old travel guides (Rendezvous, Aroma, Texas Cafe), but unfortunately all of these places have been forced to close their doors.

Coffee Shops/Bars

Coffee is a burgeoning fad in Xinjiang and while there are plenty of places that sell coffee, most of them aren't great. I'll only mention a couple of the best here:

- **Caffe Bene** (Urumqi Map C1, C4 - 14): South Korean chain that has multiple locations across the city, including one near Hong Shan Park.
- **Meseta Coffee** (Urumqi Map C6 - 15): A small coffee shop under the ring road nearby the Grand Bazaar. Nice atmosphere and good coffee.
- **Tous le Jours** (Urumqi Map A1, A2, B3 - 16): While this is technically a French bakery, this chain offers some pretty good coffee as well. Their bread and sandwiches are great to purchase as a meal for the train.
- **DaWan Coffee Shops**: A number of new Uyghur-run coffee shops have popped up around the Dawan area in southern Urumqi. A few such coffee shops can be found on Fukan Jie (富康街) south of Dawan (大湾北路).

There are numerous bars in Urumqi, most of which are clustered together in different spots. The most popular has been Fubar (0991-581-4698) located along a street full of bars beside People's Park (the northern entrance on Urumqi Map B4). While it was established by a foreigner it is now under local management.

Turpan

吐鲁番

Turpan Top Sights

Emin Minaret – Pg 142
The most iconic building in all of Turpan is this mosque whose minaret boasts some incredible Uyghur brick patterns.

Jiaohe Ancient City Ruins – Pg 143
Within the ancient ruins of Jiaohe ("Yarkhoto") you can still see homes, temples and government offices from 2,000 years ago!

Tuyoq Valley – Pg 151

Step back in time to witness what life for the Uyghur has been like for centuries.

Sand Dunes Park – Pg 158

Ride a camel, walk through the dunes or bury yourself in the "healing" sands of Sand Dunes Park.

Introduction to Turpan 吐鲁番

Turpan, also known as "Turfan" or "Tulufan", is one of my favorite places to tour in all of Xinjiang. Not only does it offer a wonderful immersion into the Uyghur culture, it's now only one hour from Urumqi, thanks to the new high-speed train.

This small Silk Road oasis can be enjoyed for a simple day trip, but I recommend you budget at least 2-3 days to fully appreciate the culture and sites in and around the city.

Aside from history and Uyghur culture, Turpan is most known for its unbearable summer heat. Because it is situated on the northern tip of the Turpan Depression, the second lowest continental point in the world behind the Dead Sea, temperatures in July and August can reach well above 40°C (104°F). If you plan to visit during that time, be sure to pack sunscreen and plenty of water!

Watch! Josh's Top 5 Turpan destinations:
www.xjtravelguide.com/turpan-intro-video

Traveling to Turpan

Turpan's smaller size, at least in comparison to other cities in China, is ideal for travelers since it doesn't require lengthy transport to get from place to place. In fact, I highly recommend you rent a bike to get around if you're up for the exercise.

For day-trippers or those who just want to visit the city, make sure to visit the **Turpan Museum**, the **Emin Minaret** and the **Jiaohe Ancient City Ruins**. If you're particularly motivated you can also make time for the **Karez** and the **Grape Valley**, although that would be pushing it for a single day.

Multi-day trips should include a few of the sites outside the city. Time permitting, the best destinations to put on your itinerary would be **Tuyoq Valley**, **GaoChang Ancient City Ruins**, and the **Bezikelik Caves**. The **Flaming Mountains** can be seen from the highway, not necessitating a tourist stop.

Other locations of interest include the **Astana Graves**, **Moon Lake** (aka "Aiding") and the **Sand Dunes Park**, although none of these are an essential addition to your itinerary.

As you plan your trip, make sure to budget enough time to just walk around Turpan. From the night market to the grape trellis street, there's a beautiful atmosphere in Turpan that can only be experienced by walking around at dusk.

Getting to/from Turpan

◄━━━━━━━━━━━━━━━━━━━━━━━━━━►

Thankfully, getting to and from Turpan is incredibly easy. There are a number of different options although the best option by far is the high-speed train.

Turpan By Train

In November 2014, Xinjiang opened up a new high-speed train that has become the most comfortable and convenient way to get to Turpan, whether you're originating in Urumqi (less than an hour) or Lanzhou (around 12 hours).

This is important: The new high-speed train station has caused a bit of confusion among travelers since there are now two Turpan train stations.

The old station, simply referred to as "Turpan Station" (吐鲁番站), is still located 50 kilometers outside of Turpan in a small town called Daheyan (大河沿). Transportation between the old station and Turpan is long and difficult, but it can be done by shared taxi (~60 RMB/pax), by private taxi (~300 RMB) or by bus (~11 RMB). Most trains that aren't high-speed trains (ones that donn't have a "D") stop at the old train station.

The new Turpan train station, referred to as "Turpan North" (吐鲁番北), is large, beautiful and much closer to the city. Instead of an hour, the new train station is only 10-15 minutes from the city center by taxi (~30-50 RMB) or can be reached by city bus (202; 1 RMB) in less than half an hour.

As you purchase train tickets, make sure you double check whether you are getting off at Turpan Station or Turpan North. It makes a difference!

Train tickets can be bought at the station, at a train booking office on LaoCheng Road (Turpan Map - C3) or online. For reference, a quick list of main cities and the the price and time to travel to **Turpan**:

- **Urumqi:** 58/49 RMB (1st class/2nd class); 55 minutes; Turpan North
- **Hami:** 196/163 RMB (1st class/2nd class); 3.5 hours Turpan North
- **Lanzhou:** 658/548 RMB (1st class/2nd class); 12 hours; Turpan North
- **Korla:** 123/69 RMB (hard sleeper/hard seat); 7 hours; Turpan Station
- **Kashgar:** 304/177 RMB (hard sleeper/hard seat); 23 hours; Turpan Station

To view train schedules or purchase tickets online, check here:
www.xjtravelguide.com/train-tickets

Turpan by Bus

If the idea of purchasing train tickets or trying to navigate a foreign train station scares you (it shouldn't!), buses are a quick and cheap alternative. Tickets are much easier to obtain and there are plenty of departure times to choose from.

The Turpan bus station can be found on the south side of the Night Market on Chunshu Road (椿树路). Below is a reference of cities and prices to travel to Turpan from each:

- **Urumqi**: 45 RMB, leaves every 20 minutes, 3.5 hours
- **Hami**: 89 RMB, one departure in the morning, 6 hours
- **Kashgar**: 292/320 RMB (upper/lower berth), leaves at 4pm, 23 hours
- **Dunhuang**: 161 RMB, one afternoon departure, 11 hours

Turpan by Air

In July of 2010, Xinjiang announced the reopening of the Turpan airport after a nearly 40-year absence. It's not practical to fly to/from Urumqi, but there are flights into the rest of China that allow you to avoid transiting through the capital of Urumqi.

These flights usually aren't cheap, though, so you'll need to do your research and count the cost.

Turpan by Car

If you'd rather hire a car to take you where you need to go, head to the Turpan bus station where there will be plenty of people asking where you want to go. You can also ask your hotel to recommend a driver and they will be happy to call one for you.

Cars are usually rented at a rate of 300-600 RMB per day depending on the type of car and whether or not your driver can speak English. If you don't pay for the entire car, expect for the driver to try to fill the extra seats.

For private drivers around Turpan, I recommend a Uyghur gentleman named Tahir who can pick you up at either train station and drive you around the city. His prices are fair and he speaks good English. Contact him using his phone number: 150-2626-1388.

Transportation within Turpan

City buses run all across Turpan and cost only 1 RMB per person. Taxis should get you most anywhere you want to go within the city for a reasonable price (10-20 RMB).

You can find bicycles to rent at John's Cafe (5 RMB/hr or 40 RMB/day) or at the Dap Youth Hostel.

What to do in Turpan

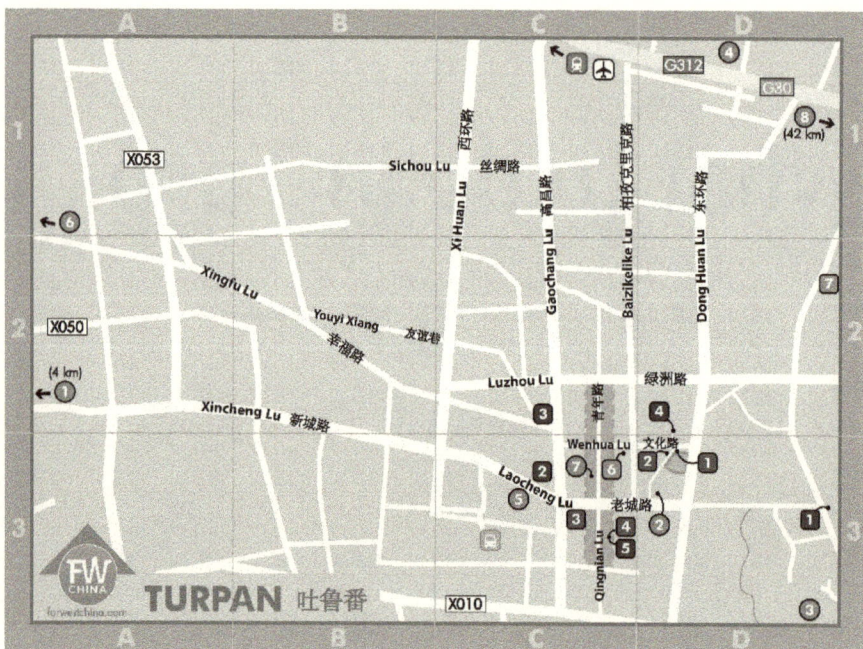

TURPAN 吐鲁番

X053
X050
(4 km)
X010

Sichou Lu 丝绸路
Xi Huan Lu 西环路
Gaochang Lu 高昌路
Baizikelike Lu 柏孜克里克路
Dong Huan Lu 东环路
Xingfu Lu
Youyi Xiang 友谊巷
幸福路
Luzhou Lu 绿洲路
Xincheng Lu 新城路
Wenhua Lu 文化路
Laocheng Lu 老城路
Qingnian Lu 青年路

G312
G30
(42 km)

TURPAN 吐鲁番

RESTAURANTS
1 Herembag -- D2
2 Ahatjan -- D2
3 Hanzada -- C3
4 John's Cafe -- C3

TRANSPORTATION
🚌 Bus Station -- C3
🚉 Train Station -- C1
🎫 Train Tickets -- C3
✈ Airport

HOTELS
1 Silk Road Lodge -- D3
2 JiaoTong Hotel -- C3
3 Turpan Grand Hotel -- C2
4 Turpan Petroleum Hotel -- D2
5 Turpan Hotel -- C3

Hostels:
6 White Camel Youth Hostel -- C3
7 Dap Youth Hostel -- D2

🏯 Mosque
✚ Hospital
E Entrance
¥ Bank

CITY SIGHTS
1 Ancient City of Jiaohe -- A2
2 Turpan Museum -- D3
3 Emin Minaret -- D3
4 Grape Valley -- D1
5 Night Market -- C3
6 Karez -- A1
7 Covered Walkway -- C3
8 Bezeklik Thousand -- C3
   Buddha Caves

To receive a free, full-resolution PDF version of this and all the maps in this guide, please register your book:

www.xjtravelguide.com/register

140

Turpan Museum

- **Name**: 吐鲁番博物馆/Tǔlǔfān Bówùguǎn
- **Hours**: 10am-7pm; closed Monday
- **Price**: Free (passport required)
- **Rating**: Highly recommended
- **Map**: Turpan Map D3 - 2

One of the first stops you should make in Turpan is the beautiful Turpan Museum. Turpan boasts one of the largest museums in all of Xinjiang, second only to the museum in Urumqi. In 2009, twenty years after the old museum was built, Turpan dedicated a new, beautiful building to hold its growing collection of over 3,200 pieces of art and history.

Within this collection there is a vast amount of what they call "Tang Dynasty artifacts" (a name referring to the time period, not the type of artifact) dug from the various ruins around the city. Most notable are the numerous, well-preserved mummies that are definitely worth a look on the third floor.

Other exhibits include artifacts excavated from Jiaohe, Gaochang and Astana. These items range from everyday pottery (from the Gaochang Kingdom period) to gold jewelry, silks and clothes possibly worn by ancient nobility.

Most signs and descriptions in the museum are translated into English and kids may enjoy the dinosaur exhibit on the second floor.

Getting There: Take bus 1 or 4 to the "Lao Cheng Dong Men" station (老城东门).

Emin Minaret

- **Name**: 苏公塔/Sūgōng Tǎ
- **Price:** 45 元 (minaret grounds only)
- **Rating**: Highly recommended
- **Map**: Turpan Map D3 - 3

The Emin Minaret is by far the most well-known of Turpan's tourist destinations. Although many beautiful and more colorful mosques exist within the city, the distinctive brick patterns and typical Uyghur architecture make this the face of Turpan tourism.

Historical Perspective | Emin Minaret

This mosque and attached minaret were constructed in honor of Emin Khoja (sometimes spelled 'Imin Hoja'), a Uyghur Turpan ruler during most of the 18th century, long after the ancient cities of Jiaohe and Gaochang had been abandoned.

Born in 1694 in the nearby town of Astana, he became a khoja (a word meaning "king" or "prince") who, according to the Chinese history books, maintained a constant and friendly relationship with the Qing Dynasty emperors.

For more than half a century, Emin Khoja remained a prominent leader in the Turpan area, maintaining peace by resisting invading Jungar troops from the outside and quelling rebellions from the inside. Toward the end of his rule, he even made trips to Beijing to meet with the Qing Dynasty emperor, at one point being asked to stay for 5 years. In 1772, while making a visit back to Turpan for holiday, his health took a turn for the worse. He remained in Turpan for five more years, cared for by his two sons, until his death at the age of 83.

Before he passed away, however, he and his son Suleman arranged for the mosque and minaret to be built in his honor. Construction began in 1777, the year that Emin Khoja passed away, and was completed in 1778.

Tips for Tourists | Emin Minaret

The Emin Minaret complex is comprised of two places you can visit: the Mosque and the Governor's Mansion. Tickets are purchased separately.

The **Governor's Mansion** is a recreation of Emin Khoja's palace depicting high-class Uyghur life during the 18th century. It's not a "must-see" but I did find it entertaining.

Along an underground tunnel you'll get a detailed history of the Khoja's life (favorable to the Chinese, of course), written in Chinese, Arabic, and poorly translated English. Artifacts are few and the place isn't well-maintained, so I don't often recommend visitors spend the money to enter the mansion.

The **Mosque and Minaret** are the heart of the complex. You can get a decent picture from the viewing deck to the south and you're allowed to enter the mosque and look around as long as worshippers are not in the middle of prayers.

Take a close look at the brickwork on the minaret. Thousands of mud bricks arranged in over 10 different repeating, geometric patterns present a good illustration of Uyghur architecture at the time. Mud is the one material they had in great supply and they knew how to use it!

Directly behind and to the side of the mosque is a traditional Uyghur cemetery. Take a walk around and notice the grave designs: cylindrical, sometimes pointed at the top, and no markings indicating names or dates. This is common in Uyghur cemeteries around Xinjiang.

Two interesting facts to note here: 1) there is a spiral staircase in the minaret that used to be open to tourists, but has sadly been closed for almost three decades due to safety concerns; 2) Look closely at the front wall of the mosque just to the right of the entrance. In 2012, this wall completely collapsed and had to be reconstructed – you can still see the outline of the old and new mud.

Getting There: There is no convenient bus that can get you all the way to the Emin complex. It's best to either hire a taxi or, if you're brave, ride a bike.

Jiaohe Ancient City Ruins

- **Name**: 交河故城/Jiāohé Gùchéng
- **Price**: 70 元
- **Rating**: Highly recommended
- **Map**: Turpan Map A2 - 1

As a tourist, few places are as entertaining to visit in Turpan as the Jiaohe Ancient City Ruins. It's usually the first place I stop when I'm showing people around and it never disappoints.

For nearly thirteen centuries, a lively city perched atop this narrow plateau 10 kilometers west of modern-day Turpan. Like most cities in Xinjiang, it bears a Chinese name "Jiaohe", and a lesser-known local name, "Yarkhoto."

Jiaohe may not be as large or as historically important as the nearby Gaochang ruins, but in my opinion, it is more visually pleasing. The two most distinctive features at Jiaohe are the absence of any city wall and the fact that many of the structures in the city, including the streets, were dug out of the ground rather than built up.

Note: Jiaohe now advertises a "Jiaohe at Night" program on Friday and Saturday evening at 9:40pm, featuring music, candlelight and a view of the ancient city by moonlight. The cost is 70 RMB (same as an entrance ticket) but it's not geared toward foreign tourists. Unless this type of experience really appeals to you, my advice is to skip it.

Historical Perspective | Jiaohe

Established early in the Han Dynasty as a garrison town, Jiaohe continued to flourish under both Chinese and Uyghur rule until it was finally abandoned at the end of the 14th century. The earliest known inhabitants were a group of people called the "Jüshi" (车师) who made the city their capital until it became a part of the Gaochang kingdom in 450 A.D.

At this point the capital was moved from Jiaohe to what is now the ancient city of Gaochang. Almost 200 years later (640 A.D.) the Tang dynasty set up their governmental offices at Jiaohe, offices that are still visible today.

Because the most thorough excavations of these ruins have been focused on the monasteries in the northern part of town, a good portion of the archeological finds are religious in nature, including painted silks, Buddhist statues and religious manuscripts. This is changing, however, as they continue to dig up the residential districts in the eastern part of town where they are finding pottery and tools.

Watch! Josh's video introduction to Jiaohe:
www.xjtravelguide.com/jiaohe-video

Tips for Tourists | Jiaohe

A wide, central street runs north towards the Great Monastery and divides the city into east and west. Along this road is where all the old workshops and businesses were located, while on the far eastern and western sides are most of the residential districts. All administrative and governmental offices were set up in the central part of the city, a short distance from the many monasteries and Buddhist stupas that occupy the northern half of the ancient city.

Although walking the entire stretch of the city is a chore, it can be rewarding if you're up to the challenge. I believe there are four places of particular interest in the ancient city of Jiaohe:

- **Residential District**: Along the eastern ridge much of the houses were carved out of the natural ground and still retain their shape.
- **The Great Monastery**: The biggest of the city's monasteries is of interest because of rock statues that are still visible in the central pillar of the main hall.
- **Government Offices**: Steps lead down to the courtyard where various caves made up the offices.
- **The Stupa Grove**: In the northernmost part of the city (i.e. the longest walk!) sits 101 of Xinjiang's earliest stupas (ancient Buddhist monuments) dating from the 5th-7th centuries.

Jiaohe

1 Buddhist Stupa Grove

2 Great Monastery

3 Government Offices

Residential District

FW FAR WEST CHINA

Exploring Xinjiang and the Silk Road

Entrance 500m

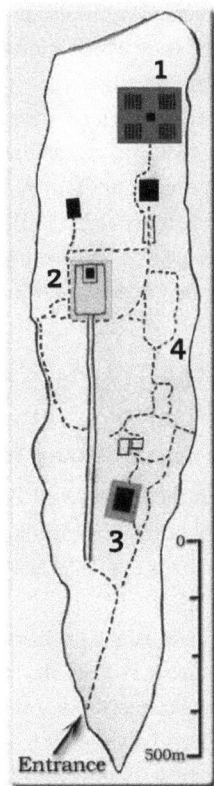

Getting There: Using public transportation, the fastest way is by taking bus 101 or 1 to its terminus at YaerXiang Village (亚尔乡). From there, hire a minibus or a taxi the final few kilometers.

Karez Ancient Irrigation System

◀━━━━━━━━━━━━━━━━━━━━━━━▶

- **Name**: 坎儿井/Kǎnrjǐng
- **Price**: 40 元
- **Rating**: Recommended if you have time
- **Map**: Turpan Map A1 & B2 - 8 & 9

If you ever find yourself wondering how a green oasis like Turpan can exist in such a hot and dry desert landscape, the answer is simple: **karez**. Heralded as one of the greatest Uyghur engineering accomplishments, this ancient irrigation system is the process by which snowmelt from nearby mountains is carried to the city through underground channels.

Because surface temperatures in the Turpan Depression can reach as high as 80°C (176°F), evaporation makes above-ground canals impractical. Instead, the Uyghur dug an underground canal from the mountains down to the city. A bird's eye view shows what looks like a neat row of gigantic ant hills, but each of these is actually a vertical shaft that connects subterranean streams of water flowing toward the city by force of gravity.

Tips for Tourists | Karez

There are two primary places to visit the Karez and they are practically next door to each other. The **Karez Well Amusement Park** (坎儿进乐园 Kǎnerjìn Lèyuán; Map A1) and the **Karez Well Folk Custom Garden** (坎儿进民俗园 Kǎnerjìn Mínsúyuán; Map B2) both offer similar experiences and have the same entry fee. My personal preference is the Folk Custom Garden but I have friends who prefer the Amusement Park.

Both tourist sites have good displays explaining the construction process with signs that are in English. Try to get yourself into the mindset of that time period and then go explore the karez. The walkable part of each karez is short, so don't rush through and make sure to snap good pictures while you can.

Getting There: Similar to Jiaohe, take the bus 101 or 1 to the terminus at YaerXiang Village (亚尔乡). The Folk Custom Garden is walkable from there but the Well Amusement Park will require an additional short taxi ride.

Grape Valley

- **Name:** 葡萄沟/Pútao Gōu
- **Price:** 75 元
- **Rating:** Enjoyable during grape season only
- **Map:** Turpan Map D1 - 4

During the months of July to September, it's pretty much impossible to miss all of the grapes falling off the vines everywhere you look in Turpan. And just in case you don't get the picture that grapes are abundant in this area, you can take a quick trip out to Turpan's Grape Valley.

At 8 kilometers in length and 2 kilometers in width, this valley covers a staggering 5,000 hectare that burst at the seams during grape season. Each year this valley produces over 6 million kilograms of grapes and almost half that amount in raisins.

There's plenty to keep you interested as you walk around including a winery that might provide good souvenirs, but there's no urgent need to stop here unless you visit during grape season. Even during grape season, there are plenty of other vineyards around Turpan that you can wander without a hefty entrance fee.

It is here, as well as throughout all of Turpan, that you'll get a close look at the mud-brick grape drying buildings. Crates of grape clusters are brought to these buildings and hung to dry into the raisins for which Turpan has become so famous.

Getting There: Take Turpan bus 4 to the front gate of the Grape Valley.

Turpan Animal Market

- **Name**: Friday Market
- **Price**: Free
- **Rating**: If you're here on Friday...go!
- **Map**: Turpan Map B3 - 10

> **Note**: There have been reports that this market - along with many others in Xinjiang - has been closed down. It's difficult to verify, so don't get your hopes too high.

In the village of Yar (亚尔) just a couple kilometers southwest of Turpan's city center, villagers gather every Friday for market. This isn't a widely-known destination so it's likely you won't run into any other tourists while you're there (unless they read this book!).

Horses, sheep, camels and other animals are bought and sold at the market in addition to all sorts of food and housewares. This isn't a place to buy a souvenir, though. Your time is best spent enjoying the festive atmosphere, doing a bit of people watching and snapping some photos.

Getting There: You'll need to hire a private car or take a taxi to this market. There's no official name for this market, but if you tell them you want to go to the 牲畜大市场 / Shēngchù Dàshìchǎng, they should know where to take you.

What to do Around Turpan

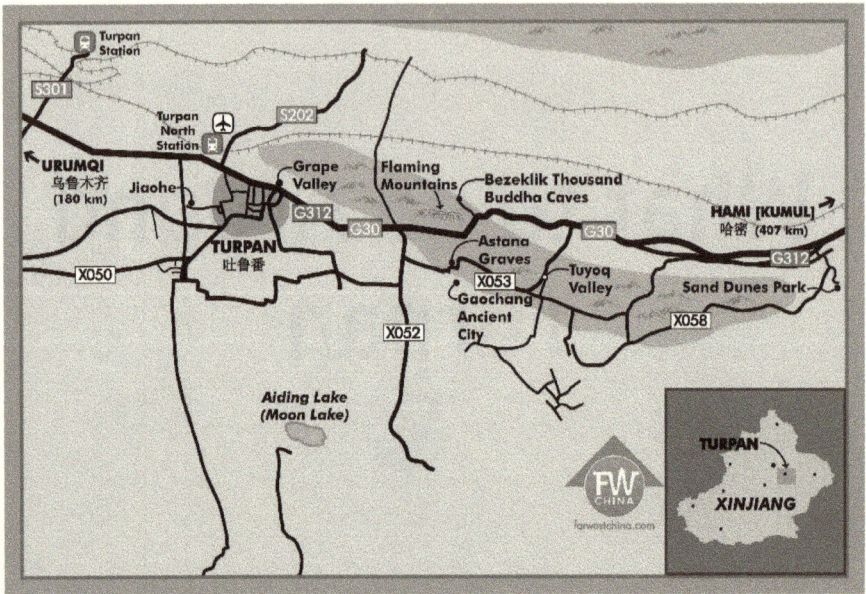

To receive a free, full-resolution PDF version of this and all the maps in this guide, please register your book:
www.xjtravelguide.com/register

Tuyoq Valley

- **Name:** 吐峪沟/Tǔyùgōu
- **Price:** 30 元
- **Rating:** Highly recommended
- **Map:** See Turpan Area Map

Hidden in a small valley between an extension of the Flaming Mountains is one of Turpan's most beautiful, yet surprisingly little-known villages. Tuyoq Valley is a living museum of Uyghur history and an example of the region's glorious mixture of dry and fertile landscape.

Within walking distance are Uyghur folk houses, an old cemetery, a Muslim pilgrimage site and a grape valley. The locals who currently live in this old village are accommodating but have become so callous to people taking their pictures that they may even ask you to pay for the privilege.

Finally, it's worth noting that while you may see signs for the Buddhist Caves, they've been closed to all visitors for years now. The caves are a dangerous climb up the cliffs and are in such a fragile state that local officials are paranoid about who can enter. I once arrived with a camera crew from CCTV (the state broadcaster at the time) and even they couldn't secure the right to view the caves.

Getting There

The biggest hurdle to visiting Tuyoq Valley is getting there. Because of its remote location, very few tours stop here. Unless you plan the trip ahead of time, a private driver may try to charge you extra while on the road.

To avoid these problems, try to work this into your schedule whenever you're visiting Turpan's eastern destinations, including the Gaochang Ancient City Ruins and the Bezeklik Caves.

Personal Endorsement

Tuyoq Valley is hands down my favorite stop in Turpan. It amazes me that travel books and tourist agencies don't push this location more. My guess is that it being 43 kilometers from Turpan could discourage prospective visitors. The valley is small enough to tour on foot yet big enough to keep your interest for the entire visit.

When you're in Turpan, chances are you'll visit the interesting, but lifeless, ruins of Jiaohe or Gaochang. I believe you would do yourself a disservice by failing to go to see this beautiful old village where people actually live and work.

Gaochang Ancient City Ruins

⬅━━━━━━━━━➡

- **Name**: 高昌故城/Gāochāng Gùchéng
- **Price**: 70 元
- **Rating**: Recommended if you have time
- **Map**: See Turpan Area Map

For nearly nine centuries, the ancient town of Gaochang ruled as a Chinese garrison and Uyghur capital of the region until it was finally left in ruins by wars during the end of the 14th century. Despite the current condition of many of its ruins, the sheer size of the city and its surrounding walls make for an awe-inspiring, albeit hot and tiring, desert walk.

A Brief History

The city of Gaochang was first established in the 2nd century A.D. as a garrison outpost for Han dynasty troops and in 443 was crowned the capital of the Western Han Empire (to the chagrin of Jiaohe, the prior capital located nearby). Later, when the Tang Dynasty occupied the area, they continued the legacy by naming Gaochang the capital of the local county and province.

It was during the middle of the 8th century that the Uyghur empire in the north of Xinjiang near Mongolia collapsed, causing large groups of Uyghurs to migrate south toward Turpan and the Gansu province. At this point, the Uyghur set up their new capital in Gaochang, which in the local language was called "Kharakhoja".

Archaeological Finds

Considering its location and traceable history of more than 1,400 years, it should come as no surprise that Gaochang is home to some of the most important archaeological finds for both the Uyghur and the Silk Road histories uncovered in Turpan. So great were the discoveries that in 1904, German explorer Albert von LeCoq spent 4 full months in Gaochang excavating and removing numerous manuscripts and sculptures.

Gaochang has often been referred to as a "cosmopolitan town" due to the variety of objects unearthed here. Traces of multiple religions, including Nestorian Christianity, Buddhism, Taoism, and Manichaeism (a dualistic religion notable for its strict vegetarian diet) have been discovered.

Texts have been uncovered written in Uyghur, Sanskrit, Chinese, and Tibetan, all of which give a sample of the ethnic changes that took place in the region's population over time.

City Layout

- **Inner Walls**: These walls, only parts of which still stand, represent the size of the town during its early existence.
- **Outer Walls**: It is believed that these walls were built by the Uyghur in an effort to extend and fortify the city around the 9th century; they measure 8-10 meters in height and thickness.
- **Palace Complex**: Although difficult to visualize now, the archaeological finds in this central area indicate all administrative offices and royal residences were located here.
- **Temple Complex**: Many temples existed in ancient Gaochang, but none were as big and impressive as this complex located in the southwest corner.

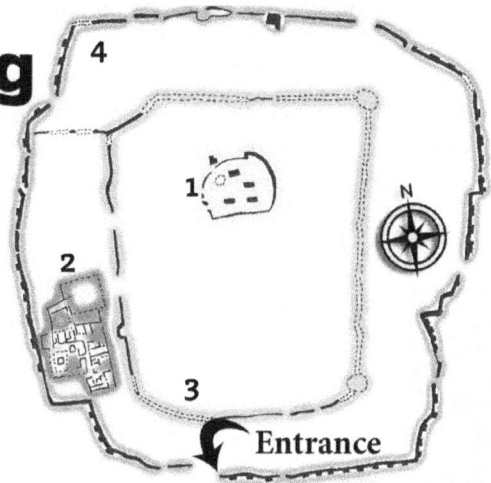

Gaochang

- Palace Complex
- 2 Temple Complex
- 3 Inner Walls
- 4 Outer Walls

FW FAR WEST CHINA
Exploring Xinjiang and the Silk Road

Entrance

Tourist Tips

- You'll have the option of walking, renting a bike or taking an electric vehicle around the ruins. Bear in mind that Gaochang covers quite a large area and might be difficult to traverse on foot, depending on your physical stamina. Expect to pay a small fee for a bike or a seat on an electric vehicle.
- Within the temple complex, take a careful look at the central post building (the square one that looks surprisingly well-preserved). The Buddhist niches on the south face of the building are of particular interest because you can still see traces of Buddhist paintings inside a few of the higher niches.

Bezekilik Caves

<——————————————————————————>

- **Name**: 柏孜克里克/Bózīkèlǐkè
- **Price**: 40 元
- **Rating**: Recommended if you have time
- **Map**: See Turpan Area Map

The Buddhist caves at Bezeklik, comfortably situated on a desert gorge overlooking the Mutougou River, used to house Turpan's most spectacular collection of Buddhist, Manichaean, and Uyghur art. Now it has unfortunately become a semi-empty monument to early-20th century archaeological extraction methods, as well as a testament to an international mud fight over which China remains bitter.

Other travel guides rashly advise travelers to "definitely skip" these caves; however, there is still something I find intriguing about Bezeklik. It might be the fact that these are one of the few ruins in Turpan where entire painted caves - despite their condition - are viewable. Even more interesting is the history of these caves, especially over the past two centuries.

A Brief History

It is widely believed, based on the basic shape of the caves and the style of painting within, that the Bezeklik caves were first built during the Gaochang Kingdom somewhere between 460-640A.D. Older history books refer to the caves as the Ningrong grottoes, a name which seems to loosely translate "the grottoes of a peaceful army."

Throughout the centuries, the caves have been rebuilt, additional caves added, and more paintings commissioned. The various pieces of art reflect this transition in both people groups and religions. From the 1st to 9th centuries, much of the art reflected the influence of Buddhism.

In the mid-9th century, when the Uyghur migrated to the area they brought with them the Manichaean religious art but converted to Buddhism in the early 10th century. Finally, in the 12th century as Mongols began to exert their influence on Asia, the painting style changed yet again. Traces of this timeline can still be seen in the caves, but the finest examples have already been cut out. Like most places in this area, the caves were abandoned in the 14th century.

It Just Wasn't Meant to Be

The tale of Bezeklik's art is a sad one to be sure. One of the primary arguments in defense of the 20th century explorers who cut out many of the beautiful murals in the caves was the obvious neglect and sometimes blatant vandalizing by the locals.

When Islam first swept through this part of Xinjiang in the 14th century, the eyes of many of the painted figures were gouged out or sometimes the entire depiction of Buddha was defaced (reproduction of the human form is forbidden in Islam). Later the locals began to believe that the paint scraped from these murals created an effective fertilizer.

Enter the European explorers, Swedish and German, to "rescue" many of these abandoned works of art. When they finally arrived at the museums in Berlin and elsewhere they were safe from destruction, right? Not quite. World War II meant bombs, a few of which destroyed the Berlin museum and half of the Bezeklik murals (not all, as China claims).

Finally, in 1916, part of the Bezeklik caves plunged into the gorge as a result of a severe earthquake that shook the area, destroying countless remaining works of art. This art just wasn't meant to stand the test of time.

Tourist Tips

- **Warning**: You can't take pictures inside the caves and more than likely a site overseer will shadow your movement to make sure you follow this rule.
- Take a stroll down the staircase toward the river if the gate is unlocked. Besides offering relief from the intense summer heat and a different angle for picture taking, you will also find the remains of a 13th century Uyghur stupa (unearthed in 1980) of minor interest.
- Site managers seem to open only a handful of caves at random each day. Be aware that not every cave contains art. Out of the 83 caves here, only 40 were actually painted in. The others were the monk's living quarters. The most distinctive cave paintings are in Cave 33 and 37, which are almost always open for viewing.
- Nearby Bezekilik you can usually find camels to ride for a small fee. Additionally, across the ravine there's an interesting staircase built up the side of the mountain that offers higher views of the valley. Mind you, it will take quite a bit of time and effort to climb all those stairs!

Flaming Mountains

- **Name**: 火焰山/Huǒyàn Shān
- **Price**: 40 元
- **Rating**: Worth a look, not a visit
- **Map**: See Turpan Area Map

The Flaming Mountains owe their name and popularity to a single Chinese novel entitled Journey to the West. This fictitious story about a pilgrim monk named Tripitaka is very loosely based on the actual journey of a monk named Xuan Zang who traveled over 5,000km to India and back in search of Buddhist scriptures.

This bizarre novel tells how Tripitaka encountered mountains of fire which under certain lighting conditions seem to flicker with the glowing light of red-hot flames. In the story, the flames were extinguished to allow for the monk's safe passage. Now the Flaming Mountains stand as a subtle reminder of how blazing hot the Turpan Depression is.

Tips for Tourist | Flaming Mountains

The Flaming Mountains are beautiful but the tourist destination is unnecessary, in my opinion. Anybody driving along the highway can see the same exact cliff face, tourist just pay to view it from a specific plot of land, on the back of a camel or on a flimsy powered glider.

If that's your thing, then don't let me stop you! I'm just warning you that I have stuck my head out of the car window to take a few photos and was more than pleased to miss the tourist trap.

Astana Graves

- **Name**: 阿斯塔那古墓群/Āsītǎnà Gǔmùqún
- **Price**: 40 元
- **Rating**: Not a "Must-See"
- **Map**: See Turpan Area Map

Throughout history, kings and leaders have usually lacked a certain sense of humility when it comes to their burial. Consider the Pharaohs of Egypt, the royalty of Europe or even the Emperors of China, each of whom built gigantic monuments to honor them after their death.

Astana was once the graveyard for the kings and nobles of the nearby kingdom of Gaochang, but unlike the aforementioned rulers, the Astana graves could easily be overlooked. Unless you know what you are looking for, you might mistake the underground tombs as bumps in the sand.

Since 1959, more than 400 excavated graves have yielding incredible murals, sculptures and a few corpses naturally mummified by the dry Turpan weather. Today, only three of these graves are open to tourists, one of which holds two mummies and the other two displaying murals.

Is It Worth It?

Here's my suggestion: if you have time to visit the Turpan Museum, which exhibits many of the mummies found in the Astana graves, then a trip to Astana is a duplicate effort. If, however, the museum is closed or you don't have time to go, a quick stop at Astana could be worth your time.

Moon Lake (Aiding)

- **Name**: 艾丁湖/Àidīng Hú
- **Price:** 30 元
- **Rating**: Optional, not recommended
- **Map**: See Turpan Area Map

Moon Lake, at 154 meters below sea level, is known as the second lowest lake in the world. You won't see too many pictures of this lake around town because, frankly, the scenery is about as picturesque as the Dead Sea in Israel, the title-holder for the world's lowest lake.

Although it may sound enticing during the hot summer to visit the Turpan region's largest body of water, don't be fooled into thinking you'll get in a good swim. Salty mud makes it a "look-only" destination.

The location is a bit out of the way and not near any other major tourist sites, so I don't normally recommend it to travelers.

Sand Dunes Park

←————————————————————→

- **Name**: 沙山公园/Shāshān Gōngyuán
- **Price**: 30 元
- **Rating**: Optional
- **Map**: See Turpan Area Map

One of the most familiar images of Xinjiang is a camel trekking along the desert dunes. While the largest and most famous desert in the province, the Taklimakan Desert, is quite a distance from Turpan, the closer Kumtag Desert does provide its own sand dunes that closely mimic that of its bigger brother to the west.

If your trip itinerary doesn't include Kashgar, Aksu, Korla, or any of the other numerous Taklamakan oasis cities and you have a desperate desire to ride a camel in the desert, Sand Dunes Park might be a worthwhile destination.

Riding a Camel

It is here at the Sand Dunes Park that you can ride a camel if you so desire. I can tell you from experience that it's not the most comfortable animal to ride on, but it's worth trying once.

Camels usually rent at about 100-200 RMB each for a short ride around a beaten path. For more information, see the chapter on Camel Treks.

Sand Therapy

Another famous activity in the Turpan area is known as "Sand Therapy." Participants bury half their bodies in the dunes in order to take advantage of the supposed healing powers of the local sand.

Take part if you wish or just enjoy the chance to take a few funny pictures. You'll likely be the only foreigner there!

Where to Stay in Turpan

Recommended Turpan Hotels

- **Best hostel**: Dap Hostel
- **Best luxury lodging**: The Vines Silk Road Lodge
- **Best mid-range hotel**: Tianhe Hotel

Turpan offers a great mix of budget lodging, luxury hotels and even a boutique bed and breakfast. Thankfully, the city is small enough that it's hard to have a bad location no matter where you're at.

Above are a few specific recommendations based on your needs with further options and detail following. This is what I recommend in Turpan for:

- **Luxury Hotels in Turpan**
- **Mid-Range Hotels in Turpan**
- **Budget Hostels in Turpan**

Luxury Hotels in Turpan

The Vines Silk Road Lodge

丝绸之路 公寓/Sīchóuzhīlù Gōngyù

Address: Muna'er Village (木纳尔村)

Phone: (0995) 856-8333

Map: Turpan Map D3 - 1

The Silk Road Lodge is the closest thing to a "boutique hotel" that you'll find in Xinjiang. It's located outside the city in the middle of a grape orchard, just a short walk from the Emin Minaret. The facilities are aging but the manager is wonderful as are the rest of the staff. If you want to experience rural Turpan life from the comfort of an air-conditioned bed-and-breakfast (with coffee in the morning!), you will love the Silk Road Lodge.

Pictures, Pricing and Booking: **www.xjtravelguide.com/turpan-vines**

Atour Hotel

亚朵/Yà duǒ

Address: Wenhua Rd (文化路)

Phone: (0995) 887-7777

Map: Turpan Map D2 – 4

Technically this is a 5-star hotel - and no doubt it's one of the nicer hotels in Turpan - but it doesn't quite compare with big city 5-star hotels. The hotel boasts large rooms and beautiful decoration. It is located on the west side of downtown, a simple taxi or long walk from most of what you'd want to see in town.

Pictures, Pricing and Booking: **www.xjtravelguide.com/turpan-atour**

Mid-Range Hotels in Turpan

Turpan Tianhe Hotel

Located on the main road in the center of town, this small hotel isn't flashy nor is it the most comfortable. It is, however, reasonably priced with an excellent location between the Uyghur market and the Turpan Museum.

天河宾馆/Tiānhé bīnguǎn
Address: 969 West Laocheng Central Road (老城中路 969 号)
Phone: (0995) 862-6999
Map: Turpan Map C2 - 2

Pictures, Pricing and Booking: **www.xjtravelguide.com/turpan-tianhe**

Turpan JinJiang Inn

Located on the north end of town, this Chinese chain hotel offers an excellent value. The beds are comfortable but keep in mind that you'll be in the Chinese part of town, away from all of the Uyghur influence.

锦江都城酒店/Jǐnjiāngdūchéng Jiǔdiàn
Address: 391 Luzhou Center Street
(绿洲中路 391 号)
Phone: (0995) 866-9666
Map: Turpan Map C2 - 3

Pictures, Pricing and Booking:
www.xjtravelguide.com/turpan-jinjiang

Turpan Hotel

Located a short walk from city life, the Turpan hotel boasts a quiet atmosphere in the central-south of town. Unfortunately, the building itself is quite old and in desperate need of renovation. Rooms aren't expensive but lack an inviting atmosphere.

吐鲁番宾馆/Tǔlǔfān Bīnguǎn
Address: 1695 Qingnian Road
(青年路 1695 号)
Phone: (0991) 856-8888
Map: Turpan Map C2 - 5

Pictures, Pricing and Booking:
Online reservations not available

Budget Hostels in Turpan

Dap Youth Hostel

吐鲁番达卜青年旅舍/Dábo
Qīngnián Lǔshě
Address: Tucked away on old Shahezi Road (老沙河子路)
Phone: (0995) 626-3193 or 186-9951-3631
Map: Turpan Map D2 - 7

Considered the best hostel in Turpan, the Dap Youth Hostel has a nice personal feel with a Uyghur-style influence. The hostel is a bit further outside of town but public transportation exists and better yet, they offer bike rentals. There are both shared and private rooms at a very reasonable price. You'll also enjoy the lovable golden retriever who lives there!

Pictures, Pricing and Booking: **www.xjtravelguide.com/turpan-dap**

Where to eat in Turpan

Where to eat in Turpan

If you need a couple suggestions on places to eat in Turpan, this short list should help get you started.

Uyghur Cuisine

It is impossible to walk a few meters in Turpan without running into a Uyghur restaurant. They're pretty much everywhere. Even though you can probably enjoy your meal at any hole-in-the-wall, if you're looking for a few suggestions, the following list of Uyghur restaurants should be helpful:

- **Hanzada Restaurant (Turpan Map C3 - 2)**: Located on the second floor on the southeast corner of the main city centre crossroads, the Hanzada restaurant is a favorite with locals. They have a picture menu but no English is spoken or written. Especially good pollo (lunch times) – order yoghurt and add sugar. Finish up your meal with local ice cream for dessert.

- **Herembag (Turpan Map D3 - 1)**: Located right next to the nice park with a lake, the Herembag is the only traditional-style Uighur restaurant in town. They feature an extensive menu, pictures of all dishes, and limited English. This restaurant is slightly more expensive than the other restaurants but is an excellent experience.

- **Night Market (Turpan Map C3 - 5)**: In the evenings, the Uyghur market turns into a food market where all sorts of grilled kebabs and noodles are available. It's a fun place to visit even if you only sample a few items.

Foreign Cuisine

Foreign food options are pretty much non-existent in Turpan. You might come across interesting fast food options boasting burgers, chicken and French fries...but sample at your own risk!

Hami 哈密

Hami Top Sights

Tombs of the Hami Kings – Pg 173
Beautiful Uyghur architecture that highlights this once-important center of trade and culture.

Introduction to Hami 哈密

◀━━━━━━━━━━━━━━━▶

Hidden behind the concrete walls of yet another ordinary Chinese city, Hami - known in Uyghur as Qumul or Kumul - boasts a rich history both for China and the Silk Road. Even as early as the 1st century, Hami was considered a key outpost in securing control of the mysterious western regions.

Of all the historical facts about Hami, probably the most interesting was shared by Marco Polo who visited Hami in the 13th century. He writes: "When strangers arrive and desire to have lodging and accommodation at [homes in Hami], it affords them the highest gratification. They give positive orders to their wives, daughters, sisters and other female relations, to indulge their guests in every wish, while they themselves leave their homes..."

Such strange "hospitality" no longer exists, of course. Still, Hami is a quaint town whose ancient stories of Uyghur kings, Silk Road travelers and constant revolts instill an air of mystery.

Traveling to Hami

That said, I personally don't believe Hami is worth more than a one-night stop, if that, which is probably why some travel guides leave this city out altogether. Anything of interest within the city can be seen in just a few hours and everything outside the city requires an allotment of time that most travelers can't afford.

From the train or bus station, a simple 15 RMB taxi ride will take you about 5km south to the section of town that includes the **Tombs of the Hami Kings** and the **Mansion of the Hami Kings**. Across the street, the **Hami Museum** and the **Hami Muqam Heritage Centre** stand side by side.

Of these attractions, you can skip the Mansion of the Hami Kings, a reconstructed Uyghur palace that feels more like the imitation it is rather than true historical restoration. The other three can be explored in just a couple hours on foot.

If you have more time to rent a car for the day, the driver can take you out to places like the **Hami Ghost City**, the **Lapuqiaoke Ancient City Ruins**, the beautiful **Barkol Lake** and the nearby **Barkol Grasslands**.

Of interest to some travelers is the fact that Hami is well-known for being one of the few places in the world that still runs steam locomotives on a frequent basis. Train spotters may enjoy sitting along the old lines near **Sandaoling City** to see these massive locomotives barrel by carrying freight of coal or other minerals. Since I have never personally made this trek, I suggest you find more Sandaoling details online.

Getting to/from Hami

Although all forms of transportation reach Hami, by far the quickest and easiest is the train. There are numerous trains that make a stop at Hami, including the new high-speed train that runs between Urumqi and Lanzhou.

Hami By High-Speed Train

Hami's brand-new rail station opened in 2014 and is located on the northern edge of town, making it easy to disembark and grab local transportation. Both the high-speed trains and regular service trains use the same station.

Train tickets are available for purchase at the station ticket office. For reference, a quick list of cities and the cost to take a train between the two:
- **Urumqi**: 196/163 RMB (1st class/2nd class), 3.5 hours
- **Turpan**: 137/115 RMB (1st class/2nd class), 2.5 hours
- **Lanzhou**: 461/385 RMB (1st class/2nd class), 8 hours
- **Xi'an**: 389/229 RMB (hard sleeper/hard seat), 21-27 hours depending on the train

As with any online train ticket purchase, I recommend using the China Highlights ticket service. www.xjtravelguide.com/train-tickets

Hami by Air

The Hami airport (哈密机场/Hāmì jīchǎng) can be found west of the city center about 10-15 minutes by taxi. There are daily flights from the capital of Urumqi as well as a few other flights from other airports in China. For flight schedules and information, check booking site Trip. www.xjtravelguide.com/trip-flights

Hami by Bus

The Hami bus station (哈密客运站/Hāmì kèyùn zhàn) is located on the eastern side of town along Jianguo Beilu (建国北路). From here you can take a bus to places such as Dunhuang (approx 7 hours) or even up toward Barkol (approx 2 hours).

Transportation within Hami

Taxis and private cars are a great way to get around Hami and are relatively cheap. Taxis run on a meter and private cars can also be rented for the day for around 300-400 RMB. Public buses run throughout the city but are an option not normally used by tourists.

What to do in Hami

Tombs of the Hami Kings

◄─────────────────────────────►

- **Name:** 哈密回王墓/Hāmì Huíwángmù
- **Price:** 40 元
- **Rating:** One of the only worthy stops in Hami

Not to be confused with the nearby Hami Kings Palace, the Tombs of the Hami Kings has a modest entrance that faces the main road. The complex isn't large but there is plenty to see inside.

The signs inside are translated into English, although it's a bit difficult to understand the history they're trying to explain amid the poor grammar. The main mausoleum was originally built in 1840 for the Uyghur King Boxier who died in 1866. Until the last king died in 1930, generations of Uyghur kings were buried here.

The complex is comprised of three sections: the main mausoleum covered in beautiful, green-glazed tile, two smaller mausoleums constructed of wood and finally the large mosque. North of the main mausoleum you can also view remnants of the old wall that extends for about 60 meters. This wall was built 28 years after the first mausoleum was finished and enclosed the area.

The main mausoleum is where King Boxier (sometimes translated as "Bixir") and 40 of the royal family members are buried. The tomb is an example of typical Islamic architecture from that time with a massive arch reaching 17.8 meters in height. The inside and outside are both covered in floral-patterned tile that alternates between a white and a green-glazed, both typical motifs in Uyghur architecture.

A few meters to the south are the smaller wooden mausoleums. Years ago, there were five wooden mausoleums in the complex, but now only two are left standing.

After exploring these mausoleums and checking out the old city wall, I highly recommend you turn your attention to the large mosque where a tall dome towers above the top. A set of rickety stairs leads up to this dome which, if you're allowed up, provide a panoramic view of the tomb complex and the city of Hami.

Hami Museum

- **Name:** 哈密博物馆/Hāmì Bówùguǎn
- **Price:** Free
- **Rating:** Possible stop if you're going to the Tomb of the Hami Kings

Originally opened in 1988 and moved to its current location in 2009, the Hami Museum is home to mummies, pottery and over 12,000 different artifacts that have been found in and around Hami.

While a visit to the museum is convenient since it's located across the street from the Tombs of the Hami Kings, don't feel compelled to visit if you're pressed for time. The Turpan Museum and the Xinjiang Uyghur Autonomous Region Museum in Urumqi are much better alternatives.

Hami Muqam Heritage Centre

- **Name:** 哈密木卡姆传承中心/Hāmì Mùkǎmǔ Chuánchéng Zhōngxīn
- **Price:** 20 元
- **Rating:** Interesting but not a must-see

It's hard to miss this building located next to the Hami Museum, with its massive Uyghur stringed instruments decorating the exterior. This is the Hami Muqam Heritage Center that pays homage to a Uyghur custom recognized as an important cultural heritage by both China and UNESCO.

This center is one of the few places where it's still possible to hear a live performance of traditional Uyghur muqam and you'll witness many of the traditional instruments that make up the Uyghur musical heritage. If Uyghur culture is part of what draws you to Xinjiang, then this might be a worthwhile stop for you.

What to do Around Hami

North of Hami

←——————————————→

Heading north of Hami on Highway S303 you'll be taking the Silk Road route to Urumqi on the northern side of the Tianshan mountain range. A bus runs from Hami to the small town of Barkol from the bus station and takes about 2 hours. You'll want to hire a car and driver if you want to stop at the Mingshan Dunes.

On your way to Urumqi, or perhaps if you just want to stay one night and return to Hami, there are a few things that are worth a visit.

Mingsha Sand Dunes
鸣沙山/Míngshāshān

Price: 20 元
Rating: Fun stop if you haven't been to Dunhuang and you're taking the northern route to Urumqi

Heading north out of Hami toward Barkol, one of the first stops is the Hami Mingsha Sand Dunes, which shouldn't be confused with the much grander Mingsha Sand Dunes near Dunhuang. You'll travel about 70km before you reach the dunes.

Dunes tower up to 100 meters in height and the translated name "Singing Sands Mountain" is derived from the sound made by the sand as it moves across the dune faces. It is here that you can ride a camel, slide down the dunes or conquer one of the sand mountains on foot.

Barkol Lake
巴里坤湖/Bālǐkūn Hú

Price: Free
Rating: Beautiful stop if you're taking the northern route to get to Urumqi

Approximately 150km northwest from Hami city by car you'll run into Barkol Lake. Although the water, described often as a "green-brown", isn't picturesque, it's location at the foothills of the Tianshan range and surrounded by lush grassland more than make up for it.

The lake is about 10km west of the town of Barkol, the county seat for the Barkol Kazakh Autonomous County. During the warmer months you'll find plenty of Kazakh yurts scattered around the lake, many of whom would happily house a paying visitor for the night as long as the police permit it.

Barkol Grasslands
巴里坤草原/Bālǐkūn Cǎoyuán

Price: Free
Rating: Enjoyable stop, time permitting

Sandwiched between Barkol Lake and the majestic TianShan peaks are the sprawling Barkol Grasslands, where herds of sheep, goats, horses and especially camels graze.

Barkol is actually quite famous for its horses and camels and you'll likely run into a herd or two if you make a visit to the grasslands. At first it may seem like a wild herd but somewhere, often at a distance, a Kazakh mounted on a horse will be watching.

South of Hami

Headed west and then a little south on multiple winding highways, you can make your way toward Wubao village where there are a few other possible places of interest.

Lapuqiaoke Ancient City Ruins
拉普乔克古城/Lāpǔqiáokè Gǔchéng

Price: 15 元
Rating: Not a must-see

Don't be surprised if you show the name of this ancient city to a Hami driver and they don't know where it is. Instead, direct them to go to Wubao (五堡乡/Wǔ bǎo xiāng) and locals there can point you in the right direction.

This ancient city is laid out into two halves that includes multiple grave sites that date back to at least the 11th century. Much of this city has already been excavated, with the archeological relics being housed in the Hami and Urumqi museums.

Despite the mummies, clothing, pottery and bronze ware that have been excavated from this site, there's not much to see as a visitor today. Little more than dirt mounds scattered around the 5,000 square meter area remain.

Hami Ghost City
雅尔当风景旅游区/Yǎěrdāng Fēngjǐng Lǚyóuqū

Price: 40 元
Rating: Nothing like the Ghost City near Karamay

Although it is literally named the "Yardang Scenic Tourist Area", most people just refer to this as the Hami Ghost City in English. It is yet another example of yardang rock formations chiseled away by years of wind.

The Hami Ghost City certainly has unique features, but the size of this destination pales in comparison to the Wuerhe Ghost City near Karamay. If you're looking to photograph yardang landforms, your first visit should still be Karamay over Hami.

As with all of these Ghost Cities, the best time to visit is during the sunrise or sunset when the colors and shadows present the area in its most beautiful form.

Where to Stay in Hami

Recommended Hotels in Hami

If you decide to stay the night in Hami, there are a number of options. Although there is plenty of lodging within the city, I think you'll be much happier if you spend the night further north, near Barkol. Unfortunately, as far as I know there is no lodging available for foreigners in the nearby Wubao village.

Hami Hotel

> **哈密宾馆 /Hāmì Bīnguǎn**
> **Address**: 4 Yingbin Road
> (迎宾路 4 号)
> **Phone**: (0902) 223-3140

Although tucked away in a small corner of Hami, this hotel has good public transportation options. There are plenty of hotel options in Hami, but this will probably be the best option that allows you to book a room online in advance. The rooms are typical for China and the hotel isn't geared toward tourists, but it is a reasonably comfortable 3-star hotel. Free WiFi is standard in all of the rooms.

Pictures, Pricing and Booking: **www.xjtravelguide.com/hami-hotel**

Recommended Lodging in Barkol City

Barkol Yurt

If you're going to be trekking all the way to Barkol, my recommendation is to at least try to spend the night in a yurt in the grasslands, which can be arranged either in person or through a local driver in Hami. Be aware: police in Xinjiang have been known to randomly disallow this, so don't be surprised if you get a visit in the middle of the night.

Barkol Hotel

If you must have a hotel, the Barkol Hotel is one of the many that can be found along Hancheng Road within the city. Don't expect high comfort or even internet access, but it is in the center of town at a good price.

巴里坤宾馆 Bālǐkūn Bīnguǎn
Address: 2 East HanCheng Road
(汉城东街育才路 2 号)
Phone: (0902) 682-2213

Pictures, Pricing and Booking: **Online reservations unavailable**

Altay 阿勒泰

Altay Top Sights

Kanas Lake Nature Reserve – Pg 191
The beautiful Kanas Lake is a popular destination, but it's also large enough to get away from the crowds. Beware the "Kanas Monster"!

Hemu Village – Pg 194

Enjoy the splendor of picturesque log cabins set against the majesty of the Altay Mountains.

Five Colored Hills – Pg 196

Enjoy the Ertix River and the colorful rocks that come to life during sunset

Introduction to Altay 阿拉泰

The Altay region in northern Xinjiang contains some of the most incredible natural scenery that China has to offer. It is, in my opinion, a hidden gem in China travel that has remained relatively undiscovered due to its remote location.

Being the northernmost point in Xinjiang, the Altay region is bordered by Russia to the north, Mongolia to the east and Kazakhstan on the west. The ethnic majority in these parts is Kazakh, although you will still run into plenty of other ethnic groups on the street.

Another ethnicity of note in Altay are the Tuvans who live in the valleys around the Kanas Nature Preserve. These are a people with Turkic roots who live a mostly nomadic life, herding their cattle through the nearby mountains. It is believed that these Tuvans were some of the first to invent skiing and can still be seen in the winter months strapping on their skis made of pinewood and horse skin.

Traveling to Altay

There's quite a bit to experience in and around the Altay region, but getting there presents the biggest problem. Most travelers opt to fly from Urumqi to Altay City or Kanas to avoid the loss of time inherent with train or bus travel (usually 8+ hours).

Around Altay, the most popular site to visit is the **Kanas Lake National Park**. This is where the majority of the region's tourism budget is spent and where you'll find the most Chinese tour groups. In addition to Kanas, I also recommending a look at **Koktokay National Park, Five Colored Hills, Hemu Village, Baihaba Village** and a few of the other small villages around the area.

Lesser-known but equally interesting around Altay is the **Beiting Ruins**, the **Qitai Ghost City**, the **Stone Men** and the **Hualin Park**. These are the places worth visiting if you plan to spend multiple days up north, but can leave off the itinerary if your time is tight.

If you have the time, hiking between Kanas Lake and Hemu village is an incredible way to experience Altay. During the winter months some tour operators can actually arrange a cross-country ski trip to make the same journey.

It's easy to get trapped in the tourism development that has occurred in Altay over the past decade. Make a point to get off the beaten path if possible. Stay a night in a village home stay. Hike beyond the wooden pathways around Kanas Lake. The more you explore, the more I think you'll enjoy Altay.

Getting to/from Altay

As I mentioned earlier, the biggest hurdle to travel in Altay is transportation. If you have the budget I recommend flying to save time. If time isn't an issue but your budget is, the overnight train will be the cheapest option.

Altay By Air

There are three airports in the Altay region: **Altay City** (AAT), **Buerjin** (KJI), and **Fuyun** (FYN). If your main point of interest is Kanas Lake, you'll want to fly into Buerjin if possible. Likewise, a flight to Fuyun will bring you closer to the Keketuohai national park if that's where you want to go.

Flights between Urumqi and Altay City (AAT) run year-round, although there are more daily flights added during the summer months. From here you're much closer to the Altay Ski Resort (see *A Guide to Skiing in Xinjiang* on page 58).

Flights between Urumqi and Buerjin/Kanas (KJI) and Fuyun/Keketuohhai (FYN) are seasonal, meaning they only operate during the summer and are a bit more expensive. The Buerjin airport is closer to Kanas Lake, Five Colored Hills and many of the other primary sites of interest than the one at Altay City. For either option, I recommend checking schedules and prices through domestic booking engine Trip.

www.xjtravelguide.com/trip-flights

Altay by Train

Although traveling to Altay by air is certainly faster, the train isn't a bad option. There are overnight trains from Urumqi to Beitun, a city about 70km southwest of Altay City. The entire trip takes about 12 hours but you can grab a relatively comfortable overnight sleeper bed option for around 200 RMB.

Again, it's worth noting that once you arrive in Beitun, you still have a considerable distance to drive before you get to Kanas, Hemu or any of the other locations. There are buses and private cars that will take you where you need to go.

Tickets can be bought both at the train station or online. As with all train ticket purchases, I recommend using a third-party provider like China Highlights.

www.xjtravelguide.com/train-tickets

Altay by Bus

Buses from Urumqi to the Altay region run daily and unlike the train or airplane, a bus can get you exactly where you want to go. Tickets are available to Buerjin (Burqin), Altay City, Beitun and many other smaller towns and villages.

For most travelers, the bus to Burerjin is the most feasible. In Urumqi, these buses leave from the NianZiGou Bus Station (碾子沟客运站). Buses leave at 11:15am, 8:10pm and 8:40pm. The sleeper bus ticket will run you ~178 RMB for a bottom berth or ~188 RMB for a top berth.

As a side note, by taking a bus you have the opportunity to get off at a few additional scenic spots along the eastern edge of the Jungar Basin (Highway 216). These include the **Beiting Ruins**, the **Qitai Ghost City** and **Keketuohai National Park** detailed below. This same route is likely what you would take were you to hire a private car, which would be more expensive but also more convenient than a bus.

Transportation around Altay

Once you arrive in Buerjin, Altay City or Beitun, you still need transportation to the various sites. Each major transportation hub (train station, bus station or airport) is located in the middle of nowhere, but there will be plenty of private drivers eager to drive you.

For those traveling in a small group, it's often best to work with a travel agency ahead of your arrival to arrange for a driver or bargain hard with these private drivers. Individual travelers may find the bus system easiest to use, which can take you directly to the gate of the Kanas Park.

Unless your schedule leaves no room for flexibility, I advise against joining a Chinese tour group. These are the easiest, no doubt, but will merely herd you from place to place without much time to explore or take anything more than the token photograph.

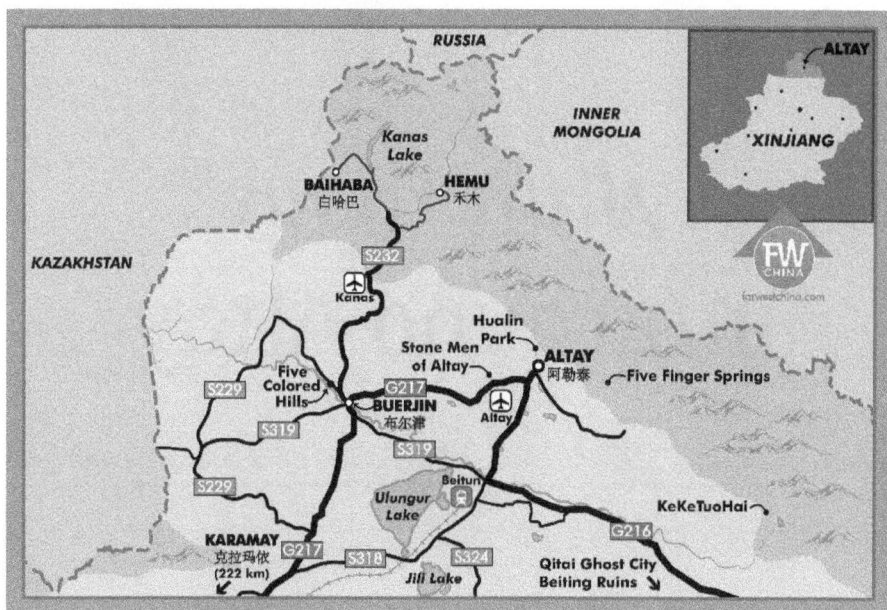

To receive a free, full-resolution PDF version of this and all the maps in this guide, please register your book:

www.xjtravelguide.com/register

What to do in/around Altay

Kanas Lake Nature Reserve

◄─────────────────────────────►

- **Name**: 喀纳斯湖/Kānàsī Hú
- **Price**: 285 元 (185 RMB Entrance ticket plus 100 RMB shuttle transport fee)
- **Rating**: Highly Recommended
- **Map**: See Altay Area Map

The most photographed section of the Altay region is the **Kanas Lake National Park**, which was deservingly named a UNESCO World Heritage Site in 2010. With so many facets to this park including forests, lakes, rivers and small villages, it has been hard narrowing it down to the most important information.

Interestingly, as recently as 1998 the Lonely Planet described Kanas as "closed to foreigners" and accessible only via an unpaved road that required hours upon hours to traverse. My how times have changed! Because of its incredible natural beauty and rising popularity among Chinese tourists, Kanas has experienced rapid development that struggles to please both tourists and environmentalists.

The three primary points of interest within the park are **Kanas Lake**, **Hemu Village** and **Baihabe Village**, although there are numerous smaller sites to visit. While it's possible to make Kanas a one-day trip, I highly recommend you budget at least one night to stay, if possible.

Exploring the Kanas National Park

Your first stop, no matter what form of transportation you use, will be at the gate to Kanas Lake National Park. Vehicles are not allowed within the park and you will be required to buy an entrance ticket that includes shuttle bus rides to the lake.

I would like to note here that as with most rules in China, there are ways to bend them. If you hire the right tour guide with enough "guanxi" (i.e. good connections), they may be able to get their vehicle into the park. While this is an ideal way to travel, it's also expensive and you would need to plan in advance.

For the rest of us common folk, a shuttle bus will lead you to the lake making stops along the Kanas River at **Dragon Bay** (卧龙湾 Wòlóng Wān), **Moon Bay** (月亮湾 Yuèliàng Wān) and **Immortal Bay** (神仙湾 Shénxiān Wān). The colorful scenery at each of these places is breathtaking, especially during the fall season. Grab the next shuttle on the road or take a walk along the river on your own for a while.

The bus will drop you off about 2km from the lake where you can either walk or hop on a shuttle that will take you to the shore. Once you finally arrive at the shores of Kanas Lake, you'll have a bit more freedom to choose what you want to see. You can hike (or take a bus or horseback ride - both an extra fee) up to the **Guanyu Pavillion** (观鱼亭/Guānyútíng) for some incredible panoramic views. Another option would be to take a leisurely walk along the shores of the lake.

The entire lake spans about 25 kilometers in length and can be seen by hiring a boat or hiking. The further north you go, the less likely you are to see another human being, much less a tourist. Views from the northern end of the lake are hard to obtain but incredibly beautiful.

Finally, with the exception of the shuttle buses to the lake which are included as part of your ticket, please note that everything else will have a fee tacked onto it. As annoying as this is, it's just how it's done. If you're physically fit and have plenty of time, you can make a lot of the hikes on your own, otherwise you should bring some extra cash to pay for some form of transportation.

Staying the Night at Kanas

Accommodation around Kanas Lake can be divided into two categories: within the park and outside the gate. The latter will on average be cheaper, but accommodation in the park will be more memorable. If you travel with a tour group, accommodations will be arranged before you arrive. Individual travelers will need to book upon arrival, as pre-booking is quite difficult.

While there are relatively comfortable hotels available in both categories, I recommend you try staying at a more rustic Tuvan home or yurt (police permitting). Prices will vary based on your ability to bargain, but I would expect to pay anywhere between 50-150 RMB per person depending on the kind of traditional home and whether or not there are meals included. Booking in advance is difficult.

Yurt: 186-6393-1935 (phone & WeChat)
Lodge: 139-9978-0535

I am often asked about camping at Kanas. Technically, camping is frowned upon if not outright banned. However, since the park is so large, there's no way to patrol even a fraction of it, making it easy to slip away. You'll need to bring all your own gear and food/water essentials upon entering the park but as long as you set up camp away from major roads and the shoreline, you should be fine (see Hiking and Camping in Xinjiang).

Adventure Tourism at Kanas

Whether you're up for rock climbing, hiking, boating, horseback riding, river rafting or even paragliding, Kanas is a great place to experience some outdoor adventure. It comes at a price, mind you, but the scenery is unparalleled.

Much of what you'll be able to do depends on the season and the weather. Ask about what's available at the park entrance and they should be able to help you.

Paragliding has become a popular offering at Kanas, which hosted a nationwide paragliding competition in August of 2012. The conditions near the lake are ideal but usually it's not something you can do without arranging prior to arrival through a tour agent.

Hiking is, as previously mentioned, another excellent way to experience this natural reserve. Don't expect marked trails or detailed maps, though, so it's best to have a guide with you if at all possible. As I mentioned earlier, it's also important to be self-sufficient, as there are few places to stock up on food within the park. One great hiking destination is the **Hemu Village**, detailed next.

Beware the Kanas Lake Monster!

At an average depth of 120 meters, Kanas Lake is the deepest glacial lake in China. Many Chinese believe that these depths hide one of Kanas Lake's greatest mysteries: **The Kanas Monster**.

Ever since the 1980s, sightings of this "monster" have intrigued people from all over the world. Now that phones can double as camcorders, videos of this monster have made the news almost every year.

There's no denying that some enormous animals live in Kanas Lake - possibly some of the largest freshwater fish in the world (local legend estimates the largest to be 10 meters in length) - but the exact species has yet to be proven. Keep your eyes open and camera ready for massive shadows in the lake or an indistinct creature making waves in the water. Your video could become the next viral hit in China!

Getting to/from Kanas Lake

Buses from Buerjin (Kanas airport), Beitun (train station) and Altay City (Altay airport) all run to the front gate of Kanas Lake National Park. Instead of taxis you'll find quite a few entrepreneurial local private drivers who tend to see tourists as ATM machines full of money.

Because of this, Kanas is one place where it may pay to hire a driver through a travel agency. The more you can arrange transportation ahead of time, the better off you will be.

Hemu Village

←――――――――――――――――→

- **Name**: 禾木乡 /Hémù xiāng
- **Price:** 60 元 (100 元 for the shuttle bus)
- **Rating**: Worthy stop, time permitting
- **Map**: See Altay Area Map

Home of the Tuvan people and located within the Kanas Lake National Park, Hemu has become a popular destination among tourists, thanks to its picturesque, backwoods atmosphere. Log cabins fill the valley surrounded by beautiful forest and rolling hills. Of course, this also means that it has become a Chinese "tourist trap," but if you come in with that expectation, it should be ok.

A visit to Hemu isn't complete without a hike up the nearby hill to get a panoramic view of the small village. Photographs from this hill during sunrise and sunset are spectacular.

If time permits, spending a night at one of the Tuvan homes can be a memorable experience. You won't have to look hard to find a place to stay. Entrepreneurial Tuvans (and Han Chinese) have taken advantage of the tourism by offering their homes as a bed-and-breakfast.

Getting to/from Hemu Village

A smooth, recently-renovated road connects Buerjin and Hemu requiring a couple hours of transport.

From the gate of Kanas Lake National Park, you can grab a bus directly to Hemu village for 200 RMB, a price which includes the entrance fee. A taxi will generally run you closer to 400-500 RMB per car.

Of course, the most scenic way to get to or from Hemu is by foot or on horseback. Horses and guides can be costly (up to 150 RMB per day) and usually make a stopover at Black Lake nearby Kanas.

Baihaba Village

- **Name**: 白哈巴村/Báihǎbācūn
- **Price**: 60 元
- **Rating**: Currently closed to foreigners
- **Map**: See Altay Area Map

> ## 2019 Update
> Unfortunately, over the past couple years, local authorities have closed off access to Baihaba to foreign travelers. I have left the description below because there's always a chance it will open up again, but it's worth noting that you likely won't be able to visit.

Approximately 17km west of Kanas Lake is **Baihaba Village**, another log cabin village that provides excellent photographic opportunities. Similar to Hemu village, Baihaba developed around the tourism industry while trying hard to maintain its rural charm.

Located just a stone's throw from the border between China and Kazakhstan where the freezing-cold waters of the Haba River mark the divide, it is primarily populated by Kazakh and Mongol peoples.

What can already be considered picture-perfect scenery during the spring and summer months turns into a majestic rainbow of colors during the fall season. If you have the opportunity, plan to visit during late September into October. Generally speaking, this is true for most of the Kanas park.

Tourism to Baihaba hasn't reached the same popularity as that of Hemu, so expect a more reserved reception from the locals. Still, it's not uncommon for a visitor to be invited to share a meal with one of the locals.

There are simple accommodations in and around the village, but it's best to see if you can arrange this through a travel agent at gate to Kanas Park or in Buerqin before you go.

Getting to/from Baihaba

A paved road connects Kanas Lake with Baihaba and is usually traversed via a taxi that costs approximately 150 RMB.

Five Colored Hills

← →

- **Name**: 五彩滩/Wǔcǎitān
- **Price**: 50 元
- **Rating**: Enjoyable stop, time permitting
- **Map**: See Altay Area Map

Wucaitan, which has been translated as either "Rainbow Beach" or "Five-Colored Hills," is a scenic Xinjiang gem worth considering as a stop on your itinerary.

Located along the Irtysh (Ertix) River in northern Xinjiang, Wucaitan is not the typical tourist destination for most foreigners. However, because it's only 24 kilometers northwest of Burqin it's a simple stop if you're already in the city.

Exploring Five Colored Hills

Wind-worn rock formations ranging from 5 to 25 meters in height line the bank of the only Chinese river whose waters reach the Arctic Ocean. Wooden pathways snake through the colorful rocks to provide various angles for incredible photographic opportunities.

The drive out to Wucaitan is quite interesting. The smooth, paved road follows the north side of the Ertix River, the side that is barren desert. Visible to the south of the river is the stark contrast of a lush, green river valley.

The buildings that welcome you to Wucaitan seem to rise up out of nowhere and, as with many places in China, the significant investment that went into the construction of the scenic spot seem ostentatious compared to the number of actual visitors.

Allotting a couple hours to walk around will be more than enough, but some of the best photo opportunities come at sunset, so plan accordingly. During the summer, mid-day can be incredibly hot so make sure you bring plenty of water!

Getting to/from Five Colored Hills

Since it's located only 24km from Buerjin, a quick jaunt over to Five Colored Hills isn't too difficult. Hire a taxi for a couple hours or jump on a mini-bus from the bus station.

Keketuohai National Park

◄─────────────────────────►

- **Name**: 可可托海/Kěkětuōhǎi
- **Price**: 90 元 (36 元 optional vehicle fee)
- **Rating**: Recommended, time permitting
- **Map**: See Altay Area Map

Nicknamed "China's Little Yosemite" after the famous U.S. national park, **Keketuohai Geological National Park** also goes by the local Kazakh name "**Koktokay**". Located east of Altay City at least a 10-hour drive from Kanas Lake, it has become well-known for its towering walls of granite rock protruding from the ground, surrounded by beautiful white birch forests and the gorgeous Irtish River.

For centuries this land has been used by the nomadic Kazakh people to sustain their cattle, sheep and other animals. Every spring many of them would pack up the family, search for green pastures and set up their yurt (ger) in the mountainous area near the river. Every fall they would retrace their route back down for the winter months.

A few entrepreneurial Kazakh have exchanged the cattle-herding life for that of business, providing the opportunity for visitors to stay in the yurt for a small fee. When the evening comes and the tourist buses leave, the sounds of a moving river and the sight of a starry heaven are paradise.

Exploring Koktokay National Park

As with many of these remote locations in Xinjiang, experiences vary by traveler. Many adventurous travelers have enjoyed hiking, camping and even climbing at Koktokay, while others have complained of being forced to lodge at the local hotels.

One thing is for sure: if you want to be herded like tourist-cattle from one scenic spot to another, feel free to join a China tourist group. If you want the option to walk around independently and veer off the beaten path, take a bus or hire a car to get you to Keketuohai and then take off on your own.

For older travelers or those with children, you'll enjoy the fact that you can be chauffeured around on a golf cart and still enjoy the beauty of the National Park.

Points of Interest

- **White Birch Forest**: Near the entrance of Koktokay there is a white birch forest that offers a spectacular splash of yellow during the fall months.
- **Shenzhong Mountain**: The centerpiece of the park. This sheer face of this mountain will remind you of Yosemite.
- **Elephant Peak**: Just beyond Shenzhong Mountain you'll run into Elephant Peak, another very picturesque granite wall surrounded by white birch.
- **Camel Peak**: Toward the end of the paved pathways is Camel Peak, named for what looks like a camel head with two humps.

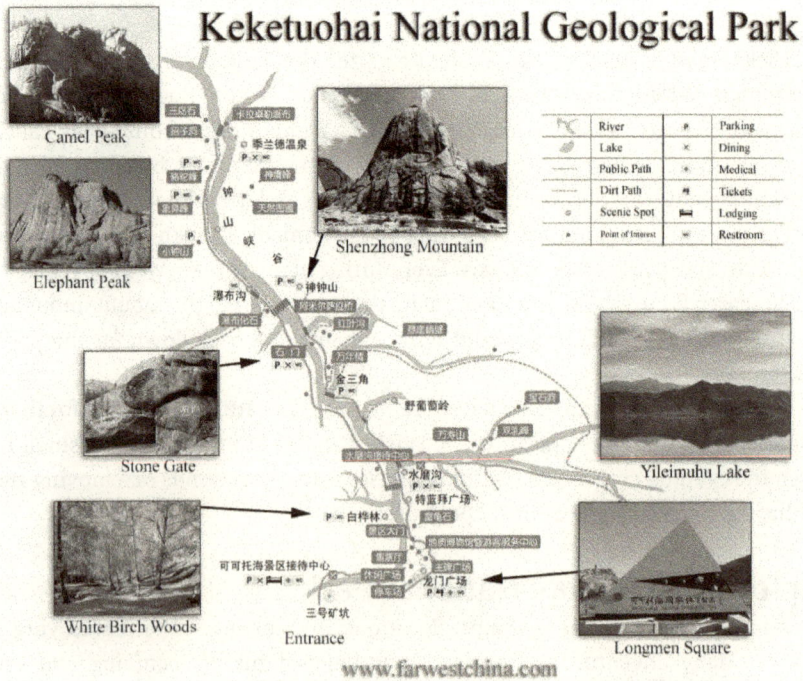

Keketuohai National Geological Park

Camel Peak

Elephant Peak

Shenzhong Mountain

	River		Parking
	Lake		Dining
	Public Path		Medical
	Dirt Path		Tickets
	Scenic Spot		Lodging
	Point of Interest		Restroom

Stone Gate

Yileimuhu Lake

White Birch Woods

Entrance

Longmen Square

www.farwestchina.com

See more detail: **www.xjtravelguide.com/keketuohai**

Getting to/from Koktokay

There is a mini-bus from Fuyun (富蕴/Fù yùn), a small town west of Altay City and just 70km from Koktokay. Because this site lies much further to the east than any of the other sites worth seeing in Altay, I recommend seeing this either on your way in or out of the region.

Buses between Urumqi and Altay City follow Highway G216 on the east side of the Jungar Basin and can stop at Fuyun. Just let the driver know that you want to be dropped off there and he'll alert you when you arrive.

Around Altay City

For all the beauty that Kanas Lake offers in the region, the lesser-known areas surrounding Altay City are also stunning. Obviously Keketuohai National Park is one of those gems but there are a few more smaller places that are fun to visit if you have the luxury of time.

Stone Men of Altay
切木尔切克墓/Qièmùěr Qièkèmù

- **Price:** Free
- **Rating:** Worth 10 minutes while driving along the road

Although a lesser-known tourist destination, if you plan to be driving between Altay City and Buerjin anyway, the Stone Men of Altay (also referred to as the "Stone Men of Qiemuer Qieke") are a fun stop along the way.

Stone figures are common throughout Central Asia, from Kazakhstan to Tajikistan to Kyrgyzstan. Often they are placed in front of ancient tombs and carved with faces and the outline of clothing. Within Xinjiang most of these stone figures are seen around the Ili Valley regions; Altay boasts over 80 of these figures and Qiemuer Qieke is the most famous.

Find these stone figures along Highway 217 near its terminus at Highway 216. It's easy to miss since only a single sign has historically marked their presence, so keep your eyes open.

Hualin Park
桦林公园/Huàlín Gōngyuán

- **Price:** 25 元
- **Rating:** Great during fall season, passable the rest of the year

Just a couple kilometers north of Altay City is a quaint little park known as **Hualin Park** filled with innumerable silver birch and poplar trees. During the fall months, the leaves of these trees turn a blazing gold and orange that contrasts beautifully with the crystal blue waters of the nearby Kelan River.

Make sure your camera is fully charged if you arrive in September or October. You'll be taking quite a few pictures here.

Five Finger Springs
五指泉景区/Wǔzhǐquán Jǐngqū

- **Price:** 5元
- **Rating:** Fun spot for nature enthusiasts and hikers who have plenty of time

About 25km southeast of Altay City is a beautiful park known as **Five Finger Springs Park**. It's not a well-known park, but for those who want a nice place to hike and camp, this is certainly an option.

The area is marked by dense forest of birch, numerous natural springs and even some gorgeous waterfalls. Locals from Altay City will come here for a day trip to picnic.

Handega Cliff Paintings
汗德尕 or 汉达尕/Hàndégǎ

- **Price:** Free
- **Rating:** Of interest to history buffs

Almost next door to the Five Fingers Springs is the Handega village where a number of ancient cliff paintings have been discovered. It was based on these cliff paintings that researchers determined ancient hunters here had developed the art of skiing.

Qitai Ghost City

⬅——————————➡

- **Name:** 奇台魔鬼城/Qítái Móguǐchéng
- **Price:** 50元
- **Rating:** Quick stop destination only if passing by

Although located quite a distance from other tourist sites in Altay, I'm including Qitai Ghost City and the Beiting Ruins here since they don't really fit in any other location category.

Qitai Ghost City is essentially a much smaller version of the more famous Wuerhe Ghost City near Karamay with a number of unique, wind-shaped rocks known as "yardang". With a bit of creativity, you can imagine many of the rock formations taking on the shape of the various animals after which they are named.

Further south from the Ghost City you can also make a stop at the **Qitai Petrified Forest Park** and **Dinosaur Valley** (新疆奇台硅化木—恐龙国家地质公园). Since the 1920s when Swedish explorer Sven Hedin documented his archeological findings in Xinjiang, dinosaur fossils have been excavated around Qitai, including some of the largest dinosaur bones in the world. Apparently, Xinjiang used to be covered with massive Tyrannosaur!

Despite how interesting I find this, the reality is that Qitai isn't worth putting on your itinerary, especially if you have time to visit the much larger Ghost City near Karamay, which is also home to a dinosaur park (see Karamay Ghost City).

Beiting Ruins

◀━━━━━━━━▶

- **Name**: Běitíng Gùchéng 北庭故城
- **Price**: 48 元
- **Rating**: Only for Silk Road history buffs who are passing by

Listed as part of the Silk Road in its UNESCO World Heritage site application, the **Beiting Ruins** (also referred to as "Bashbaliq") date back as far as the 8th century. Only two hours from Urumqi and about 10km from the smaller town of Jimsar, it was once part of the northern Silk Road route that branched off from Hami.

Although visitors once viewed these ruins in the open air, they have now been enclosed in a protective shed similar to the Terracotta Warriors in Xi'an. Scholars believe that the Beiting fortress, with its rammed-earth walls towering up to 20 meters in height, was abandoned in the mid-15th century. It wasn't until 1979 that the site was rediscovered by Chinese troops who accidentally dug out a mural from the ruins.

Archeological excavation and preservation of the Beiting Ruins continue to this day and visitors are invited to visit the nearby museum housing many of their discoveries. Of course, you can also see some of these relics displayed at the Xinjiang Uyghur Autonomous Region Museum in Urumqi.

If you have a desire to visit the Beiting Ruins, you can grab a bus or private car to Jimsar (吉木萨尔 Jímùsàěr) where you can then hail a taxi to take you north to the ruins.

Where to Stay in Altay

Recommended Hotel in Altay City

If you won't be staying in a yurt or small home near Kanas Lake, here are a few other accommodations to consider. Options for foreigners in each of these towns and cities is limited so you can't be too choosy.

Altay Sunshine Hotel

There aren't many hotel options in Altay suitable for foreigners, but this one is the best available. The advantage of this hotel is its location across the street from a small park along the river. Rooms are typical of Chinese hotels and include WiFi.

阳光酒店/Yángguāng
Jiǔdiàn
Address: 400 Jiefang Road
(解放路 400 号)
Phone: (0906) 288-8889

Pictures, Pricing and Booking: **www.xjtravelguide.com/altay-sunshine**

Recommended Hotel in Buerjin

Mystic Lake Grand Hotel

A reasonable hotel at a very good price. The hotel is located in the center of town and accepts online booking prior to arrival.

Pictures, Pricing and Booking:
www.xjtravelguide.com/buerjin-mystic

神湖大酒店 /Shénxiān Wāndà
Jiǔdiàn
Address: 32 Shenhu Rd
(神湖路 32 号)
Phone: (0906) 652-0808

Note: you may find leftover advertisements for a "**Pigeonhouse Youth Hostel**" in Buerjin laying around other hostels in Xinjiang. This hostel no longer exists.

Recommended Hotels at Kanas

⬅——————————➡

Although it might be best to arrive at Kanas to see your options for sleeping, if you're the type of traveler that needs the peace of mind that a confirmed booking can provide, here are two options to consider at Kanas.

Spruce Manor

云杉庄园/**Yúnshān Zhuāngyuán**
Address: 57 Laocun Road (老村 57 号)
Phone: 150-0306-9999

Of the many options you'll see catering to tourists inside the Kanas Lake area, the Spruce Manor is different in pretty much only one way: you can see pictures and book online. Like everything else you'll run into around Kanas, it's going to be surprisingly expensive, especially during the tourist season.

Pictures, Pricing and Booking: **www.xjtravelguide.com/kanas-spruce**

Linhai Resort

林海山庄/**Línhǎi Shānzhuāng**
Address: Near all the other Kanas hotels
Phone: (0906) 632-6333

A less luxurious - but also less expensive - option nearby is the Linhai Resort. Modest log cabins connected by wood plank walkways are more than comfortable enough.

Pictures, Pricing and Booking: **www.xjtravelguide.com/kanas-linhai**

Recommended Hotels at Hemu

◀━━━━━━━━━━━━━━━━━━▶

Hemu Hotel

Another log cabin-styled accommodation built specifically for tourists in Hemu. You'll find comfortable rooms at a relatively high price, but the scenery is beautiful.

禾木山庄/Hémù Shānzhuāng
Address: Within Hemu village
Phone: (0906) 651-5666

Pictures, Pricing and Booking: **www.xjtravelguide.com/hemu-hotel**

Ili (Yili) 伊利

Ili Top Sights

Narat Grasslands – Pg 225
There are numerous grasslands throughout the Ili region worth visiting, including the Kalajun, Narat and Bayanbulak.

Sayram Lake – Pg 219
One of Xinjiang's largest and most beautiful lakes. This is a great place to cycle, hike and stay the night.

Fruit Valley – Pg 220

Just west of Sayram Lake is the gorgeous Fruit Valley, marked by both incredible natural scenery as well as this engineering marvel of a bridge!

Baytulah Mosque – Pg 216

A place where the old and new architecture come together in Yining's city center.

Introduction to Ili 伊利

The Ili region of Xinjiang (also written as "Yili" or referred to by locals as "Ghulja") is another one of those places that offers more to see than any traveler could dream to visit in one trip. Gorgeous lakes, grasslands, and wetlands spread endlessly in front of a beautiful mountain background. Fields of lavender, rapeseed, and apricot trees bloom in spectacular form for only short periods of time throughout the year.

That's just what you can see with your eyes. The region also hides a long history of Central Asian power struggle that at one point in the early 1940s made Ili its own nation-state. The independence movement lasted for only a short while, but the Soviet influence is still strong in this corner of Xinjiang. Today, a mix of Hui, Kazakh, Uyghur, Russian and Han ethnic groups populate different parts of Ili Valley.

Traveling to Ili

A visit to Ili usually requires a number of days set aside for travel between the various places of interest.

The beautiful **Sayram Lake** is worth an overnight stay (tent camping or a stay in a yurt), as is a short trip down to the nearby **Fruit Valley**. A number of sites of interest exist around the town of Bole (Bortala) northeast of Sayram Lake, including the **Aiding Lake** and the **Arixiate Stone Men**, but they're usually too much of a detour to add to most itineraries.

Most tourists come to Ili to visit the lush grasslands; to this end, the **Narat** and **Bayinbulak Grasslands** do not disappoint. These two are the most popular, of course, while smaller, less-touristy parks exist including the **Kuerdine Nature Reserve** and the **Kunas National Forest Park**.

The city of **Yining** is a nice place to take a break while enjoying a stroll along the beautiful Ili River or a stop at the old **Baytullah Mosque**. A short drive to the west you can explore the history of **Huiyuan Ancient City** or venture south toward **Tekes**, the world's largest octagon city.

If you happen to be in Ili during the latter part of April you may want to visit the **Apricot Valley Park** which would be filled with beautiful, pink apricot blossoms. During the month of June you can stop by the **Lavender Park** to view the rolling fields of purple. If you'd like a 3-minute snapshot of what there is to see in Ili, check out this video on the FarWestChina YouTube channel.

Watch the video: **www.xjtravelguide.com/yili-intro**

Getting to/from Ili

Ili covers a vast region that includes multiple airports, train lines and international land ports. Because of this, there are a number of different options to get you into and around Ili.

Ili By Air

There are currently three airports in the region: the Yining Airport (伊宁机场 Yīníng Jīchǎng), the Bole Airport (博乐机场 Bólè Jīchǎn) and the Narat Airport (那拉提机场 Nàlātí Jīchǎng). Of the three, Yining Airport is the largest with the most flights to and from Urumqi.

Yining Airport (YIN): Conveniently located just a few kilometers from the city center, the Yining Airport hosts multiple daily flights to both Urumqi and Kashgar all throughout the year.

Narat Airport (NLT): Despite the name, the airport is actually a good 120km away from the Narat Grasslands. Still, that's 180km closer to Narat than flying into Yining City. At this point, flights from Urumqi only run 3 times a week so you'll need to check ahead and probably book directly with China Southern.

Bole Airport (BPL): The newest of the three airports (2009), the Bole Airport is about 20 kilometers east of Bortala City.

For up-to-date flight schedules and ticket prices, check Trip.
www.xjtravelguide.com/trip-flights

Ili by Train

Traveling by train between Ili and Urumqi is an excellent option for two reasons: 1) it's cheaper than flying and 2) there are a few overnight trains so it will save you paying for one night in a hotel.

You'll likely be traveling at night which means you won't be able to look out at the scenery passing by, however unlike taking a bus, the train doesn't pass by the gorgeous Sayram Lake, Fruit Valley or other such visually stunning locales. The Yining train station (伊宁站/Yīníng Zhàn) is located just north of the city center with a number of public bus and taxi options available.

By train to and from Urumqi, you have two options: either to Yining City (continuing to Horgas Port) or up to the Alashankou border crossing with Kazakhstan. There are multiple departure times between 8:30pm and 11pm.

- **Urumqi - Yining**: ~172/81 RMB (hard sleeper/hard seat), 7-10 hours
- **Urumqi - Alashankou**: ~115/61 RMB (hard sleeper/hard seat), 7-10 hours

Schedules and up-to-date pricing on all train routes in Xinjiang can be found on China Highlights:

www.xjtravelguide.com/train-tickets

Ili by Bus

Buses to Ili from Urumqi leave from Urumqi's Main Bus Station on Heilongjiang Rd (Urumqi map - A4) and take between 11 and 12 hours in transit. Since you'll be taking highway G312, you're going to pass right beside the Sayram Lake and run across the amazing Fruit Valley Bridge.

The Ili Bus station, named the "Ili Passenger Transport Center" (伊犁州客运中心 /Yīlízhōu Kèyùn Zhōngxīn), is on Jiefang West Rd (解放西路) but has moved further northwest than what you may find on older maps. You're still right in the middle of the city though, and getting taxi or public buses won't be a problem.

It's also possible to get a bus to Bole (aka Bortala), Tekes, Xinyuan (near Narat) and other smaller towns. Likewise, you can take a long-distance sleeper bus to Almaty (Kazakhstan), Altay, and even down to cities in southern Xinjiang.

It would be hard to list out pricing for each city so instead here is a list of the most important destinations:

- **Urumqi**: 178/188 (top/bottom berth), 11 hours, hourly departures
- **Bole (Bortala)**: 45 RMB, 4 hours
- **Horgos Port (toward Almaty)**: 15 RMB, 1.5 hours
- **Almaty**: 198 RMB, 12 hours

Transportation around Ili

There are plenty of buses and taxis available to get you around Yining City, Bole (Bortala) and any other city in Ili. To go between cities, the buses would be easiest while a car would be most convenient. Connect with an Ili Travel Agency or a travel agency in Urumqi if you'd rather arrange a private car and driver to take you around.

International Border Crossing in Ili

Of the eight countries that share a border with Xinjiang, Kazakhstan certainly has the longest. While there are a few different ports, the only two that allow foreigner travelers through at this time are the Horgas Port and the Alashankou Port.

For many travelers, you'll have to secure a Kazakh visa in Urumqi or elsewhere before you make an attempt to cross the border since you can't get one in Ili (see Visa Issues FAQ). For those United States citizens who want to make the trip, an agreement between the U.S. and Kazakhstan currently means that you get a visa-free entry for 15 days. It's a sweet deal and hopefully it will continue for years.

Horgas Port

About an hour and a half west of Yining City is the Horgas Port (霍尔果斯口岸 /Huǒěrguǒsī Kǒuàn). You may also see this spelled "Horgos" or "Khorgas". Most people who use this port are headed to Almaty, Kazakhstan although it could technically be used as a "visa run" location as well.

There is a passenger train that runs between Urumqi and Almaty through Horgas port. In addition, you can find a direct bus that travels through the Horgas Port (198 RMB, approx 12 hours). Either way you come through the port, processing times have been reported anywhere between 40 minutes to 5 hours. Just be prepared to wait.

Backpackers can also take a bus or train from Ili to Horgas (the city), a taxi to the port for an addition 5 RMB and then hitch a ride across the 3km border. You'll have to find a bus on the Kazakh side that will pick you up and take you where you need to go, but that shouldn't be a problem as most buses pick up people on the road regularly.

Alashankou Port

Headed north of Yining City past Bole (Bortala) you reach the Alashankou Port (阿拉山口口岸/Ālāshānkǒu Kǒuàn). This port represents the only current rail link between China and Kazakhstan and therefore remains open year-round.

There are a few ways for a traveler to cross into Kazakhstan via the Alashankou Port but the most common is via the international train from Urumqi to either Almaty or Astana (see "International Trains" in the Urumqi Train Station Guide). The only problem with this option is that train tracks in Kazakhstan have a different gauge than those in China, meaning passengers have to wait for 5-8 hours at the border while the train cars change their wheel base. For reference, this means the bus from Urumqi is 10 hours faster.

It has been suggested that it is faster to take a train to Alashankou Port, grab a shuttle bus across the border and then hop on a Kazakh train on the other side. I have been unable to verify whether this is possible.

What to Do Around Ili (Yili)

Within Yining

More than likely, the reason you are visiting Ili has very little to do with Yining City. Even so, you might decide to spend a night or two in Yining, so it's good to know what's worth seeing in the city.

Ili Kazakh Museum
伊宁哈萨克自治区博物馆/Yīníng Hāsàkè Zìzhìqū Bówùguǎn

- **Price:** Free
- **Rating:** Highly recommended

The full name of this museum is actually the Ili Kazakh Autonomous Prefecture Museum but since that's a mouthful, most prefer to just refer to it as the "Ili Museum". It is open every day from 10:30am to 6:30pm.

Although it's a relatively small museum, it's well worth a visit if you have the time. In contrast to all of the Silk Road history you'll find at the Urumqi or Turpan museums, the Ili Museum focuses heavily on the history and culture of Xinjiang's northwest, which includes Ili all the way up to Altay (since so many Kazakh populate the Altay region as well).

You will find three different exhibit halls in the museum. The first two cover the history and various artifacts of the region while the last exhibit highlights the culture and customs of the Kazakh people in Xinjiang. While the museum may not be able to provide an English-speaking guide, the signs have fairly good English translations.

As you prepare to immerse yourself in the nomadic culture that permeate the valleys and grasslands around Ili, this museum is a good introduction.

Baytula Uyghur Mosque
拜吐拉清真寺/Bàitǔlā Qīngzhēnsì

- **Price:** n/a
- **Rating:** Worthy of a picture, not much more

West of People's Park on Xinhua Road you'll run into an interesting architectural mixture of buildings known as the Uyghur Mosque or simply "Baytula". An 18th century, Chinese-style structure greets visitors while a much larger white mosque with two minarets and a central dome tower behind it.

This mosque was originally built back in 1773 and at one point it housed a madras where Islamic scholars from all across Central Asia came to study. Now its primary use is to host up to 3,000 Muslim worshippers every Friday for prayers.

Yining River Bridge
伊犁河特大桥/Yínínghé Tedàqiáo

- **Price:** n/a
- **Rating:** Just cross it to say you did

In Yining, the Ili River is a destination in itself. People go here to hang out in the cool evenings, take a walk and get pictures taken.

For the longest time there was only one bridge that connected Yining with the land to the south but that all changed in 2006 when the new Yining River Bridge was opened. Reaching almost 2km in length (1,820m), it is believed to be one of the longest bridges in China.

If you have time in the cool of the evening, take a walk along the bridge and enjoy the sunset over the Ili River.

Uyghur Parts of Town

Perhaps you've heard the name "Ghulja" in reference to Ili. This is the Uyghur name for the town and technically speaking the old town of Ghulja is located a little outside of the modern Yining City.

Although Yining City has become a booming Chinese metropolis, there are still places where you can find old Uyghur neighborhoods to walk around. The city has designated a few "Cultural Streets" such as the **Kazanqi Handicraft Street Market** (喀赞其 /Kāzànqí) that you can ask a taxi driver to drive you to or just go exploring yourself.

If you find yourself spending some time in Yining City, I highly recommend you wander around and try to find these old neighborhoods that are still paved with dirt. It's a unique aspect of the city you'll be happy you experienced.

Huiyuan Ancient City
惠远古城/Huìyuǎn Gǔchéng

- **Price:** 40 元 – museum

- **Rating**: While there is historical significance, it's all rebuilt

It comes as a surprise to most people to learn that Huiyuan, a small town about 30 kilometers west of Yining City within Huocheng (霍城), used to be the center of Chinese authority over the entire region of Xinjiang. Beginning in 1762, Qing forces built a fortress in Huiyuan that lasted until the Muslim Rebellion in the 1860s.

At that point, much of the fortress was either destroyed or left in disrepair. It wasn't until the past couple decades that the area has been rebuilt to reflect its historical past.

Today, you can view the (mostly) original bell tower (20 元), the city museum (40 元), the residence of Lin Zexu - a famous Chinese scholar once exiled here (20 元), the Ili General Mansion (45 元), the Confucius Temple (10 元) or the East Gate (10 元).

As you can tell, this place has been highly commercialized and all of the ticket booths suck the fun out of a visit. If you're passing by Huocheng, the museum with all of its English translations might be worth a quick stop; otherwise, I don't consider this a "must see" place in Ili.

Sayram Lake

- **Name:** 赛里木湖/Sàilǐmùhú
- **Price:** 70 元
- **Rating:** Highly recommended for a stop, if not a night

The stunning views of Sayram Lake (Salimu Lake) set against the towering, snow-capped TianShan are not to be missed when traveling out to Ili. Sayram, Xinjiang's highest alpine lake, is fed by snowmelt coming down the mountains and is certainly not a lake where you'll want to swim (nor are you allowed!).

Now that the new highways are complete, it's impossible to miss the lake if you're headed to Yining City by car or bus. During the spring and summer months, the fields leading up to the shores of the lake blossom with multi-colored wild flowers and Kazakh yurts litter the southern end of the lake.

While it's possible and most convenient to take a private car or tour bus out to Sayram Lake, the cheapest transport is to get a long-distance bus that will drop you off near the south shore. Be prepared to be bombarded by plenty of people trying to sell you a ride on a horse, a meal in a yurt or a place to sleep. It can be overwhelming.

The only inconvenience of choosing public transportation is finding your way back to Yining City or toward Urumqi, which may require you to wait beside the road for a bus that is willing to pick hitchhikers up.

Along the highway from Sayram Lake to Yining City there are a few additional sights that might catch your interest as well which I'll dive into later.

Exploring Sayram Lake

More than likely you'll begin your journey at either the southwest or southeast corners of Sayram Lake where all of the tourism facilities are set up (or still being built). It's here that you can arrange for a night's stay at a yurt (50-80 RMB/night/pax average), a horseback ride or just find something to eat. For those who desire a little more comfort, hotel facilities are also available, although they don't usually live up to international standards.

Since Sayram Lake covers a total of 450 square kilometers, don't expect to be able to walk around the entire lake. It is, however, advisable to do some hiking to get away from the crowds and capture a few beautiful pictures, particularly during sunrise or sunset. You can also hire a motorcycle starting at around 50 RMB to take you a distance out.

If you're lucky, there are times during festivals like Nadam (based on the lunar calendar so it changes every year) and special occasions like a wedding that you can witness horse races, a special Kazakh game known as "buzkashi" or even Kazakh wrestling. The Kazakh people are generally quite open to allowing foreigners to observe but you should always be respectful to ask before intruding into any large gathering.

Fruit Valley Bridge
果子沟大桥/Guǒzigōu Dàqiáo

- **Price:** n/a
- **Rating:** Worthy of stopping to take a picture if you can

One of the most stunning bridges you'll ever cross is located just a few kilometers southwest of Sayram Lake. Even if you're not particularly interested in a bridge, while heading toward Yining City on highway G30, you have no choice but to cross the bridge.

Opened in 2011, this bridge is considered one of China's most beautiful bridges and reaches a stunning height of 200 meters.

Fruit Valley
果子沟/Guǒzigōu

- **Price:** Free
- **Rating:** You have to drive through it...so enjoy!

Departing from Sayram Lake heading west, Highway 312 begins to descend through the meandering valley known as Fruit Valley. The passage through Ili Valley is almost 28 kilometers in length.

There's no tourist center to visit here or special scenic lookout (other than the bridge mentioned above). It's just a beautiful drive, one that will have you glued to your window the entire time. If you have a private car I recommend you make a stop at some of the stalls you see along the side of the road. The famous "Ili Apples" are grown here in Fruit Valley and they're certainly worth trying.

Lavender Park

- **Name:** 薰衣草园/Xūnyī Cǎoyuán
- **Price:** 35 元
- **Rating:** Only worth a visit in June when in season

While not a major tourist spot, if you happen to be making a journey between Yining and Sayram during the month of June, you might have the opportunity to witness the gorgeous sea of purple that covers these parts of the Ili Valley. Rows of lavender provide 95% of China's lavender-based products.

There are numerous "parks" that offer tourists a chance to walk and take photos in the fields of purple, so choose what looks best to you. The park I visited cost 35 RMB but also includes a visit to the nearby Lavender Museum. It is located on Highway G218 (not the bigger national highway) just south of where you get off of Highway G312.

Whether you visit these parks or just drive by, you'll find plenty of stalls selling lavender goods, which can make great gifts for people back home (think lavender soap, lavender hand cream, lavender-filled pillows, etc.).

Bortala City

For some travelers, a visit to Ili actually begins in the city Bole (Bortala), which is located northeast of Sayram Lake. It's possible to start your journey from Bole toward Sayram Lake, into Yining City and then up into the grasslands of the TianShan.

Before you reach Sayram Lake, however, Bole offers a few places of interest including the **Mysterious Stone Valley**, the shrinking **Aibi Lake**, and the **Arixiate Stone Men**.

Bole has an airport to the east of the city and the port of Alashankou (阿拉山口) to the north crossing into Kazakhstan. From the city you are able to hire a private car or take a bus that can drop you off at Sayram Lake.

Mysterious Stone Valley
怪石峪/Guàishíyù

- **Price:** 50 元
- **Rating:** Interesting but inconvenient to visit

Located northeast of Bole and a few kilometers west of the Alashankou Port, the Mysterious Stone Valley is a 230 square kilometer collection of oddly-shaped rocks. Although these rock formations are formed by wind erosion similar to the many "Ghost Cities" in Xinjiang, the result is entirely different.

Massive granite rock has naturally been molded into all sorts of shapes that include interesting bowl-shaped holes and arches. In addition to the rock formations, this valley is also home to a number of petroglyphs, the rock carvings of the early inhabitants of this region.

Ebinur (Aibi) Lake
艾比湖/Àibǐhú

- **Price:** Free
- **Rating:** Not worth a stop

Approximately 50km east of Bole City is the Ebinur Lake, known as "Aibi" in Mandarin. The lake is Xinjiang's largest salt lake and really isn't much to behold. In fact, the lake has been shrinking at an alarming rate over the past decade.

What makes this place worthy of note is the surrounding Aibi Lake Wetland Nature Reserve. Established in 2007 and covering a total of 615 square kilometers, this wetland reserve is home to a number of different plants and animal species that are unique to this region.

While there are Chinese tour groups that make a trek into the wetlands, most foreign tourist will have a hard time visiting.

Arixiate Stone Men
阿日夏特石人/Ārìxiàtè Shírén

- **Price:** Free
- **Rating:** Interesting but quite an inconvenient distance away

Headed west for about 40 kilometers out of Bole on S304, you can find a number of interesting stone men guarding an open grassland near the Arixiate township. A few are short and stubby and a couple stand tall, but each is carved with a unique face.

These types of stone men are scattered all across Central Asia and while it's definitely an adventure to see them in their original surroundings, you can also get a look at some of these stone men at the Ili Museum or even the Xinjiang Autonomous Region Museum in Urumqi if you don't have time to make this side trip.

Tekes County

From the Ili River, a tributary flows south through the beautiful Tekes County before crossing into Kazakhstan. The region is not highly trafficked by tourists, and the Tekes River is bordered on both sides by gorgeous terrain.

This journey south of Yining City is a potential detour on your way toward Narat and other locations to the east. I wouldn't recommend it for the majority of travelers and even those who do decide to make the trip shouldn't plan more than a day to do so.

Tekes Octogon City
特克斯八卦城/Tèkèsī Bāguàchéng

- **Price:** Free to enter the city, 20 元 to ascend the tower
- **Rating:** How many octagon cities have you seen?

At the heart of Tekes County is the city of Tekes - which just happens to be the world's largest octagon city. The plans for the city were laid back in 1938, a time when cattle were used to plow the city design and bundles of cloth were tied together to demarcate where the roads would be.

As interesting as the city layout is, it's quite difficult to appreciate it without being over a thousand feet up in the air. There is a tower in the middle of town (八卦观光塔/Bāguà guānguāngtǎ) where you can pay to get a view from above but it barely allows you to see past the 2nd ring road.

As an alternative, look out the south-facing window of your airplane when you're flying into or out of Yining Airport. Weather permitting, you should be able to get a brief glimpse of the city about 15 minutes outside of Yining City.

Qiongbola Forest Park
琼博拉森林公园/Qióngbólā Sēnlín Gōngyuán

- **Price:** 12 元
- **Rating:** Beautiful park that might be attractive to an eco-tourist

About 60 kilometers south of Yining City on Highway S237 is the entrance to the Qiongbola Forest Park, a great opportunity to experience a beautiful blend of Ili's grasslands, mountainous terrain and natural springs without the hassle of major tourism.

The park covers an area of 3,000 acres and like most places around Ili, is populated by a majority Kazakh. Qiongbola is open year-round and even has simple ski slopes and ski lifts for the more adventurous winter traveler. Check with people in Yining City to make sure the ski lifts are running before making a special trip to the park, though.

From Yining City, it is possible to hop on a bus for 15 RMB that will head a few kilometers south to CheXian (察县). From here you can hire a car for about 250 RMB to do a return trip to the park for the day.

Xiata Travel Area (w/ Stone Figures)
夏塔旅游景区/Xiàtǎ Lǚyóu Jǐngqū

- **Price:** Unknown
- **Rating:** Beautiful park but not a foreign tourist-friendly location

While the Xiata Travel Area is an incredibly beautiful park, it's an addition 130 kilometers southwest of the city of Tekes, deep into the heart of Tekes county. While I have never personally been here, I am including it here because of the famous Stone Men that are present and available to photograph.

Narat Grasslands

◀————————————————————▶

- **Name:** 那拉提草原/Nàlātí Cǎoyuán
- **Price:** 95 元 (plus 100 元 for transportation)
- **Rating:** Some of Xinjiang's most beautiful grassland

Once you've seen Sayram Lake, a visit to Ili isn't complete without trying to make it out to the Narat grasslands (also spelled "Nalati"). Although crowded with Chinese tourists, it is a glorious view of nature that will make you almost wish you could change careers to become a nomadic herder.

The legend goes that Genghis Khan once led his army toward the Narat grasslands from the TianShan to Ili. The weather had been so bad and his men had become so stricken with hunger and cold that the thought of crossing more mountains was inconceivable. Stumbling into such beautiful grassland was like paradise and upon seeing it they all shouted "Narat! Narat!" which means "sunshine" in the Mongolian language.

Today, a paved road will lead travelers right up to massive tourist center that acts as the entrance to Narat. After paying your entrance fee, buses take you along the winding road up the mountain until you reach the grasslands.

There are a number of hotels along the highway near the tourist center where you can stay, or you can find a yurt to rent while meandering through the grasslands. Officials at the tourist center told me that foreign visitors are only allowed to stay at the hotels, but while walking through the grasslands a police officer I asked laughed and shared that they were just trying to make money with hotel kickbacks.

Whatever the case, these are the kinds of problems I run into all the time in Xinjiang - I never know who to believe! My advice for Narat is to stay where you feel most comfortable.

Exploring the Narat Grasslands

The best time to visit Narat is between the months of June and September, when fields are in bloom and the weather is cool.

Because tourism is such an economic driver among the locals here, you can expect there to be plenty of opportunities to ride horses, motorcycles, join guided hiking tours, eat in a yurt, take photos, etc. None of this is included in the price of admission, of course, so make sure you have enough cash handy.

While a single night stopover is more than enough to experience Narat, a multi-day excursion would allow for an even deeper appreciation for this little paradise. Guides can be arranged or you can try to explore on your own as long as you've brought all you need.

As with Sayram Lake or any of these grasslands populated by a majority Kazakh, festival times are an excellent time to experience the horse races, games and general festivities that offer a meaningful introduction to the Kazakh culture (see Festivals and Holidays in Xinjiang for more details).

Getting to the Narat Grasslands

If you were to look at a map, you'd quickly realize that Narat isn't very close to Yining (Ili). In fact, it's almost 5 hours worth of driving to get there!

While many tourists tend to join a tour group or hire a private driver, it's also worth noting that there are at least three daily public buses that depart from the Yining bus station at 10:00am, 12:30pm and 2pm. The cost of a ticket is 45 RMB.

The same transportation is available to return to Yining.

Near Narat Grasslands

◄────────────────────────────►

While you're headed east on Highway 218 from Yining City toward Narat, there are a few places along the way that can make fun stopovers, especially during specific seasons.

Apricot Valley
新源县野杏沟/Xīnyuánxiàn Yěxìnggōu

- **Price:** Free
- **Rating:** Recommended only in late April/early May

Apricot Valley is one of those places where photographers from all over China flock once a year, a time when the beautiful pink flowers of the Apricot tree are in bloom. Unfortunately, timing your visit here might be difficult as the flowers only bloom for 3-7 days before falling to the ground.

The valley covers over 30,000 acres of land and usually comes into bloom around late April or early May. If you want to make a stop here, just head toward the Jurgen Village (吐尔根乡/Tǔěrgēnxiāng). The Apricot Valley is 3km north of the village.

Kuerding Nature Reserve
库尔德宁自然保护区/Kù'ěrdéníng Zìrán Bǎohùqū

- **Price:** 30 元
- **Rating:** Beautiful but distance prohibitive

Unlike the throngs of tourists that flood the Narat Grasslands during the summer, the beautiful scenery of Kuerdine Nature Reserve is a much quieter destination. If eco-tourism is your thing, this might be a place you'd enjoy.

From Xinyuan (新源), which is where the Narat Airport is located, you'll have to head approximately 45km southwest to reach Kuerding.

Kunas National Forest Park
巩乃斯国家森林公园/Gǒngnǎisī Guójiā Sēnlín Gōngyuán

- **Price:** 10 元
- **Rating:** Beautiful but distance prohibitive

Continuing east on Highway 218 from the Narat Grasslands for another 20 kilometers, tourists can enjoy the enchanting ecological beauty of the Kunas National Forest Park. The waterfalls here are beautiful and there are even some hot springs you can visit.

Again, because of distance and the need for a private car to get here, only the hardcore outdoorsmen and adventurous travelers will likely be interested.

Bayinbulak Grasslands

- **Name**: 巴音布鲁克/Bāyīnbùlǔkè
- **Price**: 160 元 (including transport)
- **Rating**: Difficult to reach but a beautiful destination

There are very few roads whose surrounding beauty matches that of Highway G217 that begins in Kuitun, cutting through the Tianshan before reaching Kuqa. The highway follows a river through rolling hills and vast grasslands, later giving way to towering mountains and rocky terrain until it finally reaches the edge of the Taklamakan Desert.

Along this highway, approximately 70 kilometers south of the entrance to the Narat grasslands, you will come across the Bayanbulak Township (巴音布鲁克镇). Nearby is the Bayanbulak Grasslands, home to the well-known Swan Lake and China's largest swan reserve.

"Swan Lake" is actually a term used to refer to a collection of small lakes and ponds as opposed to one massive body of water. Between the months of May and June, thousands of swans from India and further west migrate here to breed, filling up this series of small lakes.

From the Bayinbulak Tourist Center, you'll be required to purchase tickets which include bus transportation. You'll need to budget at least half a day for this visit because the bus ride alone is about 30-45 minutes. Buses run regularly with stops at the Swan Lake, a pointless tourist temple, and finally "the hill".

I say "the hill" because this is where any picture you see of Bayinbulak is taken from. It's a place where hundreds of professional, amateur and "I-just-have-an-iPhone" photographers gather every evening to snap a shot of the sun setting over the grasslands. It really is gorgeous.

The bus will drop you off at a tourist center at the base of the hill where you can buy some food or use the restroom. From here you can either hike up "the hill" (20-30 min) or pay for an electric vehicle to take you up and back.

During the summer festival of Nadam, Bayanbulak becomes a spectacle of games, competitions, food and other cultural entertainment.

Where to Stay in Ili

Although I highly recommend you take advantage of the traditional housing available along the Sayram Lake and throughout all of the grasslands of Ili, should you need to stay in Yining City before making your next trip out, here are my recommendations.

Yizhan Youth Hostel

伊栈国际青年旅舍/**Yīzhàn Guójì**
Qīngnián Lǔshě
Address: 9th West Lane, Lijun Road
(利群路西九巷)
Phone: (0999) 899-0222

Even though it has been the only hostel available to foreigners in Yining City, the Yizhan Hostel isn't a bad option. Rooms are spacious and they offer free wifi. Unfortunately, they don't rent bicycles but they are a close walk to public transportation where you can get to the train station, airport or river within 15 minutes.

Pictures, Pricing and Booking: **www.xjtravelguide.com/Yining-Yizhan-Hostel**

> **Note**: you may find advertisements for the **Hourglass Youth Hostel** or the **Doppa Youth Hostel** in other hostels around Xinjiang. While these hostels exist, they did not accept foreigners when I went through.

Hotel Yili

伊宁伊犁大酒店 **Yíníng**
Yīlí Dàjiǔdiàn
Address: 23 Sidalin
Street (斯大林街 23 号)
Phone: (0999) 802-6666

Certainly one of the nicest properties in Yining City, the Yili Hotel is a large building set within spacious grounds that offer peace and quiet. Rooms are a bit pricey but offer 4-star comfort in the heart of the city.

Pictures, Pricing and Booking:
www.xjtravelguide.com/yili-hotel

Karamay

克拉玛依

Karamay Top Sights

Karamay Ghost City – Pg 237
An impressive collection of yardang land forms in the middle of the desert.

Introduction to Karamay 克拉玛依

⬅━━━━━━━━━━━━━━━━━━━━━━━━➡

When you drive along the wide streets and walk though lush-green parks of Karamay, it's hard to imagine that the whole city was a desert wasteland less than six decades ago.

The story goes that a Uyghur man named Sayram (Salimu in Chinese) used to ride his donkey up to the hills of Karamay, fill his jars with the black liquid that literally bubbled out of the ground and sell it. Decades later this barren landscape on the edge of the Jungari Desert became littered with small tents as China moved in to extract the precious oil from the ground.

At first, camels were used to ship in water for the workers but eventually a canal was dug and reservoirs were built. Buildings were slowly erected and now, almost fifty years later, an unusually gorgeous Chinese city has emerged.

In the midst of all this progress on the east side of the city a small monument still stands. A statue of an elderly Uyghur man sits on his donkey joyfully playing the rawap, a traditional Uyghur instrument. In front of him, a pool of oil still bubbles up from the ground. Behind him, thousands of oil rigs now teeter back and forth, driving the wealth that makes this city in the desert possible.

Getting to/from Karamay

If you're planning to head straight to Karamay, there are a number of ways to get there. As the city continues to expand and develop, transportation to and from Urumqi continues to improve as well.

Karamay by Air

There are two to three flights daily between Karamay and Urumqi which are only 50 minutes in length as well as flights to/from Beijing. The only problem is that the Karamay Airport, a beautiful building that was obviously built with scalability in mind, is quite a distance from the city center. Expect an additional half hour to get from the airport into the city.

For up-to-date flight schedules and ticket prices, check Trip:
www.xjtravelguide.com/trip-flights

Karamay by Rail

Beginning in 2014, a dedicated "fast train" between Urumqi and Karamay was launched. I put "fast" in quotations because it still takes almost 4 hours, but that's speedy compared to the Urumqi-Beitun train that you could also ride (so make sure you buy tickets for the right train!). Stops along this line include Shihezi and Kuitun.

The train is a quite comfortable and a convenient way to get to Karamay, which I highly recommend. There is a first and second class, but since the price difference isn't great you should opt for the roomier 1st class seats. Currently, there are two trains leaving to/from Karamay every day in the morning and afternoon with a ticket price of under 90 RMB for 1st class and under 60 RMB for 2nd class.

Up-to-date schedules and ticket pricing can be found here:
www.xjtravelguide.com/train-tickets

Karamay by Bus

Buses leave every hour between Urumqi and Karamay. The bus station in Urumqi is located just south of the Xinjiang Autonomous Region Museum (Urumqi Map - A2). Ask the taxi driver to take you to the "MingYuan KeYunZhan on XiBei Lu" (明园客运站在西北路). Tickets are usually around 100 RMB and the entire trip takes a little more than 4 hours.

Karamay by Private Car

Ask most any hotel or head to the Karamay Bus Station and you'll easily find private cars that are willing to drive you to Karamay. You can hire the entire car or just one seat. If you choose the latter, expect the driver to wait until he fills the car before he leaves.

What to do in Karamay

◄──────────────────────────►

Practically speaking, there's really not much to see in Karamay. It's a wonderful city, don't get me wrong, but from a traveler's point of view it's not worth the four hours on a bus or train to get there.

That said, if you will be traveling up to the Altay region and want to make a stop in Karamay, there are a few things I can recommend as places to see during your visit. I'll start with a couple sites within the city and then move to the more well-known tourist destinations outside the city.

Century Park
世纪公园/Shìjìgōngyuán

Karamay's multi-million dollar Century Park, first opened in 2009, is absolutely incredible. During the warmer months it's a great place to walk around and enjoy the scenery, particularly in the cool evening. Climb the hill in the middle of the park to get a nice panoramic view of the city or sit next to the river and watch the nightly water show.

There's a river walk, boat rentals, shopping, and dining all next to the park. For a moment, you might forget that you're in China, much less the middle of the desert.

Black Oil Hill
黑油山/Hēiyóushān

To the east of the city you can visit what is known as Black Oil Hill or 黑油山. As I mentioned in the introduction to Karamay, this is where you can walk the boardwalk around pools of oil still bubbling up from the ground and take your picture next to the statue of old man Salimu and his donkey.

Keep in mind that this not a "wow" place to visit, just something that makes this part of Xinjiang unique. With that in mind, it is hard to justify the 40 元 entrance fee.

Nine Dragons Park
九龙潭/Jiǔlóngtán

Not far from Black Oil Hill on the eastern side of Karamay, water first enters the city at a place called Nine Dragons Park. It is from here that a man-made river snakes through the city and ends at the reservoir.

I mention this place not because it's a particularly interesting visit but because when you see pictures of Karamay, this monument is usually a part of the collage. There are nine dragons whose heads on this Chinese monument spit out water, hence the name.

Karamay Ghost City
魔鬼城/Móguǐchéng

About an hour north of Karamay next to the smaller city of Wuerhe (乌尔禾 /Wūěrhé), there is a natural phenomenon the locals have named Ghost City. The rock formations, known as yardang, are formed from the intense wind that sweeps across the desert here. The eerie noise this wind makes as it moves through the site is what prompted its name.

Believe it or not, you may have already seen the Wuerhe Ghost City on the silver screen. Do you remember the movie Crouching Tiger, Hidden Dragon? Scenes from that movie along with many other Chinese movies were filmed here.

You can take a Chinese tour group here but the best option is to just hire a car or ask your driver to stop here on the way up to Altay. There is an entrance fee for the park (46 元) at which point you can take a shuttle (52 元) or walk the paths on your own.

Dinosaur Park
恐龙公园/Kǒnglónggōngyuán

While traveling to or from the Wuerhe Ghost City you'll likely pass by a strange-looking park with a number of dinosaur statues. This is Dinosaur Park and although this area has become well-known for the dinosaur fossils that have been unearthed, the park itself is only of interest if you have small kids who need a break from the long car ride.

Tacheng City
塔城/Tǎchéng

Tacheng is a small town northwest of Karamay only 10 kilometers from the border of Kazakhstan. The city is an important trade link between China and Kazakhstan but doesn't offer much for tourists unless you're an avid hiker. There are a number of Chinese hiking groups that enjoy coming up to Tacheng.

The Baketu Port is a border crossing 17 kilometers away from Tacheng City but don't expect to be able to cross here. It's an unreliable port and considering how much time is required to get to Tacheng it's not one you want to get stuck at.

It's also worth noting that Tacheng has its own airport with flights to and from Urumqi.

Dushanzi, Kuitun, Wusu

Heading south of Karamay before you reach the Tianshan range you'll run into three cities that are all less than 50km from each other.

Kuitun (奎屯), which is on the rail line, acts as a hub for the region while Wusu (乌苏) is a town best known for its production of the Wusu Beer. Dushanzi (独山子) is a small town where all of Karamay's crude oil is sent for refinement.

For the most part, there's not much worthy of note here. The only exception would be the Dushanzi Grand Canyon (独山子大峡谷/Dúshānzi Dàxiágǔ), a beautiful natural wonder located about 20 minute's drive south from Dushanzi. You can hire a taxi to take you there but you won't need to spend more than 30 minutes to an hour taking pictures.

Shihezi 石河子

Introduction to Shihezi 石河子

◀──────────────────────▶

Situated at the foot of the TianShan a couple hours west of the Xinjiang capital of Urumqi, Shihezi is a city that wouldn't exist were it not for Chinese soldiers-turned-farmers.

Shihezi was first established as a base for the Xinjiang Production and Construction Corps (XPCC) in 1953, an organization that has been described as a "semi-military governmental organization." The soldiers of this corps were tasked with the job of developing the land to become a massive agricultural center, pushing back the sands of the desert to the north and turning it into fields of cotton and sunflowers.

It wasn't until 1976 that Shihezi was officially designated a "city," yet even to this day the XPCC remains in administrative control.

Traveling to Shihezi

The city of Shihezi doesn't offer much beyond what you'll find at any other Chinese city. More than likely you'll just pass through the city.

While Shihezi can often be used as a jumping off point for hiking through the Tianshan, by far the most culturally interesting site is the nearby Kangjia Shimenzi Rock Sanctuary. Once you've had the opportunity to see this, you'll likely want to continue on your way to other parts of Xinjiang.

Getting to/from Shihezi

Because of Shihezi's close proximity to Urumqi, there are plenty of options for travel. The city is situated along National Highway G30 and the adjacent train line, so it's possible to stop here on your way toward Ili, Karamay or up north to Altay.

Shihezi By Air

While there is an airport in Shihezi, located 11 kilometers southwest of the city, at this time there is no passenger transport available.

Shihezi by Train

By train it only takes an hour and a half to arrive at Shihezi from Urumqi. The train leaves from the Urumqi south station and arrives at Shihezi Station just south of the city.

Transport to and from Shihezi by train is usually the most convenient, although getting through security at the Urumqi train station can often be stifling.

From the Shihezi train station you can head in a few different directions:

- **Urumqi**: 25 RMB, 1.5 hours
- **Ili**: 147/69 RMB (hard sleeper/hard seat), 8 hours
- **Altay (Beitun)**: 166/78 RMB (hard sleeper/hard seat), 9.5 hours

For up-to-date train schedules and ticket pricing, visit this site:
www.xjtravelguide.com/train-tickets

Shihezi by Bus

Buses to and from Shihezi run frequently at the Shihezi Bus Station (石河子汽车站/Shíhézǐ Qìchēzhàn). In Urumqi, your point of arrival or departure is the bus station just a couple hundred meters north of the Urumqi South Train Station (Urumqi Map - A5). Tickets usually cost 25-30 RMB.

Transportation around Shihezi

There are plenty of buses and taxis available to get you around Shihezi. Cars can be hired near the bus stop to take you down to the Kanjia Rock Sanctuary, although don't be surprised if the driver has never heard of the place.

Kangjia Shimenzi Rock Sanctuary

◄━━━━━━━━━━━━━━━━━━━━━━━►

- **Name:** 康家石门子旅游景区/Kāngjiā Shíménzi Lǚyóujǐngqū
- **Price:** 20 元
- **Rating:** Fascinating historical site but hard to justify the distance

Amid the jagged rocks, hills and prairies that make up this northern edge of the TianShan range, a special set of rock carvings was discovered in the 1980s that has come to be known as the Kangjia Shimenzi Rock Sanctuary.

It's easy to see why it took so long for these carvings to be discovered. Without a sign pointing visitors to this particular cliff towering 100 meters into the sky, it would be incredibly easy to walk past it unaware. Over 300 figures, including both humans and animals, are depicted throughout various times in history, a history that researchers believe extends back 2,500 years.

What makes these particular carvings unique, however, isn't its length of history or number of figures. It is the fact that within these carvings is a section that depicts a sexually explicit fertility ritual.

One writer called this the "World's Oldest Pornography" with its depiction of erect penises and women dancing around. That said, it takes quite the imagination to see all of this, especially on the side of a rock.

At one point in time, tourism infrastructure was built around these rock carvings, but it has all since been left to rot. Nobody waits to collect money for an entrance ticket and the poorly translated signs are faded and hard to read. In fact, it's likely the only person you'll run into there is a local herder.

See what it looks like for yourself by following along my road trip to discover the Kangjia Shimenzi ancient rock carvings.

Watch the video:
www.xjtravelguide.com/kangjia-shimenzi

Where to stay in Shihezi

There isn't much in Shihezi to justify a long stay but if you do need to overnight in the city here are two options that will work.

Super 8 Shihezi

The Super 8 brand provides the assurance of reasonable comfort without the high price of a 5-star hotel. The rooms aren't large but the bathrooms are generally clean and it's in a great location in the center of Shihezi.

速 8 酒店/Sùbā Jiǔdiàn
Address: 74-15 Beisan Road
(北三路 74-15 号)
Phone: (0993) 270-0696

Pictures, Pricing and Booking: **www.xjtravelguide.com/Shihezi-Super8**

Left Bank Sunshine Hotel

One of the nicer hotels in Shihezi is the Left Bank Sunshine Hotel, a name that doesn't really translate well into English. Standard rooms are comfortable and are available as two full-size beds or one king-size bed.

左岸阳光宾馆 Zuǒ'àn Yángguāng Bīnguǎn
Address: At Beisi Road and Dongwu Road (北四路与东五路)
Phone: (0993) 270-5111

Pictures, Pricing and Booking: **Online reservations unavailable in English**

Korla 库尔勒

Korla Top Sights

Tarim Poplar Park – Pg 251

It's fascinating that these diversiform-leaved poplars can survive in the desert, but it's even more beautiful in the fall when they all turn bright yellow.

Introduction to Korla 库尔勒

←――――――――――――――→

Despite being less than an hour flight from Urumqi, the city of Korla is situated within the Tianshan range such that it takes at least five hours by car or train to reach. From here, the road splits between the northern and eastern edges of the massive Taklamakan Desert.

Benefitting from an abundance of oil money, Korla has quickly developed into one of the nicest and most wealthy cities in Xinjiang, rivaling Karamay. A number of beautiful parks, tall buildings and a river walk with water shows are just a few of the perks residents of this city enjoy.

Aside from oil, Korla is most well-known for its fragrant pears, a particular variety of pear that have been cultivated in this region for over 1,300 years and are now being exported all over the world.

Traveling to Korla

For most travelers, Korla will be just a stop along the way toward Kashgar to the west, Turpan to the east or Ruoqiang to the south. While the city is definitely a refreshing break from the crowded Urumqi streets, there's not much of interest within the city. The Uyghur people make up just a small percentage of the population and once you enter Korla it begins to look like every other Chinese city.

Korla is used as a jumping off point for trips to **Bosten Lake**, a stop at the **Iron Gate Pass** as well as multi-day excursions into the **Narat (Nalati)** and **Bayinbulake Grasslands**. Traveling further west from Korla you will reach **Luntai**, the starting point of the world's longest desert road - the Tarim Highway. Taking this highway (312) or the cross-desert highway from Korla (281), it is possible to make a day trip to one of the **Tarim Poplar Parks** along the Tarim River.

Since Bosten Lake doesn't rate alongside such beautiful Xinjiang gems like Kanas Lake, Karakul Lake, Sayram Lake and others, it's an easy one to cross off your itinerary. The same goes for the Iron Gate Pass which, despite its history, isn't much of a place to visit for passing tourists.

For those traveling during the autumn months (September to October), a stop at one of the Tarim Poplar Parks is very rewarding. Also, in every other season except winter, the grasslands are an amazing excursion explained in further detail in the Ili chapter of this guide since they can be accessed from both the Korla and Ili sides.

Getting to/from Korla

◄─────────────────────────────►

The fastest way to reach Korla from the capital of Urumqi is to jump on an airplane, although there are plenty of buses and trains that make the trip every day. From Korla, travelers have multiple options to head further south and west.

Korla by Air

In 2007 the Korla Airport (库尔勒机场/Kù'ěrlē Jīchǎng) officially began operation at its brand-new location approximately 18 kilometers south of the city center. It now runs multiple flights throughout the day to Urumqi as well as a number of different cities around China.

The prices quoted below are approximate and will change based on the discount for the particular day you choose to fly.

- **Urumqi**: multiple flights daily, 200-400 RMB one way
- **Beijing**: daily flights, approx. 1,400 RMB one way
- **Chengdu**: daily flights, approx. 600-800 RMB one way
- **Chongqing**: daily flights, approx. 300-500 RMB one way
- **Zhengzhou**: daily flights, approx. 600-900 RMB one way

For up-to-date flight schedules and ticket prices, check here:
www.xjtravelguide.com/trip-flights

Korla by Rail

The Korla train station (库尔勒站/Kù'ěrlē Zhàn) is conveniently located on the northeastern edge of the city and is part of the rail line that goes west through Kashgar to Hotan or east through Turpan to Urumqi. Although the train is slow, it's a relaxing and comfortable way to travel around southern Xinjiang.

There are a number of trains you can board heading in both directions. Tickets can be purchased either online or at the train station ticket hall. For reference here are a few destinations alongside the average ticket price and length of journey.

- **Urumqi**: 147/69 RMB (hard sleeper/hard seat), 4.5 hours
- **Turpan**: 115/50 RMB (hard sleeper/hard seat), 3.5 hours
- **Kuqa**: 107/43 RMB (hard sleeper/hard seat), 3.5 hours
- **Kashgar**: 249/114 RMB (hard sleeper/hard seat), 12 hours

- **Hotan**: 340/156 RMB (hard sleeper/hard seat), 18 hours, one daily in the evening.

To view schedules or purchase train tickets online, check here:
www.xjtravelguide.com/train-tickets

Korla by Bus

Buses leaving from the Korla Bus Station (库尔勒客运站/Kù'ěrlē Kèyùnzhàn) south of the river on Tuanjie Road can get passengers to most any city in southern Xinjiang, far more than would be reasonable to try to cover here.

Sleeper buses connect to Urumqi (8 hours), Turpan (5 hours), Kuqa (3.5 hours), Aksu (8 hours), Kashgar (14 hours) and many others along the northern and southern rims of the Taklamakan Desert.

Getting around Korla

Taxis in Korla run on the meter and there are a number of nice city buses that can get you throughout the city.

What to do in/around Korla

←——————————————————→

Within the City

Within the city limits of Korla, you're limited on what you can do, but that doesn't mean you should just sit in your hotel room and surf the internet.

Korla is home to great **science and cultural museums** (on 延安路 Yanan Rd) as well as kilometers worth of paths along the river. There are a couple bike shops in town that rent bicycles and it's enjoyable to bike along these paths, stopping in the evening to watch a water show (every evening during the warmer months starting on the hour). Rumor has it that Korla is home to the tallest water cannon in China. Who wouldn't want to see that?

It's also worth a visit to the Bazaar (大巴扎/Dàbāzhā) or the "Bosten Bazaar" (博斯腾巴扎/Bósīténg Bazhā) to enjoy a bit of the Uyghur culture in Korla. There are plenty of snack stalls or places to eat within these bazaars as well.

Bosten Lake
博斯腾湖/Bósīténghú

- **Price:** Free at most places
- **Rating:** Not one of Xinjiang most scenic lakes

Bosten Lake lies about 60 kilometers northwest of Korla along Highway G3012 toward Turpan. At 1,228 square kilometers in size, it is by far Xinjiang's largest freshwater lake, even though it is only 16 meters at its deepest point.

From an ecological standpoint the lake is fascinating, with a number of different fish species, a fishery, reed beds and water birds.

From a tourist standpoint, there isn't much to see or do. Other than speedboat rides, a large sandy beach resort on the north end of the lake that is usually filled with Chinese tourist (金沙滩旅游风景区/Jīnshātān Lǚyóu Fēngjǐngqū) and some places to fish, this lake doesn't quite measure up to Kanas, Karakul, Sayram or even Heavenly Lake. Unless you need a place to set up tent for a night, you can likely cross Bosten Lake off your itinerary.

Tarim Poplar Park
塔里木胡杨林公园/Tǎlǐmù Húyánglín Gōngyuán

Alternative Name: 塔里木河胡杨林保护区/Tǎlǐmùhé Húyánglín Bǎohùqū

- **Price:** 45 元 (additional costs within the parks)
- **Rating:** A difficult detour but gorgeous during the Fall months

Flowing down from the Himalayas, the Tarim River and its many tributaries snake their way like a lost highway through the Taklamakan Desert in Xinjiang. It has never been a deep or particularly strong river; regardless, it has seen a significant shortening over the past few decades. Its former terminus, the famous Lop Nor Lake, is now nothing but a dry lake bed.

One beautiful byproduct of the Tarim's presence in the desert is the collection of poplar trees that line the banks of the river. These diversiform-leaved poplars, with their jagged trunks and golden leaves, present some of the most striking photography that Xinjiang has to offer.

While these forests exist all along the Tarim River, there are two places which offer easiest access for visitors who don't have the time or money to jump on a camel caravan. The more well-known but furthest distance away is the Tarim Poplar Park (塔里木胡杨林公园) which requires a short trip from Luntai down the cross-desert highway, a total of 250 kilometers. An alternative is the Tarim Poplar Reserve (塔里木河胡杨林保护区), a smaller but significantly closer site to Korla on Highway G218.

Each will require a day trip that can be organized from Korla. Keep in mind that additional fees exist in the parks such as a shuttle bus (30 RMB), a touristy train ride (100 RMB) and a viewing tower (20 RMB). These are all at your discretion, although the latter is recommended if you want some good pictures.

Iron Gate Pass
铁关门/Tiěguānmén

- **Price:** 8 元
- **Rating:** Historically significant but not worth visiting

Even though one branch of the ancient Silk Road required merchants to travel through a ravine pass that became known as the Iron Gate Pass, what remains leaves much to be desired. The old tower guarding the gate is a rebuilt version of what was destroyed years ago and leads into a park where you can walk around.

I mention this site primarily because of its location less than 10 kilometers north of Korla. It's not a place I highly recommend unless you somehow get stuck in Korla with nothing else to do.

Narat and Bayinbulak Grasslands

A multi-day trip from Korla to the lush grasslands of Narat and Bayinbulak can be made from Korla. I go into further detail of these locations and many others in the Ili (Yili) chapter.

Where to stay in Korla

⬅━━━━━━━━━━━━━━━━━━━━━━➡

The growing city of Korla offers a multitude of options for accommodation, but since this city is not a hub for tourism only two will be mentioned here, both of them higher-end hotels.

Loulan Hotel

The Loulan Hotel is an affordable hotel located across the street from the People's Park. There's plenty of places to walk and eat nearby, as well as the riverwalk a few minutes away.

Pricing, Pictures and Booking:
www.xjtravelguide.com/korla-loulan

> 梨城花园酒店/**Líchéng Huāyuán Jiǔdiàn**
> **Address:** 2 Guangchang Road (广场路 2 号)
> **Phone:** (0996) 203-1566

Pear City Garden Hotel

Located just off the bank of the Kongque River (Peacock River), the Pear City Garden Hotel is a comfortable, 5-star luxury option in Korla. Rooms are well-adorned, bathrooms are very clean and they offer free wi-fi. A workout room and pool are available.

Pricing, Pictures and Booking:
www.xjtravelguide.com/korla-pearl-garden-hotel

> 梨城花园酒店 /**Líchéng Huāyuán Jiǔdiàn**
> **Address:** 20 Binhe Road (滨河路 20 号)
> **Phone:** (0996) 206-6666

Kangcheng Jianguo Hotel

Further north is yet another luxury 5-star hotel that is a great option for those who are willing to pay for comfort. Similar to Pearl City, Kangcheng offers a pool, a workout room and free wifi. Transportation is readily available and there are a number of food options just outside the front door.

Pricing, Pictures and Booking:
www.xjtravelguide.com/korla-kangcheng-kotel

> 康城建国国际酒店 /**Líchéng Huāyuán Jiǔdiàn**
> **Address:** 618 East Jiaotong Road (交通东路 618 号)
> **Phone:** (0996) 208-8888

Kuche (Kuqa)

库车

Kuqa Top Sights

Kizil Thousand Buddhist Caves – Pg 263
A captivating collection of Buddhist caves that house plenty of Silk Road art and history.

Kuqa Grand Canyon – Pg 264
Similar to the Antelope Canyon in Arizona, USA, this canyon is a photographer's paradise.

Introduction to Kuqa 库车

◄─────────────────►

Although it doesn't receive the same kind of attention that Turpan and Kashgar do, the small town of Kuqa (also spelled "Kuche" or "Qiuci"), bordering the northern edge of the Taklamakan Desert, is a true diamond in the dunes. Its historical importance is matched only by its unique topography.

Despite how small the modern city seems, it once held a prominent place in Silk Road history as the center of the largest of the 36 kingdoms in China's Western Regions. At the time, it was one of the most populous regions along the Tarim Basin and its music, known as "Kuchean music," became so popular that it is believed to have heavily influenced Chinese music.

As merchants made their way along the ancient Silk Road to stop in Kuqa, not only did they sell many of their wares, they also passed along their system of beliefs. Kuqa became an important center of Buddhism in the 3rd century, the remnants of which can still be seen today at places like the **Kizil Thousand Buddhist Caves**.

As with many cities in Xinjiang, the clash of history and modern development can be seen in the division of the city between the Uyghur "old city" and the Chinese "new city". Ruins of the ancient Qiuci City and its walls can still be visited near the river on the west side of town.

Traveling to Kuqa

While Kuqa is just one of many Silk Road oases along the northern rim of the Taklamakan Desert, it's an important intersection for travelers who want to get off the beaten path.

Highway G30 and the southern rail line pass through Kuqa, but from here travelers can also begin a trip up north on the narrow and winding Highway 217 into the TianShan toward the grasslands of Ili (Yili). For those coming down this incredibly scenic journey, Kuqa will be your first stop to spend the night.

While it may be tempting to think of Kuqa as an unimportant waypoint on your journey, I urge you to consider at least one full day of exploring. At the very least you should rent a taxi to visit the **Kizil Thousand Buddhist Caves** and the **TianShan Grand Canyon**, during which time you'll also pass through the fascinating geological rock forest known as the **Salt Water Valley**.

This itinerary should be sufficient to get a taste of what Kuqa has to offer, but an additional day will afford you the time to explore the **Old City** with its crumbling walls, the **Friday Bazaar** and places like the **Kuqa Grand Mosque**.

The entire region is ripe with ancient Buddhist caves, rock formations and ancient city ruins - more than are possible to list out here. The most important of these, should you have the time and inclination, are the **Subashi Ancient City Ruins**, the **Beacon Tower** and the **Kizil Ghost City**.

Getting to/from Kuqa

Kuqa acts as an important crossroads halfway between Urumqi and Kashgar on the east-west line and between Dushanzi and Khotan on the north-south Highway 217. As such, there are a number of transportation options available to travelers.

Kuqa by Air

The small Kuqa airport (库车机场/Kùchē Jīchǎng) services multiple daily flights to Urumqi. Located about 12 kilometers southwest of town, the airport is a simple 25 RMB taxi ride away.

A flight to Urumqi should cost between 300-500 RMB and the journey takes just a little over an hour.

Flight schedules and pricing can be checked here:
www.xjtravelguide.com/trip-flights

Kuqa by Rail

The Kuqa train station (库车站/Kùchē Zhàn) is located in the southern part of the city, about 6 kilometers from the People's Square. There are a number of trains you can board headed in both directions and tickets can be purchased either online or at the train station ticket hall. For reference here are a few destinations, the average ticket price and length of journey.

- **Urumqi:** 178/102 RMB (hard sleeper/hard seat), 11 hours
- **Turpan:** 152/86 RMB (hard sleeper/hard seat), 8 hours
- **Korla:** 90/43 RMB (hard sleeper/hard seat), 3 hours
- **Kashgar:** 170/98 RMB (hard sleeper/hard seat), 12 hours
- **Hotan:** 218/112 RMB (hard sleeper/hard seat), 20 hours leaving at 10:45pm

Check train schedules and ticket pricing here:
www.xjtravelguide.com/train-tickets

Kuqa by Bus

Buses depart and arrive from the Kuqa Bus Station (库车汽车站/Kùchē Qìchē Zhàn) on TianShan Road (天山东路) just southeast of the People's Park.

Sleeper buses can get you to Urumqi (12-13 hours) for between 145-220 RMB depending on the bus. Your terminus in Urumqi is the south bus station. Departures are usually only in the evening and run overnight.

Buses to Kashgar (12 hours) are 260 RMB and run three times daily. Your terminus in Kashgar is the International Bus Station across the street from Kashgar's train station. Additional buses to Korla, Turpan and Khotan are also available at this same bus station.

Getting around Kuqa

Taxis in Kuqa are cheap and run on the meter. As always, there are city buses that only cost 1 RMB.

What to do in Kuqa

Although the most spectacular sites to visit in this region are outside of the Kuqa city center, the city itself still offers a few interesting places worth a visit.

You should reserve time to walk through what is considered Kuqa's "Old City." While modern development has occurred around the People's Square on the eastern side of town, a few kilometers down Tianshan road leads to a primarily Uyghur side of town where the old way of life is still alive and well.

Qiuci Ancient City Ruins
龟兹故城/Kùchē Gùchéng

- **Price:** Free
- **Rating**: Mostly just mounds of dirt, but still of interest

Although remains of the old wall, cemeteries and dirt mounds are scattered throughout the older, western part of town, the official "Ancient City Ruins" is located off of Tianshan Road before you even reach the old city.

Unlike other ancient cities in Xinjiang, these mounds of dirt are difficult to tell apart and the layout of the city has been lost in the erosion over time. You're more likely to find a cow grazing among the ruins now than an actual tourist.

Qiuci Palace Museum
库车王府/Kùchē Wángfǔ

- **Price:** 55 元
- **Rating**: High expense for a lot of replicas

As far as I can tell, this is the only museum in Kuqa and it leaves much to be desired. A residence of the kings of Qiuci until the 20th century, it was originally built in 1759 and covered an area of 40,000 square meters. Of course, this, like many religious buildings in this area, was rebuilt in 2004, making it more of a tourism attraction than historical palace.

There are a number of Buddhist frescos from Kizil and other areas around Kuqa, but these are also replicas. Considering the high price tag and the fact that better museums in Urumqi and Turpan are free, this one may not be worth your time and money.

Kuqa Friday Bazaar
库车巴扎/Kùchē Bāzhā

- **Price**: Free
- **Rating**: Not to be missed if you're in Kuqa on a Friday

Every Friday thousands of people gather along the small streets east of the dry riverbed near the old city to take part in one of Xinjiang's great bazaars. Livestock, silks, sheep skins, medicines and other wares are sold along the dusty roads providing ample opportunity to witness a centuries-old Silk Road tradition.

Kuqa Grand Mosque
库车大寺/Kùchē Dàsì

- **Price**: 15 元 to enter, free to view from outside
- **Rating**: A worthwhile destination if you're walking the old city

As Xinjiang's second largest mosque behind the Id Kah Mosque in Kashgar, the Kuqa Grand Mosque is an impressive building worth visiting while you're walking around the old, western portion of the city.

Built in 1559 as Islam was sweeping through the region, the mosque later burned in a fire in 1925. The building you see now with its towering minarets, brick walls and green doors was rebuilt in 1928. Within the complex are the main prayer hall and a few smaller prayer halls, all of which can accommodate up to 3,000 people for Friday prayers.

Finding the mosque is a bit tricky as it is set back in the old part of town, just south of the Tianshan West Road (天山西路). You can ask most people and they'll be able to point you in the right direction but once you get close enough you should be able to see the spires jutting out above the surrounding homes.

Unless you have a particular interest in taking a look inside, I recommend you save your money and just take a few pictures of the beautiful mosque face.

What to do around Kuqa

If you have the time, a day or two spent touring the cliffs, caves and giant rocks north of Kuqa can be a memorable addition to your Xinjiang itinerary.

The two most visually dramatic sites around Kuqa are the Kizil Thousand Buddhist Caves and the TianShan Grand Canyon, but the unique topography and history of the region offer some additional detours that are certainly worth considering.

Kizil Thousand Buddhist Caves
克孜尔千佛洞 Kèzīěr Qiānfódòng

- **Price:** 55 元
- **Rating:** Recommended for those interested in Silk Road history

Located about 75 kilometers northwest of Kuqa are the impressive caves known as the Kizil Thousand Budhist Caves. These caves, carved into the side of a massive cliff face overlooking the Muzalt River to the south, contain frescos that date back as early as the 3rd century.

Historians believe that the Kizil caves predate the more famous Dunhuang caves in the neighboring Gansu province by at least a century and perhaps even influenced them. The most popular photo of Kizil shows a single broad face of the western cliff; however, the caves extend almost three kilometers in length and include 236 preserved caves, most of which we as tourist aren't permitted to visit.

As a relatively new member of the World Heritage List, the Kizil Caves have undergone extensive research and preservation over the past decade. Fragments of paintings remain in only 80 of the caves today and of these, only 10 are open for public viewing.

Experts describe the murals as a melting pot of influences spanning both time and culture. The development of the Kizil Thousand Buddhist Caves occurred over the course of five centuries and include traces of ancient India, Greece, Rome and Persia. Albert von Le Coq, a German explorer who excavated the Kizil caves in 1906 and 1913, made the interesting observation that the caves lacked any Chinese elements common among other Buddhist sites.

As with many archeological sites in Xinjiang, the presence of the German expedition and others is a source of grief for the Chinese. Explorers like von Le Coq and others carted off a number of sculptures and murals back to Europe, leaving only patches that can still be seen on the walls today.

As a tourist, you'll want to take advantage of the opportunity to not only visit the caves but to also walk along the Muzalt River valley. Getting to the Kizil Thousand Buddhist Caves will require either joining a tour group or hiring a private car from Kuqa (~250 RMB for a taxi round trip). Along the way, you'll pass by the Salt Water Valley (盐水沟/Yánshuǐgōu) whose weird rock formations situated at odd angles makes for fascinating photos.

Side Note: This is one place in Xinjiang where you will absolutely not be allowed to bring your camera. Your phone is fine (go figure), but they'll search your bag for any type of DSLR and force you to put it into a locker while you tour the site.

Kizil Ghost City
克孜尔魔鬼城/Kèzīěr Móguǐchéng

- **Price:** 20 元
- **Rating:** Possible camping spot but not as nice as the Wuerhe Ghost City in Karamay

As part of your trip to Kizil Thousand Buddhist Caves you can also make a stop at the Kizil Ghost City, sometimes referred to as the "Baicheng Ghost City". Situated north of Kizil Village about 20 kilometers from the Kizil caves, these are yet another example of Xinjiang's yardang landforms, the most popular of which can be found at Wuerhe near Karamay.

There's no history behind this "city", it's merely a collection of wind-formed rocks that make for interesting photo subjects.

Tianshan Grand Canyon
天山神秘大峡谷/Tiānshān Shénmì Dàxiágǔ

- **Price:** 45 元
- **Rating:** Visually intriguing; great stop for photographers

Aside from the Kizil Thousand Buddhist Caves, the Tianshan Grand Canyon has become one of Kuqa's most popular locations thanks to its beautiful red color and towering sandstone walls reminiscent of Antelope Canyon in Arizona (USA).

The entire canyon is 5 kilometers in length and includes a Buddhist cave dug out during the Tang Dynasty (7th-8th century). The natural walkway varies in width between 5 meters down to .4 meters with sandstone walls whose twists and texture capture the imagination.

The Tianshan Grand Canyon is located 65 kilometers north of Kuqa along Highway G217, which means that this could potentially be your first stop as you head north to the grasslands of Ili or your last stop coming down from the mountains. It's possible to include this as the second half of your day trip to the Kizil Thousand Buddhist Caves to make the best use of the car you hire for the day. The canyon is open from 9:30am-7:30pm during the summer and 10am-7pm in the winter.

Subashi Ancient City
苏巴什古城/Sūbāshi Gǔchéng

- **Price:** 25 元
- **Rating**: Worth a stop, time permitting

The Subashi Ancient City is a collection of ruins and temples located 25 kilometers north of Kuqa that date back to the 1st century. The city and its Buddhist traditions survived until the 13th century when Islam was making its way through the Xinjiang region.

Local legend says that Subashi was known as the "Kingdom of Females" because something in the water caused only girls to be born here. They say it was a matriarchal society where females held positions of authority while the men were only good for manual labor.

Since it covers an area of approximately 5 square kilometers, there's a bit of walking that visitors will do to get around but the ruins, with the mountains in the background, are picturesque. The ancient city walls jut up from the ground and the temple structure has many windows and caves visible. This temple, the Zhaoguli Temple, is one of Xinjiang's best surviving Buddhist temples and is stunning when set against the mountainous background.

Kizil Kara Buddhist Caves and Beacon Tower
克孜尔尕哈石窟/Kèzīěr Gǎhā Shíkū

Price: 15 元

Rating: The caves can be skipped but the Beacon Tower is a nice, quick stop

Just 16 kilometers north of Kuqa is another collection of caves and ruins known as the Kizil Kara Buddhist Caves. Compared to the Kizil Thousand Buddhist Caves, the Kara Caves are fewer in number, totaling only 47, and aren't as well-preserved. In short, unless you're a die-hard Silk Road art buff, these can be skipped.

The Beacon Tower, on the other hand, is worth a quick visit. There's nothing here except the 13.5-meter-high rectangular tower that was once used as a warning signal of invading armies, but it is an impressive structure that has somehow survived centuries of erosion.

Kumtura Thousand Buddhist Caves
库木吐拉千佛洞/Kùmùtǔlā Qiānfodòng

Price: Free at most places

Rating: Historically interesting but harder to reach than the Kizil Caves

As if there aren't already enough ancient Buddhist caves to keep historians busy (far more than are being mentioned in this guide), the Kumtura Thousand Buddhist Caves also overlook the Muzalt River near Kuqa. Located about 30 kilometers from the city center, these caves are closer but not nearly as well-known as the Kizil Thousands Buddhist Caves.

Because tourism to these caves is not heavy and roads are not well-built, a 4WD rental is required from Kuqa for access to the Kumtura Caves.

Where to stay in Kuqa

Kuqa International Hotel

The Kuqa International Hotel is one of the best options for foreigners in Kuqa. The rooms are nice, the price is right and they have internet in the rooms.

库车国际酒店/Kùchē Guójì Jiǔdiàn
Address: 377 Tianshan Rd (天山东路 337 号)
Phone: (0997) 731-0099

Pricing, Pictures and Booking:
www.xjtravelguide.com/kuqa-international-hotel

Kuqa Hotel

The advantage of the Kuqa Hotel is that it offers both a 3-star option and a 5-star option right next door to each other. Both are just a couple kilometers from the train station, although that means they're a bit further from the western, Uyghur part of town. Public transportation is readily available. Both hotels offer varying degrees of comfort and free in-room wi-fi.

库车饭店 /Kùchē Fàndiàn
Address: 266 TianShan Middle Road (天山中路 266 号)
Phone: (0997) 723-3158

Pricing, Pictures and Booking:
www.xjtravelguide.com/Kuqa-Grand-Hotel

Golden Bridge Hotel

The Golden Bridge Hotel is another 3-star option that is by no means luxurious but it is comfortable, at least by Chinese standards. The location right near Wenhua Road, a main artery in Kuqa, means that you'll have close access to the nearby park, plenty of banks and a number of dining options.

库车金桥宾馆 /Kùchē Jīnqiáo Bīnguǎn
Address: 1 Youyi Road (友谊路 1 号)
Phone: (0997) 712-5888

Pricing, Pictures and Booking:
Online reservations unavailable in English

Aksu 阿克苏

Introduction to Aksu 阿克苏

About 260 kilometers east of Kuqa along the dusty highway G30, the relatively small town of Aksu appears along the arid, sandy shores of the Taklamakan Desert. Thanks in part to this dry climate and some unusually rich soil, crops of cotton, corn and other such plants continue to drive the growing Aksu economy.

The area has been referred to by a couple different names before the locals started calling it "Aqsu". During the first century writers called the region "Gumo" while the famous Chinese monk Xuanzang wrote of it as "Baluka".

Control of the Aksu region has exchanged hands multiple times throughout history. Chinese, Tibetan and Uyghur armies conquered and reconquered cities throughout the latter first century until the Mongolians decided to jump in the game in the 13th century.

Yakub Beg, the brutal ruler of Kashgaria and leader of the anti-Chinese rebellion, took command of Aksu in the 19th century after senselessly massacring the Chinese Muslims who had previously inhabited the city. Within a decade the Qing army squelched the rebellion and established dominance in a region that, despite attempts at further rebellion, has remained under their control to this day.

Traveling to Aksu

In spite of all its history and the number of cultures that have had influence over the region, Aksu offers little value for travelers. Unlike Kuqa to the east, which is surrounded by Buddhist caves and fascinating rock formations, the area surrounding Aksu is surprisingly barren.

The only site worthy of note is the **Tumor Peak Nature Reserve** (新疆托木尔峰 自然保护区/Tuōmùěrfēng Zìrán Bǎohùqū) about 80 kilometers northeast of Aksu, although it's quite a detour just to see beautiful mountain scenery.

At 7,439 meters, Tumor is the highest peak in the Tianshan range and is home to the **Tumor Glacier**, the rare snow leopard and even the snow lotus plant. The mountain straddles the Chinese border with Kyrgyzstan and it is usually from the Kyrgyz side that climbers summit the peak. Since there's not much in the way of tourism infrastructure here, it's good to be prepared before making a visit and even better to hire a professional guide to visit the glacier.

Heading west from Aksu there are plenty of small villages but nothing worthy of mention here until you reach the great Silk Road city of Kashgar.

Getting to/from Aksu

←————————————————————→

As one of Xinjiang's smaller oases along the northern rim of the Taklamakan Desert, transportation to and from Aksu is available but not plentiful.

Aksu by Air

Another one of Xinjiang's many small airports, the Aksu Airport (阿克苏机场 /Ākèsū jīchǎng), serves daily flights to and from Urumqi. The airport is located about 15 kilometers north of the city center and only requires a 20-40 RMB taxi ride.

Flights to and from Urumqi will cost approximately 300-800 RMB per ticket with multiple flights to choose from.

For up-to-date flight schedules and ticket prices, check here:
www.xjtravelguide.com/trip-flights

Aksu by Rail

In the opposite direction of the airport, the Aksu train station (阿克苏火车站 /Ākèsū huǒchē zhàn) is situated on the southern side of town about 7 kilometers from the city center. There are a number of trains you can board headed in both directions and tickets can be purchased either online or at the train station ticket hall. For reference, here are a few destinations, including average ticket price and length of journey:

- **Urumqi:** 222/128 RMB (hard sleeper/hard seat), 14 hours
- **Turpan:** 194/112 RMB (hard sleeper/hard seat), 11.5 hours
- **Korla:** 133/75 RMB (hard sleeper/hard seat), 6 hours
- **Kashgar:** 123/69 RMB (hard sleeper/hard seat), 6.5 hours
- **Hotan:** 185/94 RMB (hard sleeper/hard seat), 15 hours

To view train schedules and purchase tickets online, check here:
www.xjtravelguide.com/train-tickets

Aksu by Bus

Buses depart and arrive from the Aksu Bus Station (阿克苏中心汽车站/Ākèsū Zhōngxīn Qìchēzhàn) on Wuka Road (乌喀路).

There are a handful of buses that originate from Aksu but often buses stop here on their way from one direction or the other. Buses to Kashgar leave every 90 minutes; buses to Hotan once a day in the afternoon and buses to Urumqi every hour.

Getting around Aksu

Taxis in Aksu run on the typical meter all through the day and city buses run during daylight hours.

Where to stay in Aksu

Aksu Pudong Holiday Hotel

Located a little more than a kilometer from the Aksu train and bus stations, this 3-star hotel is quite convenient for most travelers even though it is a little distance from the city center.

阿克苏浦东假日酒/
Ākèsū Pǔdōng Jiàrì Jiǔdiàn
Address: 1 W. Jiaotong Road (交通西路 1 号)
Phone: (0997) 268-8888

Pictures, Pricing and Booking:
www.xjtravelguide.com/Aksu-Pudong-Hotel

Chenmao Hongfu Hotel

To enjoy a more comfortable 4-star hotel experience in Aksu, check out the Chenmao Hongfu Hotel just east of the People's Square. The rooms are pricier but much more comfortable and the location in the city center has its advantages.

阿克苏辰茂鸿福酒店/
Ākèsū Chénmào Hóngfú Jiǔdiàn
Address: 32 Dongda Street
(东大街 32 号)
Phone: (0997) 228-3555

Pictures, Pricing and Booking:
www.xjtravelguide.com/Aksu-Hongfu-Hotel

Kashgar 喀什

Kasghar Top Sights

Id Kah Mosque – Pg 286
The iconic yellow-tiled mosque is not only the most popular in Kashgar, it's also the largest in all of China.

Livestock Market – Pg 292
Every Sunday, Uyghur from all over Kashgar gather to buy and sell animals while enjoying the market atmosphere.

Apak Khoja Mausoleum – Pg 289
The design and colors of this 17th century Uyghur building are worth the short trip right outside of town.

Kashgar Old City – Pg 287
Whether you wander the "new" Old City or the "new" Old City, the alleys provide a Uyghur charm unique to Kashgar.

Introduction to Kashgar 喀什

⬅————————————➤

Very few cities in China can claim such allure and mystery like the city of Kashgar. Considering a history that spans at least 2,000 years and a future continuing to grow as one of Central Asia's most important trade hubs, the clash of "ancient" and "modern" in Xinjiang is never more apparent than in Kashgar.

Although China has always been a major player in Kashgar's long history, they have never ceased to battle for control of the region. Chinese General Ban Chao marched through Kashgar in AD 73, subduing it from the Xiongnu tribes who had ruled before. The walled fort Ban Chao established for him and his men has been reconstructed for visitors (mostly Chinese) to walk through today.

Over the next few centuries the region changed hands between various Chinese dynasties, the Tibetan Empire, the Mongols and a band of Uyghur/Turkic tribes called the Karakhanid Khanate.

One of Kashgar's most famous rulers was a man named Yakub Beg. Although his reign covers only 11 years in the history of Kashgar, it was a violent period of insurrection among various Muslim groups that was eventually quelled by the Qing dynasty.

Since that time and the later establishment of the Peoples Republic of China in 1949, China has continued to develop and fortify Kashgar. Twenty years later, in 1969, the statue of Mao was erected in the center of town as a visual reminder of who was - and still is - in control.

Kashgar is now a city of nearly 400,000 inhabitants, a majority of whom are Uyghur despite a growing population of Han Chinese.

Traveling to Kashgar

Kashgar is one of those cities that can be enjoyed on a two-day itinerary but won't be fully appreciated without at least a week. I personally love being able to leisurely stroll around the city, but one could just as easily hire a taxi to speed up the process.

Within the city center there are only a handful of "must-see" sites to put on your itinerary such as the **Id Kah Mosque**, particularly during Friday Prayers or a big Muslim festival, wandering around the **Kashgar Old City**, the **Apak Khoja Mausoleum** and finally the **Sunday Bazaar**. All of this could be managed in a day if needed, although it would be better to spread it out over a couple days.

For those who want to dig deeper into Kashgar's history, you can also check out the **Tomb of Yusuf Has Hajib, Pantuo City** or even the **Kashgar City Planning Museum** (if it's open). Don't worry if time limits you from visiting any of these places, though, as proper context is required to appreciate them. The same goes for the **old British Consulate**, the **old Russian Consulate** and the **Laining Ancient City Walls**.

There are a number of great day trips you can make around Kashgar including to one of the many **Village Markets**, the most popular of which is at **Opal**. Another day could be spent driving and hiking up to the spectacular **Shipton's Arch** northwest of Kashgar or in the opposite direction you could ride a camel along the undulating dunes at **Dawakul Lake Desert Park**.

Unless you have specific reason, I wouldn't add places like the **Three Immortals Caves**, the **Ancient City of Hanoi** or the **Mahmud Kashgari Tomb** to your itinerary, even though they are detailed within this chapter. The effort and expense required to visit each of these locations is not met with sufficient visual reward in my opinion.

Finally, a visit to Kashgar isn't complete without at least a day or two spent traveling along the famous **Karakoram Highway**. This trip will be covered in more detail next chapter, just be prepared to budget enough time and money to make the journey.

Getting to/from Kashgar

At one point in history, Kashgar was only accessible by arduous and life-threatening journeys across either a desert or over a mountain pass. Today that has all changed, of course, and Kashgar offers both domestic and international transportation that now take mere hours, not weeks.

Kashgar by Air

The Kashgar Airport (喀什机场/Kāshí Jīchǎng) is Xinjiang's second-largest airport behind Urumqi and is located 10 kilometers north of the city. It is possible to take a taxi to and from the airport (40-50 RMB) but the number 2 city bus runs from the center of town to the airport gate.

Likewise, when you exit the airport, you can opt to either take a taxi/shuttle waiting in the parking lot or just walk out the front gate and wait near the road. Taxi drivers who enter the airport refuse to use a meter and will charge up to 50 RMB per person. If you get a taxi on the road, it is possible to rent the whole car for 20 RMB.

There are a number of domestic flights that depart from Kashgar Airport, the majority of which land in Urumqi and then may head off to other cities like Beijing, Xi'an, Guangzhou and more. The prices quoted below are approximate and may change based on the discount for the particular day you choose to fly.

- **Urumqi**: multiple flights daily, 500-1000 RMB one way
- **Yining (on to Urumqi)**: daily flights, 500-1300 RMB one way
- **Beijing (via Urumqi)**: daily flights, approx. 1,000-1,300 RMB one way
- **Shanghai (via Urumqi)**: daily flights, approx. 1,400-2,000 RMB one way
- **Chengdu (via Urumqi)**: daily flights, approx. 1,000-2,000 RMB one way
- **Ngari (Tibet)**: Tuesday & Friday only, approx. 1,500-2,000 RMB one way
- **Xi'an (via Urumqi)**: daily flights, approx. 1,000-1,300 RMB one way

For up-to-date flight schedules and ticket prices, check here:

www.xjtravelguide.com/trip-flights

Kashgar by Train

The Kashgar Train Station (喀什火车站/Kāshi Huǒchēzhàn) is on the far east side of town. City bus number 28 will take you from the People's Park the entire six kilometers to the station in under an hour but you can also hire a taxi for under 20 RMB to arrive much quicker.

Multiple trains daily originate or terminate at the Kashgar Train Station, all of which go to the capital Urumqi. Starting in 2011, a few passenger trains stopped in Kashgar on their way south to Khotan (Hotan).

Train tickets can be bought at the train station, a city ticket office (火车票代售点 /Huǒchē Piàodài Shòudiǎn) or at the many travel agencies around town. For reference, below is a quick list of popular destinations with prices and the length of the journey:

- **Urumqi:** 304/177 RMB (hard sleeper/hard seat), 17 hours
- **Khotan (Hotan):** 115/61 RMB (hard sleeper/hard seat), 6 hours
- **Kuqa:** 171/98 RMB (hard sleeper/hard seat), 8 hours
- **Turpan:** 280/163 RMB (hard sleeper/hard seat), 15 hours
- **Korla:** 222/128 RMB (hard sleeper/hard seat), 11 hours

To view train schedules or purchase tickets online, check here:

www.xjtravelguide.com/train-tickets

Kashgar by Bus

There are two primary bus stations in Kashgar, the International Bus Station (喀 什国际汽车站/Kāshi Guójì Qìchēzhàn; Map - B1) located south of town and the Kashgar Main Bus Station (喀什汽车客运站/Kāshi Qìchē Kèyùnzhàn; Map - C2) located across the street from the train station on the east side of town.

Each station serves different locations so be sure you know which one you need to travel through.

Kashgar International Bus Station
喀什国际汽车站

To arrive at the Kashgar International Bus station, your best bet is to take a taxi, although you can also hop on the #4 city bus. It's quite a distance outside the city, so give yourself at least 30 minutes to get through traffic and arrive at the station followed by another 15 minutes to get through security and to your boarding gate (and even more time if you still need to stand in line to purchase your tickets!).

Despite the fact that it's "international", this is the station you'll use to go south along the Taklamakan Desert.

- **Hotan**: 154/199 RMB (bottom/top berth), run every 1.5 hours, 8-hour journey
- **Yengisar**: 28 RMB, throughout the day, 1.5-hour journey
- **Yarkand (Shache)**: 68-88 RMB, throughout the day, 1.5-hour journey
- **Kharghilik (Yecheng)**: 93-118 RMB, throughout the day, 4-hour journey
- **Tashkorgan**: 89-119 RMB, every morning, 4-6-hour journey
- **Osh (Kyrgyzstan)**: 570 RMB, only Mondays and Fridays at 9am, 2-day journey
- **Sost (Pakistan)**: 270 RMB, leaves at noon only if there are 10+ passengers; journey takes 2 days and overnights in Tashkorgan

Kashgar Bus Station
喀什客运站

You'll find the Kashgar bus station just across the street from the train station. Unlike the international bus station, this one is closer to the city and easier to access via public transportation. From the city center it should take you only 10 minutes by taxi or 20-30 minutes on buses 6, 18, 26 and 28. This bus station services all of the cities north and east of Kashgar.

It's also worth noting that in many cases you'll be given the choice of a mid-level bus (中级/Zhōngjí) or a higher-end bus (高一/Gāoyī). Usually, the former are older buses while the latter are newer. Below, I quote pricing for the newer, slightly more comfortable buses.

- **Urumqi**: 408/373 RMB (bottom/top berth), one almost every hour, 24 hours
- **Yining (Ili)**: 410/376RMB (bottom/top berth), 24+ hours
- **Kuqa**: 260 RMB, departs at 11am, 4pm and 7pm, total 12 hours
- **Korla**: 259/283 RMB (bottom/top berth)
- **Aksu**: 100 RMB

> **Special Note**: Because of heightened security over the last few years in the Kashgar area, it is not uncommon for buses to be delayed by multiple checkpoints along its journey. For this reason, if there is an option to take a train, this is advisable.

Hiring a Car in Kashgar

There are a number of reasons you might want to hire a car in Kashgar, whether to take multi-day trip up the Karakoram Highway or a simple day trip to Shipton's Arch.

Most hotels and hostels can provide you with the phone number of a local driver or you can work directly with many of the travel agencies in the city (see list of Approved Xinjiang Travel Companies). The average going rate of a car and driver starts at about 500-600 RMB and goes up depending on the size of the vehicle.

Headed to Tashkorgan: It is possible to find an official private driver to Tashkorgan at the International Bus Station as well as near the Tashkorgan Administrative Office (塔什库尔干办事处/Tǎshikù'ěrgàn Bànshìchù) located on the far west side of town on Xiyu Dadao Road (西域大道).

Renting Bicycles in Kashgar

Kashgar is one of only a few cities in Xinjiang where renting a bicycle is not only possible, it's quite fun. Be advised that the summer heat can be almost unbearable, but during the spring and fall, it's perfect.

Bicycles can be rented at the Old Town Youth Hostel (40 RMB/day) or at a Giant Bike Shop (50 RMB/day) south of the People's Park on JianKang Road (健康路).

Transportation within Kashgar

Taxis in Kashgar can be found everywhere and are usually quite helpful when it comes to understanding which tourist spot you want to visit.

Should taxis be unavailable, the city bus system in Kashgar is also nice and if you'll be spending any length of time here they are worth figuring out. The main buses to know are bus #2 to the airport, bus #28 to the train station, and bus #20 to both the Apak Khoja Mausoleum and Sunday Bazaar.

What to do in Kashgar

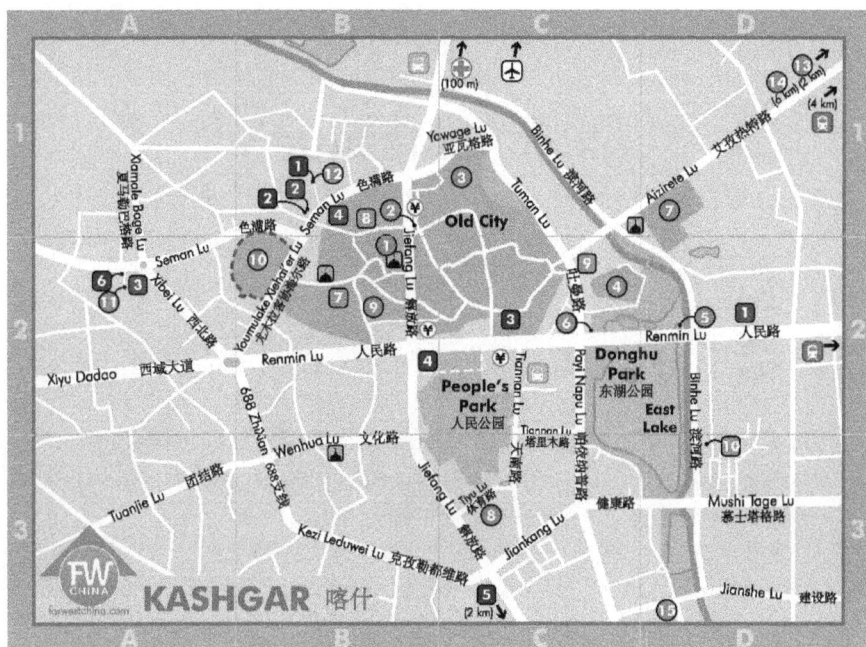

KASHGAR 喀什

RESTAURANTS
1. Altun Orda -- D2
2. Eden Cafe -- B1
3. John's Cafe -- A2
4. Karakoram Cafe -- B1

TRANSPORTATION
- Long-Distance Bus Station -- B1
- International Bus Station -- C2
- Train Station -- D1, D2
- Airport -- C1

PARKS
- East Lake -- C2, D2
- Donghu Park -- C2
- People's Park -- C2

HOTELS
1. Chinibagh (Qinibagh) -- B1
2. Eden Hotel -- B1
3. Super 8 -- C2
4. Tianyuan International Hotel -- B2
5. Radisson Blu -- C3
6. Seman Hotel -- A2

Hostels:
7. Old Town Hostel -- B2
8. Pamir Youth Hostel -- B1
9. Kashgar Camel Hostel -- C2
10. MaiTian Youth Hostel -- D3

- Mosque
- Hospital -- C1
- Entrance
- Bank -- B1, B2, C2

CITY SIGHTS
1. Id Kah Mosque -- B2
2. Night Market -- B1
3. Old City (Scenic Entrance) -- C1
4. "Old" Old City -- C2
5. Lookout Point for Old City -- D2
6. Ferris Wheel -- C2
7. Grand Bazaar -- D1
8. Tomb of Yusuf Has Hajib -- C3
9. Kashgar Uyghur Instruments -- B2
10. Laining Ancient City -- B2
11. Old Russian Consulate -- A2
12. Old British Consulate -- B1
13. Apak Khoju Mousoleum -- D1
14. Sunday Livestock Market -- D1
15. Pantuo City -- D3

To receive a free, full-resolution PDF version of this and all the maps in this guide, please register your book:
www.xjtravelguide.com/register

Id Kah Mosque

◀━━━━━━━━━━━━━━━▶

- **Name**: 艾提尕尔清真寺/Àitígǎěr Qīngzhēnsì
- **Price:** 45 元
- **Rating**: Highly recommended to see, not necessarily enter
- **Map**: Kashgar Map B2 – 1

The true heart of Kashgar lies not in the people's square guarded by China's second largest Mao ZeDong statue, but in the square and alleyways that fall under the shadow of the yellow-bricked Id Kah Mosque.

The entire mosque covers an area of 16,800 square meters, making it the largest mosque by land area in China (there is another mosque in Qinghai whose physical building is larger). Inside the Id Kah prayer halls, close to 20,000 worshipers can cram together to worship during the major Muslim festivals, although during a normal Friday that number is usually between 2,000-5,000.

If you're in Kashgar on a Friday, make note that weekly prayers begin at 1:15pm local time (3:15pm Beijing time). You won't be able to enter the mosque during prayers, but it is interesting to see all of the activity surrounding the area during this time.

Historical Perspective | Id Kah Mosque

Interestingly, the familiar yellow mosque face we easily recognize today only dates back to the early 19th century. Officially, the Id Kah Mosque was built in 1442 as a simple prayer hall by the ruler of Kashgar at the time, Saqsiz Mirza, for the purpose of saying prayers for the souls of his deceased relatives. Prior to this, part of the plot of land was used as a cemetery while the rest was dotted with older structures that can be dated back to 996 AD.

The mosque endured severe damage during the Cultural Revolution and has been renovated throughout the last few decades as an attempt by the government to appease the Kashgar residents and try to show the international community that they care. They "care" so much, in fact, that they installed security cameras to keep a close eye on worshippers. During major festivals a large unit of military are stationed nearby to remind worshippers who is really in charge. Imams (Muslim religious leaders) at Id Kah are government appointed, as are imams all across Xinjiang.

Exploring the Id Kah Mosque

Most people enter in through the front gate, however the smaller north and south gates are sometimes open throughout the day as well. Entering through the latter is a simple way to avoid paying the entrance fee, although it seems that the money is desperately needed for upkeep.

The truth is that it's not really worth paying money to see the inside of the Id Kah Mosque. It's not particularly pretty and the 45RMB ticket price is, in my opinion, quite high.

Inside the mosque grounds you will find tree-lined walkways with murky ponds and prayer halls scattered throughout. Outside in the square there are plenty of places to have someone take your picture in front of the mosque and the small shops all around sell everything from Uyghur hats to local snacks

Women are certainly allowed to tour the Id Kah Mosque although they ask that you don't do so during prayers. It is respectful to be conservative in your choice of clothing, which means at the very least covering your legs and arms.

Kashgar's Old City

- **Name:** 喀什老城/Kāshí Lǎochéng
- **Price:** Free to enter
- **Rating:** Highly recommended
- **Map:** Kashgar Map B1-2; C1-2

Kashgar's Old City has been the subject of heated debate and international criticism ever since the local government decided to update a majority of the buildings in 2009. Years later the process is still ongoing and it is increasingly clear that it won't stop until the "old" Old City is replaced by a "new" Old City.

The tourist appeal of the Old City, which is basically a 1.6 square kilometer community of Uyghur mud-brick homes and confusing alleyways, is the opportunity to jump back in time to see how Kashgar's inhabitants have lived for hundreds of years. Despite a very romantic view of this way of life, the reality is that it was quite dirty, smelly and lacked basic needs like plumbing and electricity. These amenities have since been added, but the local government decided that the buildings still presented a safety risk for earthquakes. The truth is that the labyrinth of alleyways was a nightmare for Chinese police to patrol.

Despite international outcry, many of the old buildings surrounding the Id Kah mosque and north of the Mao statue were razed and have been replaced by a more modern take on old life which includes wide streets, different architecture and sewage. A lot of what you see now might look old but was built as recently as last year.

Surprisingly, this new Old City is pleasant to walk through. Little shops populate the streets and now there's enough room for street vendors to set up and sell their wares. The true heartbeat of Kashgar's Old Town is the Uyghur people and thankfully these alleys are still full of life.

Walking around the Id Kah Mosque is where you will see most of the new buildings being erected and it continues once you cross JieFang Road headed east. The only place within Kashgar proper where you can still get a glimpse of the quickly disappearing "old" Old City is on a hill just north of the East Lake, right behind the Sunday bazaar. Access to the alleyways has now been closed and walls are being torn down every day, but before it's completely gone, you can still get a feel for what Kashgar's Old City used to be.

If you happen to be in the Old City in the evening, you'll find a night market geared towards tourist set up across the street east of the Id Kah Mosque. The market used to be located next to the main street but has since been moved deeper into the Old City past the security. The new night market is sadly a shadow of its former glory, but since it's one of the only night markets still permitted to exist in Xinjiang, it's worth a visit.

A Different View | Kashgar's Ferris Wheel

◄─────────────────────────►

- **Name**: 喀什摩天轮/Kāshi Mótiānlún
- **Price**: 15 元
- **Rating**: Worthwhile birds-eye view of Kashgar
- **Map**: Kashgar Map C2 - 6

It's hard to ignore the sight of Kashgar's ferris wheel, an awkward contraption that feels like an anachronism beside the Old City. Regardless of your personal feelings here, I was pleasantly surprised to find that the ferris wheel offers some great photo opportunities.

The entire ride takes about 10-20 minutes and the wheel runs from noon until midnight Beijing time.

Apak Khoja Mausoleum

⬅━━━━━━━━━━━━━━━━━━━━━━━➡

- **Name**: 阿巴和加麻札/Ābāhéjiā Mázhá or 香妃墓/Xiāngfēimù
- **Price:** 30 元
- **Rating**: Highly recommended
- **Map**: Kashgar Map D1 - 13

Located about 5 kilometers northeast of town, the Apak Khoja Mausoleum is another must-see site in Kashgar. Built in 1640, the entire complex is comprised of the mausoleum, gardens, and multiple prayer halls, some of which are open and of interest, some of which are falling into disrepair.

Apak Khoja was a Uyghur leader of Kashgar and many of the surrounding regions back in the 17th century. The land on which the complex stands was originally donated to Apak Khoja's father Yusuf, a well-respected teacher of the Koran during his time, who built a school here as well as the mausoleum. However, due to his son Apak Khoja's rise to power and the fame that followed, it was renamed after him following his death in 1693.

Five generations of this family were eventually entombed in the mausoleum, a total of 72 people. Unfortunately, an earthquake in the 19th century damaged much of the mausoleum, decreasing the number of tombs to only 58 which can still be seen today.

The mausoleum itself is a beautiful structure with four minarets and a large dome that measures 26 meters in height. Much of the building is covered in a green-glazed tile mixed with various other designs. The aging of the building over the years meant that many of these tiles would randomly fall off the building. Signs warning visitors of falling tiles used to be a common sight. In 2013, however, the building was remodeled and all of the tiles have been replaced.

Surrounding the mosque is a massive cemetery where you can see above-ground tombs numbering in the thousands. It used to be that this cemetery circled to the front of the mausoleum but once tourism became the main attraction, it was later covered over by a rose garden.

Take note of the intricate designs of both the tiles and the minaret window screens. Both are examples of 17th century Islamic art and if you take a close look you'll notice that each window screen is a unique geometric design.

You might notice that signs throughout the complex refer to this as the "Tomb of the Fragrant Concubine". This is no mistake. The legend, detailed below, adds intrigue to an already interesting historical site.

The Legend of the Fragrant Concubine

During Emperor Qianlong's quest to expand the borders of China, he became entranced by the beautiful wife of his recently defeated Kashgar nemesis, a woman who was famed for the intoxicating scent her body gave off without the use of perfumes or powders. She was carefully transported to Beijing to become the emperor's newest concubine, reportedly transported in a cart wrapped in silks like a precious porcelain.

According to the Chinese, she was granted every one of her desires, including a miniature oasis outside her new quarters in the Forbidden City where she happily lived out the rest of her days. Among the Chinese, the Fragrant Concubine is a symbol unity between the Han and Uyghur ethnic groups.

The Uyghur, however, insist on a different version. They remember Iparhan (her Uyghur name) forever pacing in the Forbidden City, never happy. When threatened by the emperor's mother to either resign to her fate or commit suicide, she boldly chose death over dishonor.

Some accounts of this story claim that upon her death, her body was taken back to Kashgar and buried in this mausoleum. Even the sign at the entrance to the Abak Khoja complex claims that "Xinafei [The Fragrant Concubine] was also buried in this tomb". The truth of the matter is that, again, nobody quite knows for sure and recent evidence suggests that she was probably buried in Beijing, not Kashgar.

Getting to/from Apakh Khoja Mausoleum

The easiest way to get to Apakh Khoja Mausoleum is by taxi, which only costs around 10-15 RMB one way. It is also possible to take bus #20 near the large statue of Mao that will drop you off at the "Xiangfeimu Stop" (香妃墓站), the final stop which is at the front door of the complex.

On your way back, make your way to the main road and grab a ride on the three-wheeled motorcycle taxis that frequently pass by. Flag them down like any other taxi and for only 1 RMB they will take you all the way back to the Kashgar Bazaar.

Kashgar Market

◄─────────────────────────►

- **Name:** 喀什大巴扎/Kāshi Dàbāzhā
- **Price:** Free to enter
- **Rating:** Recommended to browse, particularly on Sundays
- **Map:** Kashgar Map D1 - 7

Every Sunday, a chaotic mess known as the Sunday Grand Bazaar fills the northeast corner of Kashgar. For the past 2,000 years, people from all nearby counties have come here to buy practical goods, clothes, food and anything else you could imagine. Once merchants wised up to the fact that tourist also enjoyed taking part in the spectacle, they began selling every kind of souvenir as well.

While you can enjoy this bazaar any day of the week, Sunday offers the unique opportunity to push through a crowd of people so dense it's a wonder anybody has a chance to make a purchase. And to think that scooters still attempt to navigate among this sea of bodies!

Be warned that each entrance to the Sunday Bazaar requires a security check that includes X-ray machines, ID checks and metal detectors. Sometimes the line to get in can take 5-10 minutes.

Grab some photos, a snack, a ride on a horse-drawn cart and a souvenir if you find something interesting. It's more about the experience than the shopping and although I love diving into a good Central Asian market, I also feel a sense of relief when I finally have a chance to exit.

Livestock Market

- **Name**: 喀什牲畜大市场/Kāshi Shēngchù Dàshìchǎng
- **Price**: Free
- **Rating**: Be prepared for smelly animals...but it's a fun visit
- **Map**: Kashgar Map D1 - 14

It used to be that the livestock market was located on the grounds of the Kashgar Grand Bazaar, but as the market grew and the stench of the animals became too much, it was moved further outside the city.

Everything starts at dawn when traders bring their horses, sheep, goats, camels and other livestock to the market for sale. The pungent smells and lively sounds mix to offer a unique atmosphere that has been a part of Kashgar's DNA for centuries.

There's not much to do here other than walk around, watch the negotiations and take photos. The whole trip need only last for a couple hours on Sunday morning, but you'll enjoy the detour.

The market has been moved several times over the years so it's best to take a taxi (50-100 RMB round trip) to avoid confusion. There isn't a good public bus that goes this far northwest of the city.

Tomb of Yusuf Has Hajib

◀━━━━━━━━━━━━━━━━━━━━━━━━▶

- **Name:** 玉素甫哈斯合吉甫墓/Yùsùfǔ Hāsī Héjífǔ Mù
- **Price:** 30 元
- **Rating:** Of interest but not a must-see
- **Map:** Kashgar Map C3 - 8

South of Kashgar People's Park, a small archway leads through a lush green garden toward the blue-tiled mausoleum of Yusuf Has Hajib, an 11th century Uyghur poet and scholar. His most well-known work, Knowledge for Happiness, is a 6,645 couplet that is still praised as one of the greatest works of Uyghur literature.

Historical Perspective | Yusuf Has Hajib

Even though Yusuf was born in modern-day Kyrgyzstan, he moved to Kashgar where in 1069 he completed Knowledge for Happiness at the age of 50. He presented it as a gift to the prince of Kashgar who immediately awarded him with the title "Has Hajib" which roughly translates to "Top Advisor".

Considering his work's importance within Turkic literature, it's surprising that it barely survived the passage of time. Only three manuscripts have been found, the most recent being in Uzbekistan in 1943. Within the mausoleum complex, imprints and translations of these remaining manuscripts are on display.

To some, the sky-blue color and intricate details of this mausoleum outshine that of the Apak Khoja Mausoleum, but the truth is that this building is no more than 30 years old. The tomb was relocated to its current spot after his original tomb near the Badige village was threatened by floods.

Visiting the Tomb

The Yusuf Has Hajib complex is comprised of a main tomb hall (mausoleum), an exhibition room within the hall, and a surrounding mosque. Unless you decide to take a leisurely stroll around the gardens, a visit to the Tomb of Yusuf Has Hajib should take no longer than half an hour.

Minor Sites in Kashgar

At the risk of sharing too much information here, I also want to point to a few historical sites that are of less importance than what has already been mentioned. Personally, I don't believe the following sites are worth putting on your itinerary, but I do find value in knowing that they exist, if for no other reason than you might accidentally run across them and think "Hey, what is this?"

Kashgar City Urban Planning Exhibition Hall
- **Name**: 喀什市城市规划展示馆/Kāshìshì Chéngshì Guīhuà Zhǎnshìguǎn
- **Price**: Possible entrance fee if open
- **Rating**: Fascinating...if it's open
- **Map**: Kashgar Map C2 - Middle of East Lake

In the eastern part of Kashgar you might see an interesting, modern-looking building jutting out into the middle of East Lake. This is the home of Kashgar's Urban Planning Exhibition Hall, a two-floor museum of sorts where you can find a scale model of the "Kashgar of the future."

The exhibition hall is an interesting place to roam for any history buff, even though most of the signs aren't in English and the history (and future) presented is certainly biased. The biggest hurdle to visiting this site is getting in. Officially, it's only opened for government-sponsored visitors, so the only time I've been able to enter is when I happened to knock on the back door while somebody was there.

Laining Ancient City
- **Name**: 喀什噶尔的徕宁城/Kāshi Láiníngchéng
- **Price**: Free
- **Rating**: You might see it while driving along Yanmulakaxia Road
- **Map**: Kashgar Map B2 - 10

Along Yanmulakaxia Rd once you reach the western end of Kashgar's Old City, you might happen upon the remains of an old wall that seem to start from the road and extend out in a curve. This is part of Kashgar's old Laining City, a city whose crumbling walls still mark its boundaries.

There's nothing to see in this city other than the wall and frankly its hard to visualize the borders without a bird's eye view. Laining only boasts a history of a couple hundred years which, at least when compared to the rest of Kashgar, is quite young.

Old British Consulate

- **Name**: 英国驻喀什噶尔领事馆/Yīngguó Zhù Kāshigáěr Lǐngshìguǎn
- **Price:** Free
- **Rating**: Only interesting to Great Game enthusiasts
- **Map**: Kashgar Map B1 - 12

Behind the old **Qini Bagh Hotel**, now home to a towering new luxury hotel, a small restaurant sits tucked away with no more than a small sign to indicate its historical significance. First established in 1908 as the only British India outpost in Xinjiang, this old British Consulate became an important part of the incredible history known as "The Great Game."

Explorers from all over the world would come here to enjoy the hospitality of British Consul George McCartney and his wife Catherine, often referred to as Lady McCartney. One of the reasons this site isn't better cared for is likely because China still holds bitterness against many of the artifacts that were taken by these guests of McCartney.

The restaurant that now occupies the old consulate isn't very fancy. A simple walk through the old corridors provides an opportunity to view the old English architecture on display and a step out onto the back porch offers a different view of northern Kashgar.

Old Russian Consulate

- **Name**: 俄国驻喀什噶尔领事馆/Éguó Zhù Kāshigáěr Lǐngshìguǎn
- **Price:** Free
- **Rating**: Stop in if you're nearby but don't make it a destination
- **Map**: Kashgar Map A2 - 11

Within the grounds of the **Seman Hotel**, one of Kashgar's oldest hotels, you can walk through what is left of the old Russian consulate. Part of the consulate has been turned into a restaurant while the remainder is part of the hotel where guests can experience some truly unique room decoration.

This was the home of Russian consul Nikolai Petrovsky, the arch enemy of George McCartney during the espionage wars of the Great Game and it remains one of the most architecturally interesting buildings in all of Kashgar.

Giant Statue of Mao Zedong

- **Name**: 毛泽东塑像/Máozédōng Sùxiàng
- **Price**: Free
- **Rating**: You're bound to see it at some point
- **Map**: Kashgar Map C2 - Across from People's Park

Driving through the center of town you won't be able to miss one of China's largest statues of Mao Zedong standing over a Tiananmen-style city square. Reaching close to 18 meters (59 ft) and stretching out his right hand, Mao welcomes every visitor who enters the city of Kashgar.

This statue of Mao is the product of China's Cultural Revolution, an event which had an impact even on the distant corners of the country. First erected in 1969 as a reminder to Kashgar residents that Beijing was keeping a close eye on them, the body of the statue was designed to reach exactly 12.26 meters in height in honor of Mao's birthday, December 26th. To say that this is a beloved monument for the city of Kashgar might be a stretch, but it has become a well-known landmark.

Attempts to take down the statue over the past few decades – either by force or through proper petitions – have failed and are not well documented; however, damages sustained by the statue did eventually force the city to refurbish it in 1997. While they were at it they decided to add a grandstand along with a 62-meter long wall on which was written many of Mao's poems.

A few tour books give the misleading quote that this is one of only a few remaining statues of Mao left in China. One look at most cities and universities around China will tell you this isn't true. What they are trying to say is that this statue is one of the few statues of Mao in this particular pose (standing with right arm extended) that still exists today.

Pantuo City (Aski Sahr)

- **Name**: 喀什的盘陀城/Kāshén de Pántuóchéng
- **Price**: 30 元
- **Rating**: Not worth the price of admission unless it holds some significance to you
- **Map**: Kashgar Map D3 - 15

Pantuo City (also known as Aski Sahr) is a memorial to the great Chinese general Ban Chao and his 36 warriors, who built a small fortress in Kashgar during their mission to re-open the Silk Road. Inside the rebuilt walls of this fortress stand 37 statues including a 3.6-meter-tall statue of Ban Chao. Behind him a stone mural depicts the story of his conquest.

In an effort to reestablish China's trade and tribute system, many Han Dynasty generals were sent to secure garrisons along the southern part of the Taklamakan Desert. Ban Chao was one of the few successful generals to do so and was able to push back the Xiongnu tribe, which was at the time controlling Kashgar, to finally capture the city in AD 94. He and his 36 men set up a garrison at this location and later tried to march even further west past the Pamirs. This memorial was established in 1996 by the local government to honor his memory.

Most literature at the site and distributed by tourist agencies will gush about how the Kashgar people welcomed Ban Chao "with tears" as a hero of the city, saving them from the oppressive rule of the Xiongnu. What you won't read is how Ban Chao was famous for using local mercenaries to fight most of his battles and how this small memorial serves as a reminder that Chinese have long been a part of Kashgar's oppressed history.

What to do Around Kashgar

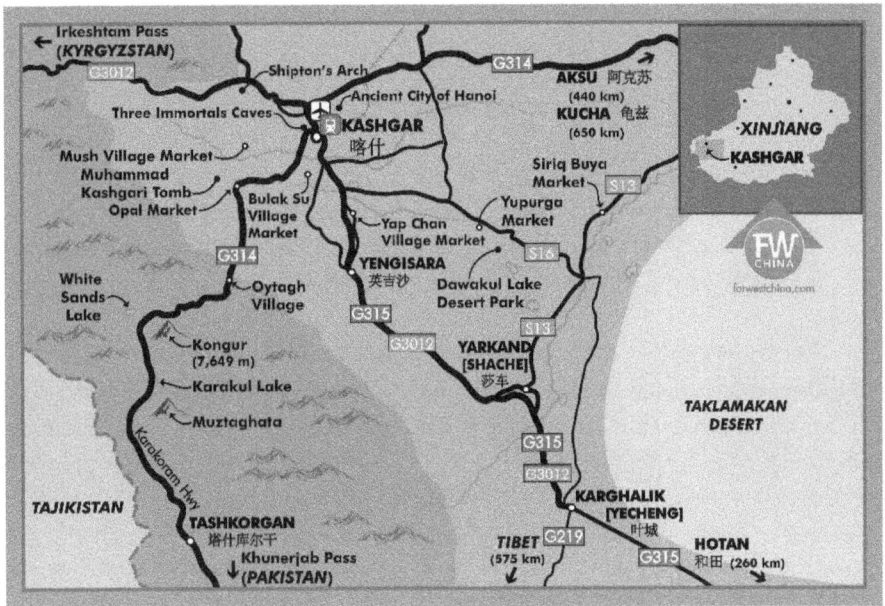

Irkeshtam Pass
← (KYRGYZSTAN)
G3012
Shipton's Arch
Three Immortals Caves
Ancient City of Hanoi
KASHGAR
喀什
AKSU 阿克苏
(440 km)
KUCHA 龟兹
(650 km)
G314
Mush Village Market
Muhammad
Kashgari Tomb
Opal Market
Bulak Su
Village
Market
Yap Chan
Village Market
Siriq Buya
Market
Yupurga
Market
S13
XINJIANG
KASHGAR
White
Sands
Lake
G314
Oytagh
Village
YENGISARA
英吉沙
G315
Dawakul Lake
Desert Park
S16
Kongur
(7,649 m)
Karakul Lake
Muztaghata
G3012
YARKAND
[SHACHE]
莎车
S13
FW
CHINA
forwestchina.com
TAKLAMAKAN
DESERT
TAJIKISTAN
Karakoram Hwy
TASHKORGAN
塔什库尔干
Khunerjab Pass
↓ (PAKISTAN)
G315
G3012
KARGHALIK
[YECHENG]
叶城
TIBET G219
(575 km)
G315
HOTAN
和田 (260 km)

To receive a free, full-resolution PDF version of this and all the maps
in this guide, please register your book:
www.xjtravelguide.com/register

Shipton's Arch

←——————————→

- **Name**: 天门/Tiānmén or Toshuk Tagh
- **Price**: 30 元 plus the cost of transportation (500-700 RMB for a 4WD)
- **Rating**: Recommended for those with time and a love of hiking
- **Map**: See Kashgar Area Map

The locals call it "Toshuk Tagh", translated to be "Mountain with a Hole," while the Chinese have named it 天门, or "Heavenly Gate." Most English guides you see call it Shipton's Arch after mountaineer Eric Shipton, the man credited with its discovery.

Shipton's Arch is the world's tallest known natural arch – so tall that it could fit the Empire State Building underneath or have a small airplane fly through it. If you have the opportunity and enjoy hiking outdoors, a day trip to this extraordinary site is worth your time. No photo does this arch justice. You just have to be there.

Historical Perspective | Shipton's Arch

In this day and age of GPS mapping and satellite imagery, it's not often that you can say that a place has been re-discovered in the year 2000. But that's exactly what happened here in Xinjiang.

Eric Shipton, an English mountaineer, first introduced the arch to the world in his book Mountains of Tartary, written while he was stationed in Kashgar as British consul. It was during this period in history that the Great Game was still afoot and this particular post along the old Silk Road was of strategic importance.

He had caught glimpses of the big arch during hikes around northern Kashgar but multiple approaches from the south proved unsuccessful. It wasn't until locals guided him to approach from the north in 1947 that he finally came face to face with this magnificent natural phenomenon:

> "At last, emerging from one of these clefts, we were confronted with a sight that made us gasp with surprise and excitement. The gorge widened into a valley which ended a quarter of a mile away in a grassy slope leading to a U-shaped col. Above and beyond the col stood a curtain of rock, pierced by a graceful arch."

Interestingly, for the half century following Shipton's discovery of the arch, no other foreigner recorded a visit to the mountain until 2000 when a National Geographic-sponsored expedition went in search.

Far better equipped and more determined than Eric Shipton, this group successfully climbed to the top of the arch and took measurements to verify that this was, in fact, the tallest natural arch in the world – 1,500 feet (457.2 meters) high, with a 1,200-foot (366 meters) opening.

Since 2000, the allure of Shipton's Arch was reignited and a path has been beaten by the feet of numerous travelers.

Visiting Shipton's Arch

From Kashgar, the first step to visiting Shipton's Arch is to hire a car with a driver who knows the way. It's only 25 miles from Kasghar to Shipton's Arch, but it will take close to an hour and a half of driving to make it to the trail head.

Currently, Shipton's Arch is being developed as a tourist destination thanks to its rise in popularity, which is both good and bad. The good is that they have built sturdy staircases and a viewing platform to make it easier (and safer) for the average tourist to see. Of course, that also means the possibility for more tourists which can take away from the spirit of adventure.

You should be prepared for another 30 minutes of hiking once you exit the car. It's not a terribly hard climb, but you should be in decent shape to make the ascent. During the entire trek you'll be guided along by monstrous canyon walls whose beautifully colored rock has been chiseled away into odd shapes by centuries of wind. The noise of Kashgar fades away into the serene sounds of a mostly-silent canyon.

When you reach Shipton's Arch, enjoy the gorgeous panorama and gaze down at the deathly 1,000-foot drop. It's unlike anything you've ever seen.

Dawakul Lake Desert Park

◄─────────────────────►

- **Name**: 岳普湖达瓦昆沙漠公园/Yuèpǔhú Dáwǎkūn shāmò gōngyuán
- **Price**: 30 元 (plus hired driver)
- **Rating**: Tourist trap, but the closest desert experience
- **Map**: See Kashgar Area Map

It's a shame that of the many people who travel out to Xinjiang, very few have an opportunity to experience a camel ride in the desert or even personally witness the undulating dunes of the Taklamakan Desert. When it comes to lasting images of the ancient Silk Road, this one is iconic.

Considering the Taklamakan's length of 1,000 kilometers, there are no doubt countless entry points into this desert. Finding a good place to experience this on the back of a camel without spending the time needed for overnight trips, however, is a bit trickier. That's where a place like the Dawakul Lake Desert Park can be useful, despite its heavy tourism.

Located about 130 kilometers southeast of Kashgar, a trip to Dawakul can be done in a day, albeit a long one. It is possible to rent a car and driver for the day, starting the day at around 9am and returning to the city around 11pm.

Dawakul Lake Desert Park offer a few different tourist experiences including camel rides (50-80 RMB), sand boarding, dune buggy rentals, a desert lake to swim in and much more. Tourism officials have created legends about the lake and the dunes to enhance the allure but the fact is that this place exists on the map purely for the sake of tourism -and mostly Chinese tourism at that.

As a tourism facility, expect to see a number of Chinese groups, cheesy activities that won't appeal to most foreign tourist and overpriced restaurants (I suggest you bring your own food). If you can look past all of this, Dawakul Lake Desert Park can be a great place to witness the sun setting over endless sand dunes while riding on a camel.

> **Note**: There are better places to ride a camel in a Xinjiang desert. For more information, jump to the chapter on Camel Treks.

Getting to/from Dawakul Lake

Unless you join a tour group, the only way to reach Dawakul Lake is by hired car. Most hotels can help arrange this or you can speak with one of the many tour agencies scattered around Kashgar (see the list of Approved Travel Companies).

You'll have to hire the car for the entire day since once you actually reach the park, there will be no other way to find transportation out unless your driver remains waiting for you.

Ancient City of Hanoi

◄────────────────────────►

- **Name**: 莫尔佛塔/Mòěr Fótǎ
- **Price**: 15 元
- **Rating**: Not worth the trip in my opinion
- **Map**: See Kashgar Area Map

Approximately 35 kilometers northeast of Kashgar, two giant structures rise from the flat desert, one of the few indications that somebody used to live here. These particular remnants, the most famous of which is the Mor Pagoda, were part of an Buddhist temple within the ancient city of Ha Noi. The limited ruins at this tourist destination are all that remain of the city after all these years.

The two remnants include a giant square edifice whose niches once held Buddhist statues while the other is the Mor Pagoda or "stupa" with its cylindrical top.

Historical Perspective | Mor Pagoda

These religious structures were part of a town built in the Tang Dynasty in the 7th century. It was abandoned in the 12th century, but frankly there isn't much known about the history of this area.

In 1957 it was designated as a historical relic protection site by the Kashgar region. It is obvious by the lack of upkeep and dedicated facilities, however, that not much money has made its way here. The only sign of upkeep is the repair that was done on the west side of the stupa where you can see recently-placed mud bricks filling a hole in the dome.

Since no buses travel out this far, a hired taxi (approx. ~300 RMB for a half-day) is a necessity. To sum up my thoughts on the Ha Noi ruins, as I stood among the ruins I watched a passenger train chugging by and thought: "You know, I think that train is more interesting than what I just paid to see."

Three Immortals Caves

- **Name**: 三仙洞/Sānxiāndòng
- **Price**: Free
- **Rating**: Not an essential part of your itinerary
- **Map**: See Kashgar Area Map

Along a small road shooting off from Highway G314, 14 kilometers north of Kashgar's city center, a set of three caves located on the side of a cliff thirteen meters off the ground.

Research suggests that these caves were dug out during the Eastern Han Dynasty (25-220 AD), each cave consisting of a large front chamber and a smaller rear chamber. No paintings remain in the western cave, with only scrapings indicating that they were removed by some early explorer.

Murals in the middle cave remain, although they were obviously repainted over centuries after the cave was first dug. This leaves the eastern cave, which is home to the only original murals from the Three Immortals Caves.

The Legend | Three Immortals Caves

According to local legend, these caves were first carved a couple thousand years ago by a king whose young princess was quite sick. Upon the advice of a fortune-teller, who informed the king that a single bee sting within the next 100 days would bring the princess certain death, the king built these caves as a sanctuary and protection during her quarantine.

Paintings and carvings were commissioned as decoration to keep the princess happy and comfortable and food was brought in to keep her alive. Apparently, bees were a big problem at the time, because on the 99th day of her quarantine a bee slipped past the food checkers by hiding in her grapes, causing death to the princess with one sting as prophesied.

After her death the caves were abandoned and its decorations left behind...or so the legend goes.

Visiting the Caves

Even though such caves are certainly not something you run across on a daily basis while driving along a highway, there's not much to see at the Three Immortal Caves other than the limited view of a few paintings on the ceiling that are peeling away.

It's free to visit the caves but I don't recommend this as a part of any itinerary. Most drivers won't even know where it is. Unless you bring binoculars or a ladder (which would still be dangerous), there are much better ways to spend your time in Kashgar.

Opal Market (Wupaer)

◀━━━━━━━━━━━━━━━━━━━━━▶

- **Name**: 乌帕儿/Wūpàer
- **Price**: Free
- **Rating**: Great for the authentic Monday bazaar
- **Map**: See Kashgar Area Map

If you found the Kashgar market a bit tainted by tourism or perhaps didn't arrive in time, the Opal Market runs every Monday and is not only a good alternative, it's also a much smaller and more authentic rural experience. This, according to locals, is what the Kashgar market used to look like 30 years ago.

The market has become famous for its camels, goats and sheep that are still sold alongside the regular goods, a practice that was ended at the Kashgar market many years ago. Folks from the surrounding villages all gather here to chat, trade and enjoy the atmosphere, a perfect opportunity for travelers to soak in the rural Uyghur culture.

Ideally, you should consider arranging your Karakoram Highway adventure to begin on Monday, making your first stop at the Opal Market which is just 45 kilometers outside of Kashgar. Even if it's not Monday, Opal is still a quaint village that offers a unique "small village" experience that you won't find in a bigger city like Kashgar. Additionally, you have the opportunity to visit the nearby Mahmud Kashgari Tomb.

For those who won't be taking a hired car to Opal (in Chinese it is known as "Wupaer") you can also consider a bus that runs from Kashgar, south of the Seman Hotel for 15 RMB.

Mahmud Kashgari Tomb

⬅————————————————————————➡

- **Name:** 麻赫穆德·喀什噶里墓/Máhèmùdé Kāshigálǐ Mù
- **Price:** 30 元
- **Rating:** Only significant site in Opal, not worth a dedicated trip
- **Map:** See Kashgar Area Map

While visiting the Opal market or passing through the village on your way to Tashkorgan on the Karakoram Highway, the Mahmud Kashgari Tomb can be an intriguing detour. The tomb, located 3 kilometers northwest of the Opal city center, sits at the edge of an old Uyghur cemetery that is equally interesting to explore.

Historical Perspective | Mohammed Kashgari

Mahmud Kashgari was an 11th century scholar from Kashgar and the tomb in Opal honors him for his contributions to Turkic linguistic studies. It was these studies that led him to compile the first comprehensive dictionary of Turkic languages.

Born in 1005, Mahmud Kashgari spent his entire life in and around Kashgar until his death almost a century later. Although locals believe that Mahmud Kashgari was of Uyghur descent, it's interesting to note that he is claimed by both the Uzbek and Kyrgyz people as well.

Scholars disagree about the exact date of his death, but most believe he passed away at the age of 97 in the year 1102. Since his passing, Kashgari's Turkish Dictionary has been translated into 26 languages and remains an important work in Turkic linguistic history.

His love of languages and books led to an interesting custom among those who come to pay their respects at his tomb. It is common for visiting Muslim scholars to contribute a book upon visiting the tomb; over the years the collection has become an unexpected library of sorts.

Visiting Mahmud Kashgari's Tomb

From the Opal city center the trip out to Mahmud Kashgari's Tomb is a simple taxi ride for 5 RMB. You can also hire a car from Kashgar for around 300 RMB for a half day.

Aside from the photogenic face of the tomb and the scenic hillside that surrounds it, make sure to check out the exhibition area where many of Kashgari's works are on display alongside archeological finds from the region.

Nearby Village Market

◀━━━━━━━━━━━━━━━━━━━━━▶

Although most people may point you to either Kashgar's Sunday Bazaar or Opal's Monday Bazaar, there are a number of village bazaars that open up all throughout the week - or at least they used to. They aren't well-known and therefore aren't often visited by foreign tourists, so as long as local police haven't shut down the markets, many travelers find the rural nature of the village market quite attractive.

To make the most of your visit, I recommend you hire a local guide to visit these bazaars, as they can introduce you not just to the market itself but also to the surrounding villages. Don't expect these markets to be big and certainly don't expect them to cater to tourism. Often, they are just selling livestock and daily necessities, so go with the expectation of experiencing Uyghur culture, not buying souvenirs.

While there are numerous village markets that could be mentioned here, I'll just name one per day to keep it simple, omitting Sunday and Monday since the obvious choices on those days would be Kashgar and Opal respectively.

Tuesday Village Market

On Tuesdays, head down south on Highway G315 for 47 kilometers until you hit **Yap Chan Village** (牙甫泉镇/Yáfǔquán Zhèn). This lively, messy market is best known for its cows and kebabs, making it a fun first stop while making your way toward Hotan (Khotan).

Wednesday Village Market

If you're looking for a village market on Wednesdays, the nearby **Bulak Su Village** (布拉克苏乡/Bùlākèsū Xiāng) is probably one of the busiest and most convenient. Located approximately 40 kilometers south of Kashgar, you'll end up crossing a narrow creek before reaching this bustling market.

Thursday Village Market

Considered the second largest market in the area behind Kashgar's Sunday Market, the Siriq Buya Market (色力布亚镇/Sèlìbùyǎ Zhèn), which you may also find referred to as "Serikbuya," comes highly praised by those who've visited. Livestock, clothing, agricultural goods and snack stalls cluster together with donkey-drawn carts and masses of people filling in the gaps.

The only drawback to this market is its location 180 kilometers east of Kashgar, which is both inconvenient and not really "on the way" to anything. I've known some travelers who stop here in transit from Aksu to Hotan while bypassing Kashgar, but this isn't something most people would consider.

Friday Village Market

From Kashgar, point your compass west and travel 40 kilometers to reach the **Mush Village** (木什乡/Mùshí Xiāng), home to a lively Friday bazaar. The livestock of choice at this market are sheep, although you'll find plenty of other goods and street snacks worth enjoying.

Saturday Village Market

Finally, to visit a good market on Saturday, look no further than the **Yupurga Market** (岳普湖/Yuèpǔhú) near the Shihit Dong Village (希依提墩乡/Xīyītídūn Xiāng). This market is recognized for its donkeys as well as the nearby Shihit Dong Village, which offers a pleasant place to saunter around.

At 90 kilometers southeast of Kashgar, the Yupurga Market is quite a distance to travel. However, since it's next door to the Dawakul Lake Desert Park, you could potentially hit two birds with one stone during this day trip.

Where to Stay in Kashgar

Recommended Hotels in Kashgar

- **Best Hostels**: Old Town Hostel and Pamir Hostel (online booking not reliable)
- **Best Luxury Hotel**: Raddison Blu
- **Best Mid-Range Hotel**: Qini Bagh Hotel

For those wishing to visit Kashgar, there is a wide range of accommodations available, suitable to every budget and comfort level. Below are a few recommendations based on specific needs with further options and detail following.

- **Luxury Hotels in Kashgar**
- **Mid-Range Hotels in Kashgar**
- **Budget Hostels in Kashgar**

Luxury Hotels in Kashgar

Radisson Blu Hotel

深业丽笙酒店/**Shēnyè Lìshēng Jiǔdiàn**
Address: 2 Duolaitebage Road
(多来特巴格路 2 号)
Phone: (0998) 268-8888
Map: Kashgar Map C3 - 5

The relatively new Radisson Blu is now the most luxurious hotel in Kashgar. It is located a bit south of the city center but is still convenient. Amenities include free internet, fitness center and a nice pool. The rooms are well-appointed and the prices aren't as high as you might expect.

Pictures, Pricing and Booking: **www.xjtravelguide.com/Kashgar-Radisson-Blu**

Tianyuan International Hotel

天缘国际酒店/**Tiānyuán Guójì Jiǔdiàn**
Address: 8 East Renmin Road
(人民东路 8 号)
Phone: (0998) 280-1111
Map: Kashgar Map B2 - 4

The advantage of the Tianyuan International Hotel is its central location. Situated next to the People's Park, it is walking distance from most of the city attractions including the Id Kah mosque and the tomb of Yusuf Has Hajib. Right outside the doors of this hotel is the famous Mao Statue, which salutes every time you enter or exit. The hotel offers the standard China amenities at a reasonable fee.

Pictures, Pricing and Booking: **www.xjtravelguide.com/Kashgar-Tianyuan**

Qinibagh Royal Hotel

皇家大酒店/**Huángjiā Dàjiǔdiàn**
Address: 144 Seman Road
(色满路 144 号)
Phone: (0998) 282-2103
Map: Kashgar Map B1 - 1

The Qini Bagh Royal Hotel (also spelled "Chini Bagh"), home to the former British Consulate in Kashgar, used to be a simple 3-star hotel until a massive, new 4-star building was built to replace it in 2014. The rooms are comfortable with a nice view and they all come with internet. Although this hotel is comparatively luxurious for most of Kashgar, it's pricing usually puts it in line with mid-range hotels.

Pictures, Pricing and Booking: **www.xjtravelguide.com/Kashgar-Qinibagh**

Mid-Range Hotels in Kashgar

Super 8 Kashgar

There are currently two Super 8 locations in Kashgar (the other one is on West Renmin Rd) but I like this particular one because it is located in the heart of the (rebuilt) Old City. It doesn't have a lot of rooms and they aren't luxurious, but the price is right and the atmosphere, especially once you step foot outside, brings to mind pictures of the old Silk Road and ancient trade routes.

速八酒店/Sùbā Jiǔdiàn
Address: 810 Areya Road
(阿热亚路 810 号)
Phone: (0998) 550-2288
Map: Kashgar Map C2 - 3

Pictures, Pricing and Booking: **Not available for online booking.**

Kashgar Seman Hotel

Like the Chini Bagh above, this hotel was also a former Consulate (this one for Russia, not Britain) and it still retains that colonial feel. The hotel offers a wide array of rooms, both expensive and budget, with architecture that matches its Russian roots. Unfortunately, its location is a bit further from the activity of the city center, but they do have John's Cafe (during the warmer season) and the offices of Old Road Tours next door, which is convenient.

色满宾馆/Sèmǎn Bīnguǎn
Address: 337 Seman Road
(色满路 337 号)
Phone: (0998) 258-2129
Map: Kashgar Map A2 - 6

Pictures, Pricing and Booking: **www.xjtravelguide.com/Kashgar-Seman**

Budget Hostels in Kashgar

←—————————————→

Old Town Youth Hostel

喀什老城青年旅馆/Kāshí
Lǎochéng Qīngniánlǚguǎn
Address: 233 Wusitang Boyi Rd
(吾斯塘博依路 233 号)
Phone: (0998) 282-3262
Map: Kashgar Map B2 - 7

Because it is situated in Kashgar's Old City, some find this a harder hostel to find, although in my experience once you've found it, it's hard to miss. It is designed as a Uyghur courtyard and has a great atmosphere, nice people and cheap beds. The hostel rents bicycles, has free wifi and a number of different room options.

Pictures, Pricing and Booking:
www.xjtravelguide.com/kashgar-old-town-hostel

Pamir Youth Hostel

帕米尔青年旅舍/Pàmǐěr
Qīngniánlǚshè
Address: 726 South Youhao Road
(友好南路 726 号)
Phone: (0998) 282-3376
Map: Kashgar Map B1 - 8

You can't miss the Id Kah Mosque when you stay at the Pamir Youth Hostel! You're practically on the doorstep and can see into the mosque from the nice balcony. It's a great location on the 3rd floor of a nearby building with an inexpensive rate. There is a bit of noise but the hostel atmosphere is worth it.

To find this hostel, face the Id Kah Mosque and look to the the buildings on the right for a green dome. There should be a sign that says "Pamir Hostel" with a set of stairs underneath.

Pictures, Pricing and Booking: www.xjtravelguide.com/Kashgar-Pamir-Hostel

Kashgar Maitian Youth Hostel

Located more toward the east of town by the East Lake, the Maitian Youth Hostel has recently undergone a renovation and looks quite nice inside. It's a quaint hostel with friendly staff, decent beds and an excellent price. The problem is that it is located in possibly the worst place you could imagine. Difficult to find, outside the center of town and no easy transportation means this isn't a highly recommended hostel.

麦田国际青年旅馆/Màitián Guójì Qīngnián Lǚguǎn

Address: East Renmin Road, First Alley (人民东路南一巷)

Phone: (0998) 280-1111

Map: Kashgar Map D3 - 10

Pictures, Pricing and Booking: **www.xjtravelguide.com/Kashgar-Maitian-Hostel**

Where to Eat in Kashgar

Where to eat in Kashgar

◀━━━━━━━━━━━━━━━━━━━━━▶

Finding a place to eat in Kashgar shouldn't be hard but it's always nice to have a few suggestions to start with. Everybody has their own favorites so my suggestion is to ask your hotel or any local you can befriend which restaurant they recommend.

The eateries listed below are the most popular with tourists and don't include the numerous hole-in-the-wall places you can find in the Old City and throughout Kashgar.

Uyghur Cuisine

There are three places that I most highly recommend for local food in **Kashgar**:

- **Orda (Kashgar Map D2 - 1)**: You'll find this restaurant recommended in practically every travel guide and it's always packed with people. There's a reason for this, though. The food is good and the atmosphere, including live music, is great.
- **Eden/Herembag (Kashgar Map B1 - 2)**: Located next to the Qini Bagh, the Eden restaurant in Kashgar is the same chain that you'll find in Turpan and Urumqi. The food is a Uyghur/Turkish mix and the restaurant is beautifully decorated. It is more expensive than average.
- **Night Market (Kashgar Map B1 - 2)**: A visit to Kashgar isn't complete without at least one visit to the night market, if not more. Every night, across the street from the Id Kah Mosque, a small square fills with vendors selling everything from goat heads to delicious Uyghur ice cream.

Western Fare

As with Urumqi and Turpan, Kashgar has its share of fast food establishments where you can get a burger, such as Best Food Burger or Marry Brown, as well as local restaurants whose menu features a few western dishes. Aside from this, there is currently only one establishment that I know of whose primary focus is western fare.

John's Cafe (Kashgar Map A2 - 3)

Located within the Seman Hotel complex, this cafe offers drinks, simple dishes and travel help if you need it.

Doing business in Kashgar has been rough and a number of small cafes have opened and subsequently closed including Fubar, the Karakoram Cafe and Gallery Cafe, although you'll find mentions of each still online and in guide books.

316

Karakoram Highway

Top Sights along the KKH

Old Stone Fort – Pg 325

This old Stone Fort in Tashkorgan is over 2,000 years old and overlooks the beautiful Aral Grasslands.

Karakoram Highway
One of the most amazing modern feats of engineering, this highway stretches 1,300km between China and Pakistan.

Taheman Grasslands
Along the Karakoram Highway, a number of beautiful scenes such as the Taheman Grasslands will keep you glued to the window.

Karakoram Highway Introduction

←——————————————————→

Seldom does one highway evoke such wonder and inspire such wanderlust like the Karakoram Highway. Officially designated as Highway 314, the Chinese portion of this road stretches 413 kilometers from Kashgar through Tashkorgan until it reaches the border with Pakistan.

No other paved highway crosses an international border at a higher elevation than the Karakoram and the entire climb up the Chinese side is equivalent to scaling a small mountain. Up until 1979, when the paved road was first constructed, this pass through the Himalayas was a treacherous and often a deadly journey for caravans. Even now the highway closes on occasion due to landslides, mudslides and snow.

The Karakoram Highway took two decades to complete; today it requires less than four hours to drive. There's no reason to rush, however, as the scenery out the window is arguably some of the most beautiful in all of China. During the warmer months, cars seems to stop around every bend to allow tourists to step out and take just one more picture.

Traveling the Karakoram Highway

Entire books have been written about the Karakoram Highway, whose level of detail I do not intend to reproduce here. While most people hire a car and driver to transport them along the highway, options are available to take a public bus from Kashgar or, if you're incredibly adventurous and well-prepared, a bicycle.

Traversing the Karakoram Highway in a single day or even with a one-night stay is doable but not recommended. This is a trip whose breathtaking beauty you will remember for the rest of your life, so it's best to take your time!

A better option would be to stay two nights in **Tashkorgan** where you can visit the old **Stone Fort** on your way up to the **Khunerjab Pass** and then leave early for **Karakul Lake** where you can hike around at the base of the grand Muztaghata mountain before returning to Kashgar.

Part of the adventure of the Karakoram Highway is exploring it for yourself, but for the sake of planning I'll share with you the five stops considered to be the most interesting along the way.

Top 5 Stops Along the Karakoram Highway

Assuming that you are beginning your journey from Kashgar, where the majority of travelers start, the following stops are listed in order and measured out as an approximate distance from Kashgar's city center.

#1 Oytagh Red Mountain Valley - 90km

It's impossible to miss the massive river valley flanked by bright red canyon walls on the western side of the Karakoram Highway. Most visitors just stop here to take a picture for a few minutes and then head along their merry way. Unfortunately, they miss out on one of the most beautiful sites this section of highway has to offer.

Following a side road into the valley westward for a distance beyond Oytagh Village is the **Oytagh Glacier Park** (奥依塔格冰川公园 /Àoyītǎgé Bīngchuān Gōngyuán), an incredible collection of scenic views that includes majestic peaks, beautiful grassland, hundred-foot waterfalls and, of course, glaciers. A 4WD and some good hiking books are necessary for this detour, so don't expect your hired taxi driver to agree to take you here.

For this glacier trip, you'll probably want to consult with a travel agency in Kashgar. Not only can they arrange a car and guide, they can also set up an overnight stay in most cases (see the list of Approved Travel Companies).

> **Important Note**: Due to some local politics, Oytagh Park has been closed off and on over the past few years. Before putting this on your itinerary, make sure you check with a local tour agency to find out if it's even open for visitors.

#2 White Sands Lake - 170km

Traveling on for another 80 kilometers, the highway snakes around a corner to reveal the **White Sands Lake** (白沙湖/Báishāhú), a tourist-given name that is known locally as Bulungkol Lake (布伦口/Bùlúnkǒu).

The tourist name is derived from the stretch of sand dunes that lay across the lake from the highway, often reflected on the water to mesmerizing effect. During the warmer months, you'll find a number of cars parked along the side of the road with their occupants out admiring the view. This, of course, attracts locals from the nearby Bulungkol Village who set up shop at the edge of the lake selling precious stones and other wares.

You may notice part of the Karakoram Highway actually leads directly into the lake. Despite its appearance as a boat ramp, this used to be a section of the Karakoram Highway until part of the lake was damned up, causing the water levels to rise. The Karakoram Highway had to be rerouted but the old pavement still emerges from the waters, making for a humorous picture.

While driving along this section of the Karakoram Highway, take note of the majestic peak filling your view, a mountain known as **Kongur Peak**. At 7,649 meters, it is the highest mountain whose entirety rests within the borders of Xinjiang (the other mountains straddle international borders). Kongur was first summited in 1981 by a British-led expedition and although it is still a dangerous ascent, climbing tours can be arranged for those wishing to summit themselves.

#3 Karakul Lake and Muztaghata - 196km

Probably the most well-known stop along the Karakoram Highway is the **Karakul Lake** (喀拉库勒湖/Kālākùle Hú), whose icy-cold waters are guarded by the snow-capped **Muztaghata** mountain. There is a debate among travelers as to which lake claims the title of the most beautiful in Xinjiang: Karakul Lake or Kanas Lake in the north. Whatever your opinion, there's no doubt that Karakul Lake is less developed for tourism than Kanas Lake.

The lake is relatively small and not difficult to circumnavigate in a couple hours on foot. Kyrgyz yurts are often set up on the western bank and are available for rent. Unfortunately, there are also concrete yurts and a small hotel which act as an eyesore among the beautiful natural surroundings.

If it is still allowed, try to schedule a night in a yurt at Karakul Lake. The locals, primarily of Kyrgyz ethnicity, often rent out space in their yurts for 50-100 RMB per person and each can hold about 10 people. The space may get cold at night, even during the summer. The nearby outhouses are disgusting but the discomfort can be worth the adventure. Another option would be to do a home stay at the nearby village between the lake the mountain, which can sometimes be arranged by tour operators in Kashgar, depending on the political climate.

Be Advised: Over the past few years, travelers have been restricted from staying in yurts overnight at Karakul Lake. It's not clear whether this is a permanent change or a temporary ban. Either way, you'll want to ask your hostel or a local travel agency to find out if staying the night is possible or if a permit can be arranged.

In addition to leisurely walking around, locals will be more than happy to provide horseback rides (50-100 RMB), camel rides (50-100 RMB) and even motorcycle trips to the base of Muztaghata (50-100 RMB). Pricing of each activity usually depends on the season and your negotiating skills.

It's best to arrange for transportation to leave Karakul ahead of time, either heading further south to Tashkorgan or north back to Kashgar. Failure to plan means you'll have to wait on the side of the road for the next bus that usually arrives in the early afternoon. Hitchhiking is also possible and either option should run you about 50-100 RMB for the trip.

For those with ample time to spare and an adventurous spirit, the area around Muztaghata is a wonderful place to peacefully hike amid beautiful scenery and numerous glaciers. Hikes usually begin at the **Subash Village** (苏巴什 Sūbāshí) and head toward the **Muztaghata Base Camp** on the western foot of the mountain where you can explore the **Kartamak** and **Kmatolja Glaciers**, two of the many that slowly descend the mountain.

Note: Officially, any person hiking up Muztaghata as far as base camp will need to pay an "Environmental Protection Fee" of 400 RMB/person through a tour agency. Permits to climb beyond base camp are based on group size and must be purchased in advance.

There's also an alternate climbing route that follows the Torbulung River around to the eastern base camp, but this road is far less traveled and much riskier. Whichever way you go, I strongly advise you connect with local tour guides who provide the much-needed direction for such hikes. Climbing expeditions can also be arranged in Kashgar but are extremely expensive for the average traveler.

#4 Tashkorgan and the Stone Fort - 295km

Although there still remains more than 100 kilometers to the China-Pakistan border, there is a sense of "arrival" when you enter the town of **Tashkorgan** (塔什库尔干镇/Tǎshikù'ěrgàn Zhèn). A large sign welcomes you to "Tashkurgan Tajik Autonomous County", the first indications that the residents you'll meet here are mostly of Tajik descent.

The town is small, numbering just over 40,000 for the entire county, and your options for food and lodging are limited. Regardless, it's a quaint town to explore and the people are shy but friendly.

The name Tashkorgan means "stone fort," so it should be no surprise that one of the main places to visit would be the old **Stone Fort** (古石头城/Gǔshítou chéng), located just on the northern edge of town. Many scholars believe that this crumbling stone castle was the one mentioned by Ptolemy in his 2nd century BC geographic guide book.

There is more to see in Tashkorgan, of course, but this will be covered in the next section.

#5 The Khunjerab Pass - 413km

Finally, the **Khunjerab Pass** (红其拉甫山口/Hóngqílāfǔ Shānkǒu) represents the highest paved border crossing in the world, a large concrete structure marking official passage onto the Pakistan side of the Karakoram Highway.

By this point, travelers have reached an elevation of 4,693 meters and it is not uncommon to be experiencing altitude sickness.

This pass is usually closed during the winter season (approximately December through April) but the guards are not keen to allow you to stick around for long no matter what time of year. Transportation can be arranged from Tashkorgan or Kashgar.

Tashkorgan

What to do in Tashkorgan

Tashkorgan is the final major town before crossing into Pakistan and it has been developed into a beautiful town with smoothly paved roads, modern-looking buildings and a monument to the eagle in the center. The eagle has become a symbol of this region, being an important part of the Tajik culture that includes eagle training and even a popular eagle dance (see the chapter on Tajik people of Xinjiang).

The more you can interact with the local culture in Tashkorgan, the better. If you need specific locations to visit, however, here are a few worthy of note.

Tashkorgan Stone Fort
古石头城/Gǔshítou Chéng

Price: 30 元

Rating: Great photo but definitely a deteriorating ruin

As mentioned earlier, the Tashkorgan Stone Fort (also referred to as the "Stone Castle") on the northern edge of town is probably the most photographed view in Tashkorgan.

This area has a 2,200-year history as a major caravan stop along the Silk Road and was once the capital of various kingdoms. During this time, it served to control these caravan routes and provide refuge for the merchants.

Now, tourist can climb up the fort and view the beautiful scenery from one of the four watchtowers. The fort isn't one of Xinjiang's most well-preserved ruins and some have been disappointed by its small size. A picture is still a must, although that can be done from the grasslands if you don't want to pay to walk the fort.

Aral Golden Grasslands
阿拉尔金草原/Ālāěr Jīncǎoyuán

Price: Free to enter

Rating: Picturesque scenery and worth a visit if in Tashkorgan

To the east of the town, the Tashkorgan River snakes through a valley of lush green grass, grazing cattle and local yurts. Wooden platforms now give visitors the opportunity to walk around and the photo opportunities, particularly at dawn and dusk, are amazing.

This area is known as the "gooz" by the local Tajik. Personally, it's one of my favorite places to wander around. I've been invited into a yurt for a meal, watched a local game of horseback known as "buzkashi" and watched as children splashed in the streams.

Don't feel like you have to stay on the wooden paths. Explore around and enjoy the grasslands!

Tajik Cultural Museum
塔吉克族博物馆/Tǎjíkèzú Bówùguǎn

Price: Free
Rating: Very small but has some interesting exhibits

This small museum of Tajik culture is located right off the circle near the eagle monument in the center of town. Most of the museum is dedicated to the clothes, culture and customs of the Tajik people and there are two mummies in the basement that are of interest.

The signs are roughly translated into English, so at the very least you'll have an idea of what you're looking at.

Transportation from Tashkorgan

There are only two ways to get to Tashkorgan: through Pakistan or through Kashgar. We've already gone into detail about getting to Tashkorgan in the chapter on Getting to/from Kashgar, so I want to briefly touch on transportation details to exit Tashkorgan.

Tashkorgan toward Pakistan

If you want to get a bus to Pakistan, you'll want to leave quite early in the morning and arrive at the Pakistan bus stop (at the Immigration Office) no later than 7:30am local time (9:30am Beijing time). Tickets will cost about 225 RMB per person.

Tashkorgan toward Kashgar

Along the east-west Tashkorgan Road in Tashkorgan, the city bus station is the place where you'll find both buses and taxis to take you back toward Kashgar.

A taxi usually costs around 120 RMB per person, assuming a full car of 4 people, and you can be let off at any point along the way (for instance, at Karakul Lake). A bus is usually only 90 RMB per person but stops often along the route.

Where to stay in Tashkorgan

⬅—————————➡

There are only a couple options for accommodation in Tashkorgan, but thankfully they are good ones.

K2 Youth Hostel

It's hard to miss the bright yellow building with a large "K2" printed on the sign. This, as far as I know, is the only hostel open to foreigners along the Karakoram Highway. It's not luxurious, but they do offer internet, bike rental, laundry and car hire.

凯途国际青年旅舍/**Kǎitú Guójì Qīngnián Lǚshě**
Address: 1 Hongqi Lafu Road
(红旗拉甫路 1 号)
Phone: 182-9965-1555

Pictures, Pricing and Booking: **www.xjtravelguide.com/k2-hostel**

Crown Inn

The foreign-owned Crown Inn at Tashkorgan is the best place to stay in the city if you're not up for a hostel experience. The rooms are comfortable and the on-site restaurant offers a variety of foods, including

皇冠大酒店/**Huángguàn Dàjiǔdiàn**
Address: 23 Pamir Road
(帕米尔路 23 号)
Phone: (0998) 342-2888

some western dishes. You won't get internet in the rooms, unfortunately, but they do have wi-fi in the common area. The staff can help arrange your visit to the Khunjerab Pass as well as vehicles and guides to anywhere else you may want to go.

Pictures, Pricing and Booking:
www.xjtravelguide.com/Tashkorgan-Crown-Inn

Hotan & the Southern Rim

Hotan Top Sights

Hotan Carpet Making – Pg 342
For centuries, women in Hotan have been making carpets by hand. See for yourself.

Desert Burial Sites – Pg 343
Dotting the sands of the Taklamakan Desert near Hotan are these strange burial sites, including the Mazar of Imam Asim.

Yarkand Top Sights

Tomb of Amanisa Han – Pg 336

Within Yarkand's Altun complex is a beautiful building that is the Tomb of Amanisa Han, the revered Uyghur woman who composed the Twelve Muqam.

Introduction to the Southern Rim

◄─────────────────────────────►

At the base of the Tibetan plateau, before you reach the sands of the Taklamakan Desert, a series of small Uyghur towns and tiny villages connect to form what was once a vibrant corridor of the ancient Silk Road. Not only was the southern route a shorter distance to travel from inland China to Kashgar, it was also less prone to roadside thieves.

Over the course of time, as both the trade routes and the Taklamakan shifted, many of these towns were abandoned or swallowed up by massive sand dunes. For hundreds of years, these buried cities remained untouched until their rediscovery in the 19th and 20th centuries by foreign explorers who were willing to risk their lives entering the Taklamakan Desert. What they found and brought back with them turned the explorers into legends abroad and despised enemies in China.

As the Hotan Museum so eloquently states:

> *"In the late 19th century and early 20th century, those so-called 'explorers' and 'archeologists' from foreign countries came to this piece of land to look for cultural relics of ancient time and took many precious ones away."*

As you can tell, they don't look kindly upon foreign involvement in the preservation of the region's history.

In spite of everything that was hauled away by the foreigners, more than likely other such abandoned towns remain hidden in the sands of the desert, just waiting to be found.

China has learned its lesson, though. Now, they strictly control who is allowed off the beaten path and required heavy fees and mandatory chaperones for those researchers who are determined to visit the ancient ruins.

Traveling the southern Silk Road is still an adventure, although now most of the exhilaration is derived from discovering the culture of small-town Uyghur life instead of searching for long-lost cities in the sand.

Traveling the Southern Silk Road

It used to be that a journey from Urumqi to Hotan (often spelled "Khotan") would take up to 2 months but, as with most transportation throughout Xinjiang, that has been reduced to just under a full day.

Hotan is now linked to Urumqi by rail, passing through Kashgar and continuing along the northern rim of the Taklamakan Desert. A new train is currently being built from Korla into nearby Qinghai and it is not out of the question to think that these trains will eventually be linked together, although not anytime in the near future.

In the meantime, the northern and southern rims of the Taklamakan Desert have been connected via three cross-desert highways that are truly modern engineering feats. The easternmost Highway 218 goes from Korla to Ruoqiang, following the ever-shrinking waters of the Tarim River.

The second cross-desert highway, Highway 312 that starts at Luntai and ends in Minfeng, is the longest paved desert road in the world. The intended use of this highway is for oil companies and most tourist will never have a need to ride it unless they're taking a short trip to the Tarim River Poplar Park.

Finally, the westernmost Highway 217, the same highway that makes a thrilling cut through the Tianshan, connects Kuqa with Hotan (Khotan). Apart from flying, this highway is now the fastest way to get from Hotan back to Urumqi via bus.

From Kashgar, the southern Silk Road begins at the small towns of **Yengisar**, home to the beautiful Uyghur knife, **Yarkand**, known in Chinese as Shache and **Karghalik**, from which begins the highway to Tibet. Finally, it's on to **Hotan**, best known for its precious jade, carpets and paper-making.

From Hotan, the road continues to **Keriya** (Yutian), **Niya** (Minfeng), **Cherchen** (Qiemo), and **Charkhlik** (Ruoqiang), where you can choose to head north to Korla or east into the Qinghai province.

The further you travel from Kashgar along the southern rim of the Taklamakan Desert, you'll find fewer and fewer locals who can speak Mandarin Chinese. Showing them the Chinese characters won't help either. Unless you have the time to learn Uyghur, this is a challenge you should expect to face regularly. Prepare to use plenty of sign language or just find somebody who can understand you. It's all part of the adventure!

Also, due to political tensions that have resulted in a number of deadly riots over the past few years, stability is not something travelers should expect from this region. Security checks, military patrols and authorities who question your passage - things which aren't unheard of throughout Xinjiang - are especially noticeable along this road.

Cities Between
Kashgar and Hotan

Yengisar 英吉沙

The town of Yengisar (英吉沙 /Yīngjíshā), 70 kilometers south of Kashgar, emerges from a number of small villages. If you've heard of Yingisar before, it is probably in connection with its knives, the most famous (historical) export of the region.

Yingisar knives are valued for their craftsmanship and design, although what is produced now often doesn't compete with what was made just a decade ago. Tighter restrictions on knives in the region, coupled with mass production, has crippled the industry in Yengisar. The old factories once buzzing with activity south of town are mostly shuttered now.

If you're able to find a knife to buy in Yingisar - and that's a big "if" - don't expect to take any knife you purchase with you, either on the bus, train or checked-in on an airplane. Even China Post won't take your knives. Special shipping arrangements have to be made, and it's not guaranteed that the knife will arrive at its final destination. It's a major inconvenience that in some cases isn't even worth the effort.

Even if you don't end up buying a knife, walk around to see there is anybody actively making knives. It's a fascinating process that is unfortunately a dying art.

Transportation

Buses/cars between Yengisar and Kashgar run 28 RMB; to Yarkand (Shache) for 42 RMB.

Lodging

While I don't recommend you stay the night in Yengisar, the only hotel I can find that claims to accept foreigners is the Tianfu Hotel (天府宾馆 362-8668).

Yarkand (Shache) 莎车

The town of Yarkand, which is referred to by Chinese as Shache (莎车), was at one point in its history a bigger and more important center of trade than Kashgar. The reason for this was the extensive commercial trade that occurred over a pass into India, a pass that has since been closed due to political disputes.

Despite its waning prominence, the Sunday bazaar is still a wonderful experience in Yarkand, as is strolling around the old city. The only big site of interest is the Altun Complex, an area that includes the Altun Mosque (阿勒屯清真寺/Ālètún Qīngzhēnsì), the Altun Mazar (阿勒屯麻扎/Alètún Mázā) and the Tomb of Amanisa Han (阿曼尼莎汗 Āmànníshāhàn).

The city of Yarkand is laid out in a fairly easy grid, whose primary east-west road makes it simple to understand where to find the old and new parts of town. On the west side of town it is called "New City Road" (新城路/Xīnchénglù) where you'll find a number of nicer hotels; heading east it changes names to "Old City Road" (老城路 /Lǎochénglù). The bazaar and old city are on this eastern side of the city as is the Altun Complex, which is located on the easy-to-remember Altun Road just off Old City Road.

The draw of the Altun Mosque, built in 1533, is its intricate Uyghur wood carving and architectural style, while the Altun Mazar houses the tombs of the kings who ruled Yarkand kingdom through most of the 16th century. The Tomb of Amanisa Han (1526-1560) pays homage to the woman who composed one of the most cherished of Uyghur musical traditions: the Twelve Muqam.

Transportation

There is a bus station and a train station that can take you from Yarkand toward Kashgar (88 RMB) or Hotan (104 RMB).

Lodging

There seem to be a number of hotels that accept foreigners in Yarkand. I recommend either the Shache Hotel (莎车宾馆) or the Shache Queen Hotel (莎车王后大饭店 0998-852-9999), both located on the main Xincheng Road.

Finally, when you decide to make your way further south to Karghalik (Yecheng), there's a detour a bit to the west known as the Golden Poplar National Forest (金湖杨国家森林公园 Jīnhúyáng Guójiā Sēnlín Gōngyuán). Accessible only by private car, this park is another example of the beautiful Xinjiang poplar tree, whose leaves burn a beautiful golden yellow during the fall months.

Karghalik (Yecheng) 叶城

← ——————————————— →

Best known as the starting point for the Xinjiang-Tibet Highway, the town of Karghalik, known in Chinese as Yecheng (叶城), is located 60 kilometers south of Yarkand.

There's not much to see in Yecheng aside from the mosque in the city center and the old town alleys behind it. Unless you're planning to make the journey into Tibet or are staging a climb of the relatively close K2 mountain (both of which require much planning and hiring of vehicles) Yecheng is probably not a place you'll need to stop.

Hotan (Khotan)

和田

Getting to/from Hotan

Historically speaking, Hotan used to be one of the most remote places in all of Xinjiang, guarded by the Taklamakan Desert to the north and the Tibetan Plateau to the south. China has invested heavily in transportation, however, which means that Hotan is now connected via air, rail and a cross-desert highway.

Hotan by Air

The small Hotan Airport (和田机场/Hétián Jīchǎng) is located about 10km south of town. A taxi to or from town should average around 20-30 RMB. The airport serves daily flights to and from Urumqi which, depending on the discount, could be cheaper than taking the train (and much faster). There are multiple flights daily to Urumqi that cost roughly 300-800 RMB and last two hours.

Hotan by Rail

From the Hotan Train Station (和田站/Hétián zhàn), located 5 kilometers north of the city center, you can travel to and from Kashgar or all the way up to Urumqi. There are now multiple trains that depart Hotan station toward Kashgar and Urumqi each day.
- **Urumqi**: 370/217 RMB (hard sleeper/hard seat), 24 hours
- **Kashgar**: 123/69 RMB (hard sleeper/hard seat), 6 hours

Check up-to-date schedules and ticket pricing here:
www.xjtravelguide.com/train-tickets

Hotan by Bus

Buses depart and arrive from the Hotan Bus Station (和田公路客运中心/Hétián Gōnglù Kèyùn Zhōngxīn) on Taibei Road (台北路). Daily buses from Khotan head in three different directions: west toward Kashgar, Yarkand (Shache), and Yengisar; east toward Keriya (Yutian), Niya (Minfeng) and Cherchen (Qiemo); and finally, north through the desert to Kuqa and Urumqi.

Getting around Hotan

Taxis in Hotan can get you most anywhere in the city usually for under 10 RMB. A bus system also operates, although it will probably be more convenient to use a taxi.

What to do in Hotan

◀━━━━━━━━━━━━━━━━━━━▶

Much of what makes Hotan famous lies hidden beneath the desert sands north of the city, but many travelers are quite enchanted by the slow pace of life that hasn't modernized at the same pace as Kashgar.

Wandering around the Uyghur neighborhoods, exploring the Sunday Bazaar and understanding a bit of the region's history at the beautiful Hotan Museum are just a few of the most interesting things to do in Hotan.

In addition to the ancient ruins and Uyghur culture, there is much to enjoy in the form of Hotan's other manufactured exports: jade, carpets, silk and paper. Pick a couple that interest you, or choose them all if you have time, and enjoy viewing the production process as it has been for centuries in this part of the world.

Hotan Sunday Bazaar
- **Name:** 和田大巴扎/Hétián Dàbāzhā
- **Price:** Free
- **Rating:** Highly recommended

Still mostly untainted by western tourism, the Hotan Sunday Bazaar is what the Kashgar Bazaar used to be - vivacious crowds of local Uyghur, dusty roads, smelly animals and plenty of street food.

Located in the northeastern portion of town on Taibei East Rd (台北东路), the joy of visiting the bazaar is taking in all the sights, smells, and tastes that are completely exotic to most tourists. Foreigners aren't as common here as they are in Kashgar, but they are still welcomed by vendors and locals alike.

Hotan Museum
- **Name:** 和田博物馆/Hétián Bówùguǎn
- **Price:** Free
- **Rating:** Highly recommended

The relatively new Hotan Museum, located in the western side of the city on Beijing West Rd (北京西路), is not a large museum when compared to the museums at Urumqi or Turpan, but it's still a great place to stop.

Here you'll find a number of artifacts from the nearby desert city ruins, including coins, pottery, clothing and much more. The mummies and the intricate wooden coffin are some of their most prized displays.

The museum is open every day except Wednesday from 10am-1:30pm and 4pm-7:30pm Beijing time.

Uyghur Neighborhoods & Grape Trellis Corridors

Hotan is still predominantly Uyghur in population, which is becoming increasingly rare in Xinjiang. Outside of the modern city center, far to the west of the city, taking a walk through the dirt streets and alleys of the Uyghur neighborhoods surrounding the city provide plenty of entertainment.

During the summer months, the 1,000+ kilometers of pathways covered by grape trellis offer relief from the beating sun and wonderful photo opportunities. Known as the Grape Trellis Corridors (葡萄长廊/Pútáo cháng láng), you'll have to get a taxi to drive you a good distance to the west of the city to find them.

Jade Carving Factory

- **Name**: 和田工艺美术玉雕厂/Hétián Gōngyì Měishù Yùdiāochǎng
- **Price**: Free
- **Rating**: Fun to watch but not a long stop

If there's one thing that Hotan is best known for all across China and even the world, it would be jade. The beautiful green and white jade that comes from Hotan is in high demand and the price continues to soar as the jade becomes scarce.

Jade is sold in shops all across Hotan but it is at the Jade Carving Factory where you can watch artisans sculpt these rough pieces of jade into beautiful works of art. The jade pieces on sale at the shop range from very simple rocks to insanely expensive collector's items. If you're looking for an authentic jade gift or souvenir, this is a great - albeit expensive - place to purchase.

The factory is located on Gujiang North Rd (古江北路) on the southeast corner of the intersection with Jiashi Rd (加实路).

Hotan Carpet Factory

- **Name**: 地毯厂/Dìtǎnchǎng
- **Price**: Usually free
- **Rating**: Recommended if you have the time

In 2009, Hotan opened up its first official Hotan Carpet Museum (和田地毯博物馆/Hétián Dìtǎn Bówùguǎn), but since the Hotan Museum already has a display of carpets, you'll probably appreciate more a visit to a handmade carpet factory.

It is at the carpet factory where you'll witness rows of women diligently weaving a carpet pattern by hand using the colorful balls of silk hanging overhead. There are a number of these carpet factories around the city, the biggest of which is the Nakixwan Carpet Factory (纳克西湾手工地毯/Nàkèxīwān Shǒugōng Dìtǎnchǎng) on the eastern side of town, across the river along highway G217.

Additional carpet factories are scattered across the region including the Lop Carpet Factory (洛浦县白城地毯厂/Luòpǔxiàn Báichéng Dìtǎnchǎng), which is approximately 20km east of Hotan, and more along the way toward Yutian (于田).

Jiya Ancient Atlas Silk Factory

- **Name**: 吉亚乡古老丝绸艾特莱斯厂/Jíyàxiāng Gǔlǎo Sīchóu Aitècàisīchǎng
- **Price**: 10 元
- **Rating**: Recommended if you have the time

About 15 kilometers northeast of Hotan in the Jiya Township (吉亚乡), a small factory still operates to manufacture the beautiful atlas pattern that you see so many Uyghur women wear. While it's more of a tourist destination than a working factory, it will give you a wonderful view into the production of silk, Hotan's most important export before jade became so highly valued.

For those limited in time, I recommend coming here instead of the more mechanized Shatou Silk Factory (和田沙驼丝绸厂/Hétián Shātuó Sīchóuchǎng, 10 元), which is what you'll see most tour groups point you toward. It's a bit further away, but the experience of watching the locals process and weave the silk by hand is worth the extra travel.

Mazar of Imam Asim (Jiya)

- **Name**: 依麻木阿斯木麻扎/Yīmámù Āsīmù Mázhā
- **Price**: Cost of transportation
- **Rating**: Memorable experience

> **Note**: As of 2019, travelers have shared with me that this mazar is no longer open - both to locals or to tourists. While I'm keeping this chapter for posterity's sake, you'll need to check with other travelers or local travel agencies to find out for sure.

Within the windswept sand dunes north of Hotan, along the edge of the Taklamakan Desert, there is a fascinating pilgrimage site that makes for a memorable visit.

Imam Asim was a respected Sufi imam and soldier who was known as being part of the army that brought and end to the Buddhist kingdom of Hotel around 1000 A.D. He was buried in the sands of the Takalamakan, a peculiar sight of sticks, flags and fences to keep the sand from completely overtaking the tomb.

What makes this so interesting is that Imam Asim's Mazar is one of the few places where a Sufi mystic version of Islam still exists. This can be seen in the animal sacrifices that are sometimes made at the tomb, the colorful flags (which aren't common with other Uyghur burial sites) and the fact that Uyghur gather to chant and pray at his tomb.

To get here, you can take a combination of public transportation, taxis or hitchhike. Most of the Uyghur you see along the way won't be able to read or understand Mandarin Chinese, so just keep saying "Imam Asim Mazar" and they should point the way.

I recommend making this mazar your last stop while visiting the Silk and carpet factories in Jiya. They are all on the same road that head north and dead end at the Taklamakan.

Mulberry Paper Making

- **Name**: 普恰克其乡桑皮纸/Pǔqiàkèqíxiāng Sāngpízhǐ
- **Price**: Cost of a guide
- **Rating**: Recommended if you have the time

> **Note:** Again, I have been told that this is another place that has been shut down since I last visited. You'll need to check with locals, travelers and travel agencies before making this hour-long trek.

The tradition of paper making from the bark of Mulberry trees is believed to date back 2,000 years and there are still a handful of families that keep the tradition alive.

One such place is at the Puqiakeqi Village in Moyu county (墨玉县), about 30 kilometers northwest of Hotan. Here visitors can witness the entire paper-making process: from cutting the bark to soaking it, beating it and molding it to become paper. Souvenirs here are a must.

Unfortunately, this paper making village isn't well-known among the locals. You'll need to instruct your driver to head toward Puqiakeqi and from there he can ask around to find out where the paper making family is located.

Ancient Cities Surrounding Hotan

◄──────────────────────────►

There are a number of ancient city ruins that surround Hotan, mostly within the sands of the Taklamakan Desert. Some of them are close to the city while others require a 4WD and a camel trek. Almost all of them require "historical preservation fees" to visit.

These fees, which are reportedly negotiable but range between a few hundred RMB to a few thousand, must be paid to the Hotan Cultural Relics Bureau.

For more information, contact the Hotan CITS (135-7968-0038 or 0903-251-5220) or visit their offices at 49 Tunken Road (屯垦西路).

Most visits to these protected sites will need to be done under the supervision of a licensed travel agency even after these permit fees have been paid. Be mindful that attempting to visit these historical sites on your own is not only dangerous, it is illegal.

Needless to say, it takes determination and deep pockets to get the opportunity to visit Hotan's ancient Silk Road ruins, whether by vehicle or on a multi-day trek between the humps of a camel.

Melikawat Ancient City Ruins
- **Name:** 玛利克瓦特古城/Mǎlìkèwǎtè Gǔchéng
- **Price:** 10 RMB
- **Rating:** Best option for low cost/minimum travel balance

Approximately 30 kilometers south of Hotan along the White Jade River are the Melikawat Ancient City Ruins. Based on the artifacts that have been unearthed here, we know that the city was a major Buddhist center and some archaeologists contend it was even a capital of the region at one point.

While the earthen ruins still protrude from the ground, it's hard to distinguish them as buildings or walls of any sort thanks to wind erosion and flooding. In fact, because of these floods, most of the city lies under a meter of sand and dirt.

That said, if you're not willing to pay a high permit fee for sites like the Rawak Stupa or Mazar Tagh (see below), Melikawat is the next best option to see a desert ruin.

Ancient City of Yotkan

- **Name**: 约特干古城/Yuētègàn Gǔchéng
- **Price**: 15 RMB
- **Rating**: Not much to see

West of Hotan 15 kilometers, the Ancient City of Yotkan is one of the closest ancient ruins to visit, even though I don't recommend them to travelers. It once occupied a large portion of land and historians believe this site used to be capital of the ancient Kingdom of Hotan.

Next to nothing remains, however, since most of the ruins are buried under sand and marsh. A few artifacts that were unearthed here are displayed at the Hotan and Urumqi museums.

Rawak Stupa

- **Name**: 热瓦克佛寺/Rèwǎkè Fósì
- **Price**: Approx. 300 RMB permit fee
- **Rating**: Of the better-quality ruins, this is the best price/time value

Considered one of the best-preserved stupas on the southern Silk Road, the Rawak Stupa is probably one of the most visually rewarding destinations to spend your money if you're determined to visit desert ruins. Located about 40 kilometers from Hotan in the deserts north of Jiya Township (吉亚乡), a journey to the Rawak Stupa will require both a 4WD and additional walking/camel riding.

Alternatively, CITS in Hotan can arrange a multi-day camel excursion, which includes all transportation, camping equipment and permit fees for a couple thousand RMB.

Aksipil Fort Ruins

- **Name**: Aksipil - Chinese name unknown and unnecessary
- **Price**: Approx. 200 RMB permit fee
- **Rating**: Not much to see to the casual observer

While the ram-packed walls of this ancient fort still tower up several meters from the sand dunes, there's not much to explore here. Even Aurel Stein, the famous Silk Road explorer and archeologist, only spent a single day surveying the site in 1901.

Mazar Tagh Ruins

- **Name**: Mazar Tagh - Chinese name unknown and unnecessary
- **Price:** Approx. 300 RMB permit fee
- **Rating**: Long distance to travel but beautiful ruins and surrounding area near Hotan River

The ruins of Mazar Tagh are located about 180 kilometers north of Hotan on the west side of the cross-desert Highway 217. The crumbling remains of a fort rest on a bluff overlooking the dark waters of the Hotan River, a fort which used to be a military outpost for the Tibetan Empire.

A number of military documents on paper and wood were discovered here, providing valuable insight into the Tibetan Empire, whose control stretched up into Hotan for a time. Most of these documents, recovered by Aurel Stein during his expeditions in 1907 and 1913, rest in the British Library today.

Where to Stay in Hotan

◄──────────────────────────►

There are plenty of places to stay in Hotan, almost all of which accept walk-ins. For the sake of convenience, the following hotels are recommended because they allow booking online in advance of your arrival.

West Lake International Hotel

One of Hotan's nicest hotels is also one of the most expensive. The West Lake International Hotel is located in the center of town and offers free internet in the room, a breakfast buffet, a few restaurant options and an attached spa.

西湖国际大酒店/Xīhú Guójì Dàjiǔdiàn
Address: 111 South Tanaiyi Road
(塔乃依南路 111 号)
Phone: (0903) 252-2222

Pictures, Pricing and Booking: **www.xjtravelguide.com/Hotan-West-Lake-Hotel**

Hotan Xiyu Hotel

Although this 3-star hotel is farther away from the city center, it has two things going for it: much cheaper rooms and close proximity to the Hotan Museum. Rooms include free wi-fi. This is one of the best mid-range options in Hotan.

和田西域大酒店/Hétián Xīyù Dàjiǔdiàn
Address: 261 West Beijing Road
(北京西路 261 号)
Phone: (0903) 251-1777

Pictures, Pricing and Booking: **www.xjtravelguide.com/Hotan-Xiyu-Hotel**

Note: For cheaper accommodation, consider the Jiaotong Hotel (交通宾馆) located right by the bus station. The rooms are run down but they are cheaper than what you'll find further into town. You can just walk in or call ahead for reservations: (0903-203-2700).

Other Cities along the Southern Rim

Keriya (Yutian) 于田

Heading further east of Hotan for 180 kilometers on the southern route of the Silk Road, you'll come across Keriya, known by the Chinese as Yutian (于田). While the town is undergoing rapid development, it is still at heart a small town that is best enjoyed wandering around on foot.

Aside from the traditional bazaar and Uyghur neighborhoods, there's not much that Keriya has to offer most travelers. The ancient city ruins mentioned below are both a good distance from the city and similar to the previously mentioned ruins near Hotan. In addition, they will require permission and a permit fee to visit, if permission is even granted.

Permission and permits will still need to be obtained in Hotan, as Keriya (and its ruins) are still under Hotan's jurisdiction.

DanDan Oilik Ruins

- **Name**: 丹丹乌里克/Dāndān Wūlǐkè
- **Price**: Approx. 7,000 RMB permit fee
- **Rating**: Incredible storehouse of artifacts but not accessible to the average traveler

Because gaining access to DanDan Oilik for the average traveler is close to impossible, I won't go into too much detail here. After being abandoned at the end of the 8th century, DanDan Oilik was rediscovered in 1896 by Sven Hedin, another well-known Swedish explorer of the region. The sheer volume of manuscripts, paintings and artifacts that have been found here are astounding and are displayed in museums in Xinjiang and around the world.

The DanDan Oilik ruins consists of not only mud-brick homes but also wooden beams and ancient temples rising from the desert sands. Discoveries are still being made at this site and it was named a protected cultural heritage site in 2006.

Karadong

- **Name**: 喀拉墩古城/Kālādūn Gǔchéng
- **Price**: Approx. 5,000+ RMB permit fee
- **Rating**: Fascinating fort ruins but cost/time prohibitive

Similar to DanDan Oilik, the Karadong city ruins are located far north of Keriya (180 kilometers) in the middle of the Taklamakan Desert. This fort, build next to the Keriya River, acted as a military outpost controlling the north-south passage along the river.

Karadong, which means "Black Sand Dunes" in Uyghur, includes ruins of a large rectangle fort with walls 8 meters in height that were first rediscovered by explorer Sven Hedin in 1896.

Niya (Minfeng) 民丰

Niya, known in Chinese as Minfeng (民丰), is another notable town on the southern rim of the Taklamakan, 120 kilometers west of Keriya (Yutian). Construction and development is ongoing, of course, but the town still retains its ancient feel, especially in the neighborhoods surrounding the newer portions of the city.

Again, there's not much to see in Niya city proper other than the traditional bazaar and mosque, but there are sites of interest further north. These include a sacred pilgrimage site and the ruins of the ancient Niya city.

Daily buses to Hotan in the west and Cherchen (Qiemo) in the east leave from Niya's only bus station.

Mazar of Imam Jafar Sadiq

- **Name**: 大玛扎瘗庠噎垞泼閽地勐/Dàmǎzā Yìmáme Cháfā Sadikè
- **Price:** 50 元
- **Rating**: Best area example of a small desert village with an interesting mazar

Located about 70 kilometers north of Niya along the Tarim Highway, this shrine to a venerated Uyghur imam offers a unique glimpse into traditional life in the desert as well as how the locals honor their "saints."

The Mazar of Imam Jafar Sadiq (a mazar is a burial place for respected leaders), isn't large nor is it built with the tourist in mind. For this reason, it can make for an enjoyable excursion that gives a very rural experience without a terribly high cost. Taxis can be hired from within town or there are reportedly minibuses that make the trip from near the Niya bus station, although I couldn't confirm this.

Ancient Niya Ruins

- **Name:** 尼雅遗址/Níyǎ Yízhǐ
- **Price:** Approx. 5,000+ RMB permit fee
- **Rating:** Home to incredible former excavations but not accessible to the average traveler

Rediscovered by Aurel Stein in 1900, the Niya Ancient Ruins rest 115 kilometers north of modern-day Niya. As opposed to the temples and forts found in many of the other archeological sites, Niya is unique in that most of what has been discovered are the residential areas of town.

A number of wooden tablets, textiles, pottery and tombs have been excavated here which are displayed in museums all over the world, including the Xinjiang Autonomous Region Museum in Urumqi.

The Niya Ruins, like DanDan Oilik and others, are another site that is not only difficult to reach within the desert, it is also highly guarded by authorities and inaccessible to average travelers.

Endere Ruins

- **Name:** 安迪尔/Āndíěr
- **Price:** Approx. 7,000 RMB permit fee
- **Rating:** Photogenic stupa but not accessible to the average traveler

The Endere Ruins are located halfway between Niya and Cherchen. The site was first excavated by Aurel Stein during his expedition here. Although crumbling walls still surround the ancient city, the most notable structure is the stupa, one of many indications that this site was once a center of Buddhist worship.

Cherchen (Qiemo) 且末

The river oasis town of Cherchen, also officially known as Qiemo (且末) on the map, is a small but interesting place to spend a day or two while passing through. It is surprisingly modern despite its remote location and like many of these southern Taklamakan towns, doesn't have the opportunity to host many foreign tourists.

Among the small, southern Taklamakan towns, Cherchen is probably the most likely to interest an independent traveler. There are a few small sites worth visiting and accommodation is cheap and relatively comfortable.

The most interesting fact about Cherchen is that despite repeated expeditions, the ancient city of Cherchen mentioned in the annals of history has yet to be discovered.

There is an airport in Cherchen (且末机场/Qiěmò Jīchǎng or airport code "IQM") with flights that take off from Urumqi five days a week. The flight takes about 2 ½ hours, which is a huge improvement from the 15+ hour bus ride from the capital city.

Still, the bus is the cheapest and most common mode of transportation to Cherchen. More than likely you'll find your way here from Korla or Hotan. Once you arrive, take a day to wander the Uyghur neighborhoods, shop in the bazaar and visit one or two of the following sites.

Zaghunluk Ancient Mummies

- **Name**: 扎滚鲁克古墓群景点/Zhāgǔnlǔkè Gǔmùqún Jǐngdiǎn
- **Price**: 30 元
- **Rating**: Recommended

Probably the most interesting of the sites around Cherchen is Zaghunluk, home of a number of ancient mummies excavated from the region in the late 1980s. The "museum" sits alone on an empty plain about 5 kilometers southwest of Cherchen, a simple taxi ride away.

There are a number of tombs all across this plain, but this building covers a particular set of graves that you can view through a plexiglass cover. In order to view this museum, you'll want to first make a stop at the Toghraklek Manor (see below) where a key to the building is often held.

Toghraklek Manor Museum

- **Name**: 托乎拉克庄园博物馆/Tuōhūlākè Zhuāngyuán Bówùguǎn
- **Price**: 20 元
- **Rating**: Short but interesting visit on your way to Zaghunluk

On your way to Zaghunluk to the southwest of Cherchen, you'll run across the Toghraklek Manor Museum, a restored traditional Uyghur villa first built in 1911. Although there's not much on display other than a few small objects, it's an interesting view of the large living quarters of a wealthy county leader.

Lalulik Ruins

- **Name**: 来利勒克/Láilìlèkè
- **Price**: 50 元
- **Rating**: Not much to see

Although you may come across Chinese literature that talks about the ancient sites of Lalulik or even Neleke, there's really not much to see at either location besides a few heavily eroded "buildings". It's a wonder that anybody even discovered these and realized that there was history behind these rocks.

Additional Day Trips

Although rarely visited by foreign tourists, I want to mention two additional places of interest around Cherchen. There is a Wildlife Park (野生动物/Yěshēng Dòngwù) and ancient petroglyphs near the town of Serikule. Both of these will require a tour guide who is familiar with the areas and they are at such a distance (230 and 180 kilometers respectively) that they might even require multiple days to visit.

I don't specifically recommend either of these sites but wanted to mention them as you might run across literature within the city that talks about them as options.

Charkhlik (Ruoqiang) 若羌

⬅━━━━━━━━━━━➡

The small town of Charkhlik, known as Ruoqiang (若羌) on a Chinese map, is the point where the cross-desert Highway 218 meets with Highway 315 heading toward Hotan as well as into Qinghai. There's not much to see within the city other than the daily lives of its Uyghur inhabitants, but the uninhabitable sands to the northeast are home to a couple ancient ruins and the remains of China's nuclear testing program.

Two of these sites - particularly Loulan and the nuclear testing base - are extremely difficult for foreigners to access. Miran is one of the few that is relatively easy to visit from Charkhlik but it still requires a sizable permit fee.

Miran Ruins

- **Name**: 米兰/Mǐlán
- **Price**: 500-1,000 RMB permit fee
- **Rating**: Recommended as a cheap but interesting option for ancient ruins

Although smaller than the Loulan Ruins (see below), the Miran Ruins are a much cheaper and easier-to-access option from Charkhlik. The site is comprised mostly of a large, circular fort that was at one point occupied by Tibetan troops as a means to control access to the southern Silk Road that came up through Gansu and Qinghai.

A 4WD is required to visit these ruins, as well as a relatively cheap permit fee from the Cultural Relics Bureau that can be obtained through a travel agency or in person in Hotan.

Ancient City of Loulan

- **Name**: 罗兰/lúo lán
- **Price**: Approx. 10,000+ RMB permit fee
- **Rating**: Impressive ruins that are far too cost/time prohibitive for the average traveler

Established as a trading city before the shifting waters of the Tarim River forced its eventual abandonment, the Ancient City of Loulan is an impressive collections of Buddhist stupas, fortified walls, homes, wooden beams sticking out of the sand and ancient dried out orchards.

It was here that the famous mummy known as the "Beauty of Loulan" was found. She is still on display in the Xinjiang Uyghur Autonomous Region Museum in Urumqi and is famous for very un-Chinese characteristics (bone structure, red hair, etc.).

Nuclear Testing in Xinjiang

On October 16, 1964, China tested its very first nuclear weapon in the desert sands around Loulan. An additional 45 nuclear tests were conducted until testing was halted in 1996.

Fallout from these nuclear tests is still unclear and likely won't be publicized in China, but the old bunkers and testing sites are still visible from satellites in space. Chinese news outlets have made mention of the fact that one of these testing facilities is now open as a tourist attraction.

While I am certain that this nuclear tourist attraction exists, I have been unable to confirm whether foreign tourists are permitted to enter, or if its doors have even remained open.

Apenddix

Recommended Reading

If you're looking for further reading on Xinjiang to deepen your understanding of its history, culture or language, below is a sampling of some excellent resources to get you started. I've provided a short description of each book, along with an external link leading to their respective Amazon pages.

Xinjiang: China's Central Asia

This Odyssey guide by Jeremy Treddinick is a great companion to this travel guide you're now reading. The beautiful photos are backed by a deeper historical context that will help you truly appreciate what you will be seeing.

Silk Road | Insight Guides

If Xinjiang is just one stop on your entire journey along the Silk Road, I recommend you check out this great guide by Insight Guides. Not only does it cover China and all the 'Stans (Kyrgyzstan, Kazakhstan, Uzbekistan, etc), it also marches you into Iran, Turkey, Syria and other such countries on the western end of the famed Silk Road. It's a hefty 2-pound book, but that beats buying a Lonely Planet for each country you're going to visit.

Eurasian Crossroads: A History of Xinjiang

If you are interested in Xinjiang history, there is no better book than this one written by James Millward, a recognized expert on the region. It's incredibly detailed, which can at times be hard to follow but, in the end, gives you an appreciation for the diversity of the region. I have a copy of this book on my shelf that I always keep on hand for reference.

Silk Road: Monks, Warriors & Merchants

For a broader view of Silk Road history, this Odyssey book by French historian Luce Boulnois was a fun read for me. Combining this book with Millward's Eurasian Crossroads mentioned above, I felt equipped with the appropriate historical context not just for the Xinjiang region but for all the regions and countries surrounding it.

Wild West China

If you don't have the patience or time to read through either of the above two history books (which are over 400 pages each), this shorter book by Christian Tyler is an acceptable alternative. It presents Xinjiang's history in more of a story format, which provides an entertaining read but I feel like the author also takes liberty to hint at his own political agenda. In other words, enjoy the book but read with caution.

Foreign Devils on the Silk Road

Before anybody travels to Xinjiang I suggest they grab a copy of this book by Peter Hopkirk. Why? Hopkirk is a master storyteller and does an amazing job piecing together the story of the Great Game and how that played out here in Xinjiang. You'll appreciate Urumqi, Kashgar and especially Dunhuang (in Gansu) so much more if you read this book before you visit.

The Mummies of Urumchi

One of the most interesting pieces of history unearthed in Xinjiang are the numerous mummies you find in the museums across Xinjiang. This book attempts to unravel the mystery of who they are and where they came from.

Under the Heel of the Dragon

As part of his doctoral thesis, Blaine Kaltman conducted over 217 interviews with Han and Uyghur in Xinjiang to get their perspective on the tension here. The results - and the quotes - are eye-opening.

The Uyghurs: Strangers in Their Own Land

Author Gardner Bovington is another highly respected member of the academic community covering Xinjiang. I found this book to be quite insightful, covering every topic from from politics to religion.

Down a Narrow Road: Identity and Masculinity in a Uyghur Community

Diving into a bit of ethnography here, this book by Jay Dautcher could be considered a more unbiased, academic view of the Uyghur people.

The Gobi Desert - The Adventures of Three Women Travelling Across the Gobi Desert in the 1920s

Anybody who studies Xinjiang's history over the last century will run across two names: Cable Mildred and Francesca French. They were the first English women to cross the Gobi Desert and this is their fascinating travelogue of the journey.

News from Tartary: An Epic Journey Across Central Asia

Many people are familiar with Peter Fleming, famous journalist, writer and explorer. In this book he recounts his journey from Peking (Beijing) to Kashgar - all 3,500 miles of it. Fascinating read!

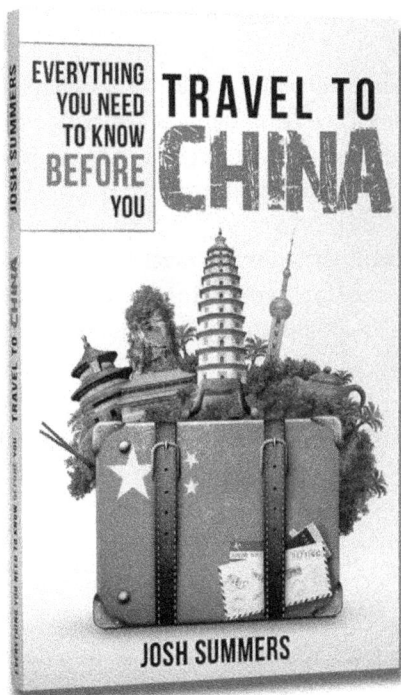

If you enjoyed this travel guide, you might also like this other China guide written by Josh Summers. Learn more:

www.travelchinacheaper.com/travel-guide

Approved Travel Companies

←——————————————————————→

The following is a list of companies that I have used or spent considerable time getting to know since I first arrived in Xinjiang. You might not have need for every service listed here but there will be at least one and these are the companies I recommend you trust with your business.

Xinjiang Travel Agencies

Old Road Tours: Abdul and the members of his family that run Old Road Tours have an office in Kashgar's Seman Hotel. They are reliable, speak excellent English and can be contacted via email (abdul@oldroadtours.com) or phone (138-9913-2103).
www.oldroadtours.com

Xinjiang Travel: Yet another company based in Kashgar (and run by a Uyghur man named Abdul), Xinjiang Travel runs tours all across Xinjiang. You can connect with them via email (xinjiangtravel@yahoo.com) or phone (158-0998-3737).
www.xinjiangtravel.com

Xinjiang Travel World International Travel Service: Based in Urumqi, this Chinese-run agency can arrange for car rental in Urumqi and tours across the region. You can contact them via email (Silkroad_Xinjiang@163.com) or by phone (135-6598-7078).

CITS: Offices for CITS are scattered all across Xinjiang. Don't expect English speakers but they can arrange most any type of tour in the region. You can connect with them via phone 24 hours a day at (0991-450-9666).
www.cits.net

Xinjiang Drivers
While all of the travel agencies listed above will be able to provide you with transportation, if you just need a driver or a car, here are my recommendations:

Urumqi: If you're looking to hire a car and driver around Urumqi, look no further than a young man named Mehsum (13999837411). He speaks good English and is very familiar with Urumqi. To rent a car to drive by yourself, I recommend Zhongpinghe (0991-485-2140; www.xjzph.com) that has locations at the airport and throughout town. Be warned: they don't speak English and they don't accept foreign credit cards.

Turpan: I highly recommend the services of a Uyghur man named Tahir (150-2626-1388). He can pick you up at both train stations and take you all around the major tourist sites in Turpan. His prices are reasonable and he offers discounts for multi-day trips.

Kashgar: Because there are so many great tour agencies whose main office is in Kashgar, I recommend you reach out to one of the companies listed above, including Old Road Tours or Xinjiang Travel. You can even arrange for a car hire through John's Cafe near the Seman Hotel.

Other Travel-Related Services

Passport Visas Express

This company has processed multiple Chinese visas for my friends and family traveling to Xinjiang. They are quick, professional and have even offered a special 10% discount to readers of this book. Visit their website and input promo code FWC10 to get an exclusive 10% discount.

www.passportvisasexpress.com

ExpressVPN

ExpressVPN has been one of the best and most reliable services to help people in China access sites like Facebook, Gmail and Twitter. Whether you're coming to China for a couple weeks or a couple years, securing your internet activity is highly recommended.

www.expressvpn.com

China Trains

To make travel easier, I find that booking train tickets online saves a lot of time and hassle. One of the best websites to book online is China Highlights and they'll deliver your tickets right to your hotel.

www.chinahighlights.com/china-trains/

Trip (Flights)

The two most popular websites to purchase domestic flights in China are Trip and eLong. I prefer Trip (formerly called Ctrip) and it is what I have used over the past decade to book almost all of my domestic and international travel. The website is in English and their service representatives also speak good English.

www.trip.com/flights

WorldNomads

Xinjiang healthcare is not great, unfortunately, so if you want the peace of mind that you could be airlifted out in case of an emergency, I recommend getting specific travel insurance before your journey. Get a free quote from World Nomads.

www.worldnomads.com

ABOUT THE AUTHOR

Josh and his wife first moved out to Xinjiang in 2006, completely unaware that they had just signed up for one of the craziest life adventures they could ever imagine. Within a year they had fallen in love with the region and began to travel together with a map and a tent on the back of their motorcycle.

FarWestChina began as a simple blog to update friends and family on this amazing adventure but has grown into a respected travel website featured by CNN, The New York Times, Lonely Planet, CNBC and many more. Josh has been interviewed on radio and TV stations all across the globe and has spoken at Peking University and Tsinghua University, two of China's most prestigious institutions.

Josh and his family, which includes his beautiful wife and two adventurous sons, consider Xinjiang to be their second home.

FarWestChina.com